THE 1956 WAR

The Cummings Center for Russian and East European Studies
The Cummings Center Series

THE 1956 WAR
Collusion and Rivalry in the Middle East
Edited by David Tal

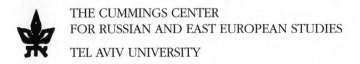

THE CUMMINGS CENTER
FOR RUSSIAN AND EAST EUROPEAN STUDIES
TEL AVIV UNIVERSITY

The Cummings Center is Tel Aviv University's main framework for research, study, documentation and publication relating to the history and current affairs of Russia, the former Soviet republics and Eastern Europe. The Center is committed to pursuing projects which make use of fresh archival sources and to promoting a dialogue with Russian academic circles through joint research, seminars and publications.

THE CUMMINGS CENTER SERIES

The titles published in this series are the product of original research by the Center's faculty, research staff and associated fellows. The Cummings Center Series also serves as a forum for publishing declassified Russian archival material of interest to scholars in the fields of history and political science.

EDITOR-IN-CHIEF
Gabriel Gorodetsky

EDITORIAL BOARD
Michael Confino
Yaacov Ro'i
Shimon Naveh
Nurit Schleifman
Igal Halfin

MANAGING EDITOR
Deena Leventer

THE 1956 WAR

Collusion and Rivalry
in the Middle East

EDITED BY

DAVID TAL

FRANK CASS
LONDON · PORTLAND, OR

First published in 2001 in Great Britain by
FRANK CASS PUBLISHERS
Crown House, 47 Chase Side
London, N14 5BP

and in the United States of America by
FRANK CASS PUBLISHERS
c/o ISBS, 5824 N.E. Hassalo Street
Portland, Oregon, 97213-3644

Website: www.frankcass.com

British Library Cataloguing in Publication Data

The 1956 War: collusion and rivalry in the Middle East. –
(The Cummings Center series)
1. Egypt – History – Intervention, 1956
I. Tal, David II. Cummings Center for Russian and East European Studies
956'.044

ISBN 0-7146-4840-X (cloth)
ISBN 0-7146-4394-7 (paper)
ISSN 1365-3733

Library of Congress Cataloging-in-Publication Data

The 1956 War: collusion and rivalry in the Middle East/edited by David Tal.
    p. cm. – (The Cummings Center series, ISSN 1365-3733)
Includes bibliographical references and index.
ISBN 0-7146-4840-X (cloth) – ISBN 0-7146-4394-7 (paper)
1. Sinai Campaign, 1956 – Diplomatic history. I. Tal, David. II.
Series.
DT137.S55 A18 2001
956.04'4 – dc21

2001017230

Typeset by FiSH Books, London
Printed in Great Britain by
MPG Books Ltd, Bodmin, Cornwall

Contents

Abbreviations

AVPRF	Foreign Policy Archives of the Russian Federation
BGA	Ben-Gurion Archive
CIA	Central Intelligence Agency
CoSD	Chief of Staff Diary (Israel)
CPSU	Communist Party of the Soviet Union
FLN	Front de Libération Nationale
FRUS	*Foreign Relations of the United States*
GAA	General Armistice Agreements
GRU	Main Intelligence Directorate (Soviet Military Intelligence)
IAF	Israel Air Force
IDF(A)	Israel Defence Forces (Archives)
ISA	Israel State Archives
LPA	Labour Party Archive
MID	Soviet Ministry of Foreign Affairs
NA	National Archives (Washington, DC)
NATO	North Atlantic Treaty Organization
PRO	Public Record Office, London
RCC	Revolutionary Command Council (Egypt)
SCP	Supreme Command Post
SEATO	South-East Asia Treaty Organization
SHAA	Service Historique de l'Armée de l'Air
SWB	Summary of World Broadcasts
TsKhSD	Centre for the Preservation of Contemporary Documentation (Russia)
UAR	United Arab Republic
UNA	United Nations Archive
UNEF	United Nations Emergency Force
UNGA	United Nations General Assembly
UNSC	United Nations Security Council
UNTSO	United Nations Truce Supervisory Organization

Acknowledgements

This book originated in an international conference held at Tel Aviv University in 1996, on the 40th anniversary of the Suez War. Experts in various aspects of the subject gathered to introduce what were at that time new findings on the war, covering the diverse issues and subjects involved in this many-faceted conflict. In the time that transpired between the conference and the preparation of this collection for publication, the contributors expanded their papers and brought them up to date as much as possible. I am both obliged and pleased to thank the following for their assistance in realizing this project. First, I would like to thank the contributors, upon whom this volume relied. I would like to thank the School of History at Tel Aviv University, which hosted the conference, and its head at the time, Prof. Shulamit Volkov. I am also grateful to Professor Marcello Dascal who, as Dean of the Faculty of Humanities at the time, provided financial support.

Professor Gabriel Gorodetsky, then head of the Cummings Center for Russian and East European Studies and currently director of the Morris E. Curiel Center for International Studies, assisted in the organization of the conference and, more significantly, in his contribution to the publication of the book. I would like especially to thank Deena Leventer, managing editor of the Cummings Center Series, who went beyond the call of duty to make the publication of this book possible.

Introduction: A New Look at the 1956 Suez War

DAVID TAL

An understanding of the 1956 Suez War entails, above all, a willingness to examine sharply divergent points of view. Six countries were involved in the conflict at different levels, each with its own separate agenda and distinctive perspective. For Israel, it was a 'fee' collected by France as a price for the nascent alliance between the two states, which was so important to the Israelis; it also offered an opportunity to extract a price from Egypt under optimal conditions. For the French it was an economic enterprise, aimed at regaining for them and the British their hold of the Suez Canal Company, as well as an opportunity to punish Egyptian President Gamal 'Abd al-Nasser for his alleged assistance to the rebellious Algerian independence movement, the Front de Libération Nationale (FLN). Britain, too, sought to reacquire the assets it lost when Nasser nationalized the Suez Canal, but also entertained the hope of regaining the influence it had lost under the terms of the October 1954 Anglo-Egyptian agreement that brought to an end more than a century of British domination over Egypt. For Nasser's Egypt, the victim of a flagrant act of aggression triggered by its decision to unshackle itself from imperialist conquest, it became a kind of a war of liberation, with Nasser emerging from the war as the prime bearer of the Arab nationalist cause and as one of the influential figures in the non-aligned bloc. Two other countries, although not involved directly, made a considerable impact and acted from their singular points of view. The United States sought to maintain Western influence in the Middle East but opposed British imperialist posturing; while the Soviet Union viewed the war as an opportunity to enhance its influence in a region it had penetrated successfully only a year earlier. The input of the two Great Powers also injected the tensions of the Cold War into the Middle East crisis. The essays in this volume underscore this multifaceted nature of the 1956 war.

1

Oddly enough, though, while the motives of the British and the French were quite clear, those of the Israelis had undercurrents that are often overlooked. The explanation that it was the newly established Israeli–French axis that brought Israel into the war, while accurate as far as it goes, is not sufficient – and not only because the Israelis themselves, both contemporary and later scholars, have adduced different explanations, all related to the Arab–Israeli conflict, and more specifically to Israeli–Egyptian antagonism, which had intensified in the two years before the war.

The Israeli leadership justified its decision to go to war by citing 'the mini-war which the Arab rulers have waged against us for eight years'.[1] Moshe Dayan, who as the Israel Defence Forces (IDF) Chief of Staff led the Israeli military campaign, described the war as the natural culmination of the reprisal raids the IDF had mounted in the years preceding the war. Following the last such raid, carried out on 12 October 1956, against the Jordanian police fortress at Kalkilya, and the most costly in terms of casualties – 18 Israeli soldiers and officers were killed – Dayan told the General Staff that 'the current method [of reprisal attacks] demands a revision'.[2] That revision materialized in the Sinai War, or in its Hebrew code name 'Operation Kadesh'. Scholars have generally accepted this version, which seeks to connect the multitude of border incidents from 1949 to 1956 with the war.[3] However, invoking the Arab–Israeli conflict as the exclusive cause of Israel's decision to enter the war is misleading. True, the Israeli–Egyptian border was an arena of armed clashes and other incidents, but these were localized events, which neither side wished to escalate into a war. A distinction therefore must be made between the border clashes and the Israeli decision to go to war. The border situation and the war were not cause-and-effect cases, although border incidents did create a bellicose climate.

The tension along the Arab–Israeli borders was in fact engendered by Israel's two major achievements in the 1948 war, apart from retaining its independence. First, by the end of the war, the demographic equilibrium in Israel had turned dramatically in favour of the Jews, as compared with the population ratio envisaged by the UN Partition Resolution. Whereas the designated Jewish state was supposed to consist of about 500,000 Jews and 350,000 Arabs, Israel in 1949 had a population of 600,000 Jews and fewer than 100,000 Arabs. The second achievement was territorial. The cease-fire lines extended beyond the Partition lines, and some parts of the designated Palestinian state, in Western Galilee and in the south of the country, were incorporated into Israel. The official Israeli position was that Palestinian Arabs who had fled or been expelled forcibly from Jewish-controlled and occupied territories would not be permitted to return, nor would Israel agree to negotiate its territorial gains.[4] The General Armistice Agreements (GAA) signed with Lebanon, Syria, Jordan and Egypt perpetuated the situation on the ground, and even though Israeli leaders stated that the GAA should be the first step towards formal peace treaties, they were in fact content with the *status quo* as it emerged from the armistice accords.

The agreements were signed under the auspices of the United Nations, and were implemented and monitored by Mixed Armistice Committees, each headed by an official of the UN Truce Supervisory Organization (UNTSO) and with delegates from Israel and the relevant Arab state. One of the serious problems the UNTSO observers encountered was cross-border infiltration into Israel from neighbouring countries. During the war hundreds of thousands of Palestinians found refuge in the Jordanian-controlled West Bank and the Egyptian-controlled Gaza Strip. Even while the fighting raged, many of them tried to cross Israeli lines, and the tide of would-be returnees swelled when hostilities were terminated. Palestinians attempted to cross the border into Israel for a variety of reasons: to return to their homes, visit relatives or reclaim property left behind; to cultivate land and grow crops so they could earn a living; or, in some cases, to steal from Israeli settlements. The armistice lines with Jordan and Egypt also produced infiltrators of another type: individuals who at the end of the war found themselves residing along the new borders. Many were cut off from their land, which was now inside Israel. Finding the situation untenable, they crossed the borders, which were not marked, to cultivate their fields or orchards. Another aspect of the same phenomenon was attempts by Arabs in the border areas to seize and till empty land on the Israeli side, or even to harvest crops sown by Israeli settlers.[5]

Few of the infiltrators from Jordan and the Gaza Strip were motivated politically. There were, however, Palestinian activists who crossed the border to carry out sabotage and murder inside Israel in order to generate constant military tension on the borders, prevent the stabilization of the *status quo* created by the armistice accords, and in general, keep the conflict simmering.[6] It should be emphasized that this 'political' infiltration represented the lesser part of the phenomenon. It was the Israeli reaction that imbued the infiltrations with a political dimension, since Israel did not treat them for what they were but linked them to the broad Arab–Israeli context and to the country's political and security problems.

Pursuing this policy, the IDF reacted forcefully against the infiltrators, applying a broad range of measures, of which the best known were the reprisal raids. These attacks had a single goal: to convince and induce the Egyptian and Jordanian authorities to enlist in the war against infiltration. Israel did not consider the reprisal raids a strategic tool for conducting its relations with the Arab states. Their primary purpose was to combat infiltration, and especially its lethal consequences. Most of the reprisal operations were mounted following raids by infiltrators that had resulted in Israeli fatalities. Indeed, this pattern characterized the entire period until October 1956. The operations bore local significance and were part of the Israeli effort to preserve the *status quo*, not to alter it.[7]

From 1949 to 1954 the focal point was the border with Jordan, but during 1954 the situation changed. Fierce Israeli military activity on both sides of the border, combined with a growing resolve by the Jordanian authorities to stamp out the phenomenon, was instrumental in bringing about a substantial decline in cross-border infiltration from Jordan and, far more important, in the number of victims it claimed. The result was a marked improvement in the situation along the Jordanian border in 1954, reflected in the cessation of IDF reprisals against Jordan from September of that year.

However, even as relative quiet prevailed on the border with Jordan, tension mounted along the border with Egypt and the armistice line with the Gaza Strip beginning in February–March 1954. Compounding the 'conventional' infiltrations, which had gone on since 1949, Egyptian soldiers now opened fire on IDF border patrols, while infiltrators from the Gaza Strip planted mines on the patrol routes.[8] The Israeli government urged Egypt through various channels to put a stop to this activity, but these diplomatic efforts were largely ineffectual. The Egyptians insisted that they were working to prevent border incidents and infiltrations, and the Israeli government knew for a fact that the authorities in Gaza were taking steps to put a stop to conventional infiltration.[9] The violence along the border continued, but Prime Minister Moshe Sharett consistently refused requests by the IDF's Chief of Staff, Moshe Dayan, to launch reprisal attacks.[10]

On 21 February 1955, David Ben-Gurion took over the Ministry of Defence again, after having been out of the government for about 15 months. A few days after his return, Egyptian intelligence agents murdered an Israeli civilian in the centre of the country. Ben-Gurion thereupon submitted to the cabinet a plan for the IDF to attack an Egyptian military camp near Gaza City. This time Sharett approved the raid, and on 28 February the IDF attacked the camp, destroying buildings and engaging Egyptian forces. The Israeli force lost eight soldiers, the Egyptians 38.[11] Despite claims by both contemporary and later scholars,[12] Operation Gaza was only one of a series of such raids, although various meanings and implications were read into it retroactively. It has already been explained that the primary reason for sending IDF units across the border was murderous activity by infiltrators inside Israel. Israeli reprisals, the first of which was carried out in March 1950, were intended as collective punishment against civilian targets; their express purpose was to cause as much damage as possible in order to induce the civilian population to pressure the government to take action. Consequently, until the beginning of 1954 the Israeli reprisals were almost always directed against civilian targets.[13] However, the negative reactions throughout Western Europe and in the United Nations to the Qibiya raid (14 October 1953) brought about a policy shift. General Dayan was sent to the United States for the Security Council debate on the Jordanian complaint, where he had an opportunity to see first-hand the impact of the operation in the international arena. The lesson was clear: 'We learned that when the Arabs attack peaceful civilians we must direct our reactions to military objectives.'[14] Operation Gaza was thus in line with the new reprisal–raid policy, its purpose being to pressure Egypt to step up its preventive action against infiltrators and to eliminate border incidents. However, the Israeli decision did not take into account the effect on Nasser, who was then experiencing serious political problems. Nasser was deeply involved in an internal power struggle within the Egyptian leadership, trying to consolidate his position after ousting Nagib from power in the summer of 1954. His authority was not universally accepted by the Egyptian political establishment and he was heavily dependent on the army for support. The Israeli attack on the army camp in Gaza was thus a blow to Nasser and his group, coming on top of his failure to prevent the Baghdad Pact. Nasser, then, was not in a position to simply shrug off the operation, even if he knew that it was a reaction to brutal infiltrations.[15]

At the same time, Nasser had no intention of going to war with Israel.[16] His reaction was limited to the ongoing situation on the ground. He refused to order his troops to cease firing at Israeli patrols – indeed, this practice was intensified after the Gaza raid – and also encouraged the establishment of groups of *fedayun* ('those willing to sacrifice themselves'). Organized by Egyptian intelligence, *fedayun* raiders were sent into Israel on two occasions (August 1955 and April 1956). From time to time they also were involved in border clashes along the Gaza Strip and other Arab territories.[17]

The escalating tension along the border set the stage for a clash between the Prime Minister and Foreign Minister Moshe Sharett and Defence Minister, Ben-Gurion over Israel's security policy. Beneath the surface, another debate, far less known, involved Ben-Gurion and his protégé, Dayan. The dispute with Sharett revolved around the means to implement the country's security policy, while the disagreement with Dayan concerned the aims. Both Ben-Gurion and Sharett maintained that Israel should adhere to the armistice regime. Where they disagreed was over how to convince Israel's neighbours, mainly Egypt, to prevent the violation of the 1949 accords and take determined action to deter infiltration into Israel from their territories and so avert border clashes. Sharett urged a diplomatic offensive, while Ben-Gurion held that only military measures would convince the neighbouring governments to implement their armistice commitments. Dayan, of course, backed Ben-Gurion's advocacy of military action; but unlike Ben-Gurion, he did not balk even at full-scale war to prevent the violation of Israeli territory. Ben-Gurion was unwilling to dismantle the *status quo* deriving from the armistice agreements, and warned in July 1955 that retaliatory attacks could deteriorate into war.[18]

THE TURNING POINT: THE CZECH–EGYPTIAN ARMS DEAL

The turning point in Israeli-Egyptian relations was Nasser's arms deal with Czechoslovakia, which was made public on 27 September 1955. The deal was unrelated either to Israeli–Egyptian tensions in general or to Operation Gaza in particular, as scholars commonly argue. There were several reasons for Nasser's turn to the East, and as Rami Ginat shows, it preceded Operation Gaza. The Egyptian–Soviet *rapprochement* had a dual background: regional developments, in which the Great Powers were involved; and Nasser's thrust to release Egypt from its past while bringing about 'the eradication of imperialism', and the 'creation of a strong national army'.[19] It was more than natural for a vigorous young leader, who was also a senior army officer, to wish to build a modern army for his country. Moreover, one of the major symbols of imperialist control in Egypt was the military's total dependence on the imperialist power, which used its control to weaken the native army. Unceremoniously rebuffed in his attempts to obtain arms from the West, Nasser could only become increasingly dismayed with the behaviour of Britain and the United States. To this one should add the tilt of the regional arms balance in Israel's favour. During 1954–55 France sold significant quantities of weapons to Israel, including 24 Mystère II fighter planes, several dozen AMX-13 light tanks, mobile 155 mm Howitzers, and additional weapons systems and spare parts. In May 1955 Israel asked to purchase 200 anti-tank missiles, 30 Mystère IV fighter planes, 15 Vautour bombers and 30 more AMX-13 tanks. France promised to consider Israel's shopping list favourably, and made good on its pledge. These acquisitions temporarily tilted the regional arms balance even further in Israel's favour.[20]

It was at this juncture that Egyptian and Soviet interests converged. The Israeli acquisitions were inopportune for Nasser, particularly as both Britain and the United States had rejected his requests for arms.[21] At the same time, Western efforts to create a regional defence organization in the Middle East were causing anxiety in the Soviet Union. Nasser's quest for arms gave the Soviet Union a strategic opportunity to gain a foothold in the region and at the same time to dissociate Egypt from the West. The upshot was that clandestine talks underway since 1953 between senior Egyptian and Soviet officials culminated in a major arms deal, strengthening Egypt militarily and shifting dramatically the regional arms balance in Egypt's favour.[22]

The news of the arms sale shook Israel and deeply worried Ben-Gurion. His initial response to the 27 July 1952 Free Officers' coup had been positive, and Israel officially welcomed the new regime.[23] However, during 1954 and 1955 Ben-Gurion changed his opinion about Nasser and began to perceive him as an enemy. His fear, frequently expressed, was that the Arab world would unite under an Ataturk-type leader. The schisms in the Arab world were its weakness, Ben-Gurion thought, and accorded Israel a strategic advantage. Nasser's rise to prominence, combined with Egypt's growing involvement in the region, led Ben-Gurion to believe that the Egyptian ruler was that self-styled Ataturk. The Israeli leader found in Nasser's book, *The Philosophy of the Revolution*, confirmation of his fears that Nasser's goal was to unite the entire Arab world under Egypt's leadership and then launch Arab armies against Israel.[24] Nevertheless, Ben-Gurion saw no reason to effect a revision in Israeli–Egyptian relations and continued to adhere to the *status quo* and abide by the terms of the armistice regime. It was the arms deal that was the turning point for Ben-Gurion: the balance was weighted so heavily in Egypt's favour, he believed, that Nasser now possessed the tool with which to put his intentions into practice.[25]

It is unclear whether Nasser actually intended to use the arms, whose purchase he had just announced, against Israel. Egyptian officials, with Nasser at the forefront, rejected Israeli accusations that Egypt harboured aggressive intentions. Despite the deterioration along the border before and after September 1955, the Egyptian leadership consistently told Western diplomats that their country had no plans to attack Israel.[26] Still, Egyptian foreign policy undoubtedly underwent a change in late 1954 and early 1955, as Nasser began to brandish the banner of Arab nationalism under Egyptian leadership.[27]

Israel viewed these events from its own point of view, narrow as this may have been. Nasser's adoption of an aggressive foreign policy, combined with his new stock of military hardware, unnerved the Israeli leadership. Sharett wrote in his diary that the Soviet bloc's entry into the Middle East was 'a frightening military factor'. Reflecting on the deal, he felt a 'deep concern for our security, the likes of which I have never experienced since the days preceding the establishment of the State [of Israel]'.[28] Israel's immediate instinct, fuelled by the militant Chief of Staff Dayan, was to initiate an attack against Egypt. The possibility was considered briefly during October–December 1955, but finally rejected. Rebuffing Dayan's military logic and fending off the pressure he exerted, Ben-Gurion steered Israeli activity towards what he then viewed as the primary goal: arms procurement. This meant taking the diplomatic channel.[29]

Attempts to purchase arms in the United States and Britain failed, but the French Prime Minister, Edgar Faure, told Moshe Sharett, who was still Prime Minister and Foreign Minister, that France would consider Israeli requests for weapons. The Sharett–Faure talks laid the foundation upon which Shimon Peres and other Defence Ministry officials were able to make progress, resulting in a massive Israeli–French arms deal in June 1956.[30] Carrying out Faure's commitment turned out to be a very complicated matter. France's internal political instability and the conflict between the pro-Arab Quai d'Orsay, and Israeli sympathizers of the defence establishment hampered the final conclusion of the deal.[31] It was only after the establishment of the Guy Mollet government that a favourable turnabout, from Israel's point of view, occurred. Two developments led to the final step. First, the Indian government had just cancelled an order for 200 Mystères, and the French Defence Ministry was eager to find new buyers. Second, the situation in Algeria was not improving for France, whose defence officials were convinced that the problems in Algeria were at least partly attributable to policies being implemented by Nasser in Cairo. This point was critical. The deterioration in Algeria, for which the French in part blamed Nasser, brought about a fundamental shift in France's Middle East policy. Israel was seen as a promising ally in the struggle against Nasser's perceived intervention on the side of the Algerian rebels.[32] The turning point came when the Mollet government concluded that Nasser was a common enemy of France and Israel and that the two countries had a mutual interest, which could be served by the French providing arms in return for Israeli assistance, mainly in intelligence and special operations, against Egypt.

Peres took the cue, and in Paris, beginning in mid-April, put forward ideas that were listened to attentively, particularly by the Defence Ministry.[33] On 31 May Peres introduced the idea to Prime Minister Ben-Gurion (he had resumed the post in November 1955 and continued to hold the defence portfolio as well), who ten days later gave his consent 'to conduct negotiations with the French, [and said he was] ready to go as far as possible in cooperation with them, even in acts of war, as long as the French are ready to share responsibility with us'. It was decided that Dayan, Peres and the Director of Military Intelligence Colonel Yehoshafat Harkabi, would visit France in late June in order to bring the negotiations to a 'practical conclusion'.[34] The details were hammered out during the weekend of 23–24 June at a secret conference in the town of Vermars, south of Paris. The French delegation consisted of high-ranking officials from the Defence Ministry, the Prime Minister's office, the secret service and the office of the Governor of Algeria. Dayan described the Israeli position, stressing the military dimension, while the French emphasized intelligence and operational aspects. The French approved the entire package of Israeli arms requests – 200 AMX tanks, 72 Mystère Mark IV fighter planes and ammunition – worth $80 million. The exact nature of the cooperation the French had in mind is still classified, but they expected Israel to provide them with intelligence about Egypt's assistance to the Algerian rebels and to conduct covert operations against Egyptian and other forces involved in the Algerian war. The Israelis had no hesitation about sharing intelligence with France, but were more reluctant when it came to military operations, fearing possible repercussions if Israel's involvement became public. Ben-Gurion, still committed to the security policy he had adopted in late 1955 – to take every possible measure to prevent Egyptian violence that would force a retaliatory attack and consequently a war – wanted to avoid any Israeli military operations that would force Nasser to respond. To assuage Israel's fears in this regard, the French agreed to cooperate in the operational activity and not to leave it to the Israelis alone.[35] If the Egyptian–Czech arms deal was depicted as one involving 'arms-for-cotton', by analogy the Israeli-French deal involved 'arms for intelligence and military operations'.

The deeper implication was that Israel, for the first time, was on the brink of signing a security pact with a Great Power, albeit one in decline. The Israeli leadership, and Ben-Gurion in particular, had always sought a formal alliance with such a power, believing that this would constitute the ultimate guarantee of Israel's security in the hostile Middle East. Persistent efforts to convince the United States and Britain to commit themselves formally to Israel's security, undertaken since the early 1950s, had been unproductive.[36] Now it seemed possible to upgrade Israeli–French relations beyond the buyer–seller level.

It is unclear whether Ben-Gurion intended to use the arms acquisitions to enable the IDF to make war with improved means that could match the new Egyptian equipment, or to deter Egypt from attacking. He himself seemed uncertain, as attested by the conflicting signals he sent and the speeches he delivered in this period.[37] Ben-Gurion's aim seemed to be to alert public opinion to Israel's serious security situation while keeping all options open: war, reprisals, or a diplomatic move such as seceding from the armistice regime.

The Vermars conference was significant not only because of its strategic implications for Israel but also because it marked the removal of the Israeli Foreign Ministry from any role in cultivating the newly developing relations with France. In early April Dayan pressed for the Foreign Ministry to be excluded from the arms procurement talks, and Ben-Gurion, over Foreign Minister Sharett's fierce protests, complied.[38] The defence establishment dominated completely the development of Israel's strategic relations with France, leaving no room for the Foreign Ministry. This was not necessarily the direct cause of Sharett's forced resignation in June 1956, but it did reflect his diminished position. Ben-Gurion's relations with Sharett were always uneasy and   complex. During the years when the two were in agreement over Israel's national aims, their disagreements stemmed from differences in character or involved specific questions of tactics. Even when they were engaged in a heated debate over the issue of the reprisal attacks during 1955, they shared the belief that Israel should adhere to the *status quo*. Ben-Gurion believed that their divergent personalities and contrasting approaches to policy served Israel's interests. He depicted his relations with Sharett as a 'coalition' in which each balanced the other.[39] As long as the two shared the belief that Israel should adhere to the *status quo*, the 'coalition' was relevant. However, developments during the autumn of 1955 produced a fundamental shift in Ben-Gurion's perception of Israel's strategic situation and needs. Unlike Sharett, he no longer felt committed to the *status quo*. Ben-Gurion was convinced that if Israel did not acquire arms Nasser would attack as soon as the Egyptian army absorbed its new weapons. Consequently, the chief priority was to build up the IDF, though Ben-Gurion did not rule out the possibility of an Israeli pre-emptive strike. On various occasions in the past, Sharett had shown his ability to effectively curb Ben-Gurion's aggressive initiatives.[40] Although Ben-Gurion was not necessarily bent on war in mid-1956, he was unwilling, under the new circumstances, to allow Sharett to curb the government's freedom of action. So, when Sharett gave him an opportunity to banish him from the government, he acted.

Sharett himself spoke of his possible ouster from the government during the middle of May 1956. Press reports in late May claimed that a government reshuffle was imminent and that Sharett would probably become the secretary-general of the ruling Mapai party. The opportunity presented itself following the setback Mapai suffered in the July 1955 elections.[41] On 3 June Ben-Gurion indeed proposed to him that he become secretary-general of Mapai – in short, that he leave the government. Sharett finally yielded to the pressure, and on 18 June submitted his resignation to the Prime Minister. He was replaced by Golda Meir (Meyerson), the Minister of Labour.[42]

On 19 July, US Secretary of State John Foster Dulles informed the Egyptian ambassador in Washington that the United States was delaying

INTRODUCTION

indefinitely its promised funding for the Aswan High Dam. Nasser responded exactly one week later, on 26 July 1956, by nationalizing the Suez Canal. Two days after that, Ben-Gurion and Dayan discussed the possibilities that seemed to have opened up for Israel. The Israeli Chief of Staff tried again to persuade Ben-Gurion to let the IDF initiate a move against the Egyptian army, but Ben-Gurion seemed to prefer a 'wait and see' policy, and decided not to take action.[43] So, even though Israel would be at war with Egypt within months, that development was not connected directly to Ben-Gurion's talk with Dayan on 28 July. Indeed, we should emphasize what is usually only intimated: the decision to go to war was not an Israeli initiative, it was the result of a proposal by France to punish Nasser in kind for nationalizing the canal. The road to war was embarked upon in August 1956, when the Director-General of the French Ministry of Defence, Abel Thomas, met with his Israeli counterpart, Shimon Peres, and informed him that 'the English and the French have decided in principle on a joint military operation to capture the canal'. Thomas added that the English objected to Israeli involvement in the military campaign, but the two nevertheless discussed 'our participation in planning and advice, and if necessary, more than that'.[44] The Suez crisis erupted at a time when Israeli–French cooperation was at its height and Israel had restored its military superiority, both in quantity and quality. The Thomas–Peres conversation in August was part of the ongoing strategic dialogue between the two states. It was also the first step in a process that eventually involved Israel in the Suez War. The question of whether even without the Suez crisis and the French initiative Israel would have gone to war against Egypt must therefore remain moot.

THE INTERNATIONAL DIMENSION OF THE WAR

As has been already noted, a proper understanding of the war requires a broad perspective. As this volume shows, the war sprang from a range of causes and interests, some of them mutually conflicting. The chapter by Aron Shai, which addresses the imperialist aspect of the war, also places it in the broadest context. Shai exposes the discrepancy between the imperial forces' self-perception of their power, and their actual material and diplomatic capabilities, as well as the irrelevance of imperialism in the post-war era and in the face of the emerging nationalist and radical governments of what would come to be known as the Third World. These discrepancies, Shai explains, while underlying the Anglo-French decision to take military action in order to restore their ownership of the Suez Canal Company, also doomed the initiative from the outset. However, as Paul Gaujac and Keith Kyle show, the British and the French also had concrete reasons for going to war, which overrode the common cause suggested by Shai. Britain, critically dependent on Middle Eastern oil, considered it vital to secure control over the major sea lane by which the oil was shipped. However, Keith Kyle explores the diversity of factors that influenced British decision-making. The decision-making process was not linear but complex, driven by conflicting factors that produced twists and turns. In a word, it was human.

One of the factors that hampered the British leadership was the military dimension. Again, the problem was internal as well as external: the military found itself hamstrung by the political aspect of the campaign, and its planning fluctuated between purely military considerations – some of which were themselves the subject of disagreement within the armed forces – and unavoidable political constraints. The situation was further compounded by the issue of Anglo-French military cooperation and the possible role that would be assigned to Israel. In short, the 1956 war was, in addition to all its other complexities, also a coalition war, and Paul Gaujac and Motti Golani explore the inherent difficulties this posed: 'Such a situation, in a coalition war, is always unfortunate if the understanding is less than perfect and if the intentions are different or opposite.' Beyond the personal friction generated by the fact that senior French officers had to operate under British orders, the complex command structure played havoc with the need to make quick decisions. The whole system was overloaded and cumbersome. And not the least of the difficulties was that the two allied armies effectively were fighting two different wars:

The British were trying to prevent another country from conquering a passage point crucial for their nation. . . . The French, in addition to their unequivocal vigorous assistance to Israel against the Egyptian threat, saw here mainly an opportunity to erase Egypt as active supporters of the Algerian rebels and to take advantage of their victory over Cairo to wipe out the rebellion once and for all.

Overlying these complexities was what Paul Gaujac calls the 'Franco-French war', referring to the internal struggles among French commanders. The question of Israel's participation in the war further strained Anglo-French relations and undermined coalition unity. All these conflicting and contradictory demands and expectations came to a head at the Sèvres conference (22–24 October 1956). Avi Shlaim explains that the Sèvres meeting was essential precisely because Israeli–French–British collaboration was impossible due to British unwillingness to enter a war together with Israel. The Protocol of Sèvres created the conditions whereby Britain could fight a war on the same side as Israel, but without being a member of an official tripartite alliance. Motti Golani shows that the British condition severed the coalition and created misunderstanding in Israel about British actions, though mainly their inaction. The British operated according to their own schedule, while the Israelis expected a different pace. The timetable discrepancy incensed the Israelis, who had not been told about it. It also affected Israeli military moves: apart from several high-ranking officers, the IDF was unaware of the Sèvres agreement, and Israeli field commanders found the resultant military planning peculiar. One outcome of this was that the commander of the Israeli operation launched hostilities at a time that seemed to him appropriate but which under the terms of the Sèvres agreement – of which he was unaware – was in fact premature. This is only one example of the consequences produced by the strange structure of the coalition, which the British insisted was a non-coalition.

It was here that the sharply divergent points of view of the belligerents converged: the underlying political considerations of the 1956 war overshadowed its military aspects. Indeed, the political aspect dictated the nature of the war and was a crucial element in enabling Nasser to turn a military defeat into a political and diplomatic triumph. As Yoram Meital argues, while the political process hampered the military planning of the tripartite belligerents, Nasser wanted to drag out the diplomatic efforts following the nationalization of the Suez Canal on the assumption that prolonging the diplomatic process set in motion by Egypt's actions would reduce the danger of an attack on Egypt. Nasser exhausted every legal, diplomatic and moral argument as a mean to justify the nationalization, but when Egypt was nevertheless attacked by Israel and confronted with the Anglo-French ultimatum, Nasser acted to capitalize on the new situation. Meital shows that the Egyptians perceived the war in a broader context than their assailants. They regarded it as an imperialistic assault designed to punish and suppress Egypt's national liberation movement. This was the springboard of Nasser's subsequent campaign against the West's claim to hegemony over the Middle East, which fomented unrest across the region and gradually eroded Western influence. Elie Podeh addresses this aspect of the war, from the point of view of the inter-Arab system. The 1956 war established Nasser's position in the Middle East, and through his promotion of the pan-Arab cause he was able to moderate inter-Arab conflicts, particularly the struggle between Egypt and Iraq, over supremacy in the Arab world. The July 1958 crisis in the Middle East was one result of Nasser's growing influence.

Paradoxically, one reason for Nasser's success was the ongoing Cold War, in which both the United States and the Soviet Union competed for

Nasser's good will. The Soviet Union was victorious, as Rami Ginat shows, owing to its lengthy negotiations with Egypt resulting in the famous 'arms-for-cotton' deal. Two crucial points made in Ginat's paper are, first, that Egypt refused to accept Western dictates and Western hegemony, both under the monarchy and under the Free Officers' regime, and second, that Egypt's foreign and regional policies were influenced less by the Arab–Israeli conflict and more by domestic and regional as well as Arab considerations. Ginat views the Cold War as instrumental in the shaping of the Soviet position towards Egypt. Laurent Rucker adds another dimension to the discussion, when, through the use of recently declassified Soviet Foreign Ministry documents, he explores the more enigmatic, internal dimension of the Soviet conduct of the crisis. Controversy over foreign affairs issues in general, and over the Suez crisis in particular, was in fact used as part of the internal power struggle within the Soviet leadership. The debate and controversy were over power and ideology although, as Rucker implies, it is difficult to determine where one ends and the other begins. As to the other major player in the Cold War, the United States, its reaction to the crisis made it clear that the Eisenhower administration sought to prevent the Arab–Israeli conflict from becoming intertwined with the Cold War; in other words, Egypt's pro-Soviet stance did not automatically bring the United States to back Israel – the contrary was in fact the case. As Isaac Alteras observes, Eisenhower's intention was to prevent the Soviets from reaping benefits by siding with the Egyptians. But there was more to it than that: Eisenhower felt betrayed by the participation of the United States' allies, particularly Britain, in the surprise attack, and his anger went a long way towards determining his response. The upshot was that Nasser's military defeat was transformed into a diplomatic victory, thanks in large measure to the unrelated and uncoordinated US–Soviet diplomatic campaign that followed the war.

NOTES

1. Israel's Prime Minister, David Ben-Gurion, in the Knesset, 23 January 1957, in David Ben-Gurion, *Maarekhet Sinai* [The Sinai Campaign] (Tel Aviv: Am Oved, 1959), p. 243.
2. Moshe Dayan, *Avne Derekh* [Milestones] (Jerusalem: Idanim, 1976), p. 250.
3. Mordechai Bar-On, *Shaarei Aza* [The Gates of Gaza] (Tel-Aviv: Am Oved, 1992), pp. 376–7; Kenneth Love, *Suez: The Twice Fought War* (London: Longman, 1969); pp. 1–2; Benny Morris, *Israel's Border Wars, 1949–1956: Arab Infiltration, Israeli Retaliation and the Countdown to the Suez War* (Oxford: Clarendon Press, 1993); Michael B. Oren, *The Origins of the Second Arab–Israel War*, (London: Frank Cass, 1992), pp. 7–8.
4. David Tal, 'Israel's Road to the 1956 War', *International Journal of Middle East Studies*, 8 (1996), pp. 60–1; see also the statement by the Foreign Minister in the Israeli

Knesset, 9 Jan. 1950, Israeli State Archives (ISA), 2380.

5. 'Infiltrations', Israel Defence Forces Archives, Givatayim, Israel (IDFA), 108/52/34; S. Ben-Elkana, head of Minorities Branch, Israel Police: 'Survey on the Infiltration Problem', 8 March 1951, ISA, 2246/51/b; Ben-Gurion Diaries (BGD), entry for 30 Sept. 1949; Baggot J. Glubb, *A Soldier with the Arabs*, (New York, NY: Hodder & Stoughton, 1957), pp. 245–6; Ehud Ya'ari, *Mitsraim ve'hafedayun, 1953–1956* [Egypt and the Fedayun, 1953–1956], (Givat Haviva: Centre of Arabic and Afro-Asian Studies, 1975), p. 9.

6. S. Bruk to Investigations Branch, Police HQ, 4 May 1950, ISA, 2181/51/1 a; Ya'ari, *Mitsraim ve'hafedayun*, pp. 9–10; Zvi Al-Peleg, *ha-Mufti ha gadol* [The Grand Mufti] (Tel Aviv: Ministry of Defence, 1989), pp. 126–7.

7. Tal, 'Israel's Road to the 1956 War', pp. 65–9.

8. Operations Branch/Intelligence, Daily reports for Feb.–April 1954, ISA, 2428/12; Memorandum of the Assistant Secretary of State for Middle East, South Asia and Africa Affairs to the Secretary of State, 7 April 1954, National Archives (NA), RG 59, 684A.86/4-754; Y. Teqoa memorandum: 'Incidents along the Gaza Strip border before the kidnapping of the Israeli soldier', 5 May 1954, ISA, 2951/11.

9. Y. Teqoa memorandum, 'Incidents along the Gaza Strip border', 5 May 1954, ISA, 2951/11; Lt. Col. A. Shalev: 'Report of a meeting with General V. Bennike on 12 April 1954', ISA, 2951/4; US ambassador to the Secretary of State, 10 and 12 April 1954, NA, RG 84, Cairo Embassy General Records, box 255.

10. M. Sharett to E. Elath (and others), 26 Oct. 1954. Quoted in Moshe Sharett, *Yoman Ishi* [Personal Diary] (Tel Aviv: Ma'ariv Publications, 1978), Vol. 2, p. 591.

11. Y. Teqoa to Israeli delegations, 28 Feb. and 2 March 1955, ISA, 2952/2; Sharett, *Yoman Ishi*, Vol. 3, p. 800, entry for 27 February 1955; ibid., p. 816, entry for 6 March 1955.

12. Tel Aviv 757, Lawson to State Department, 4 March 1955 in Department of State, *Foreign Relations of the United States, 1955–1957 XIV (FRUS)* (Washington, DC: US Government Printing Office, 1990), pp. 86–8; Keith Kyle, *Suez* (London: Weidenfeld & Nicolson, 1991), p. 64; Kenneth Love quotes in similar words Nasser's response to him in Love, *Suez*, p. 83. See also Mohammed Abd el-Wahab Sayed-Ahmed, *Nasser and American Foreign Policy, 1952–1956*, (London: LAM, 1989), p. 107.

13. Moshe Dayan, who was the head of Southern Command, explained the rationale that led the IDF to attack civilian targets. Protocol of Mapai's Political Committee meeting, 18 June 1950, Labour Party Archive (LPA), 11-1-3.

14. Dayan, *Avnei Derekh*, p. 115.

15. Mohammed Heikal, *Nasser: The Cairo Documents* (London: New English Library, 1972), p. 5; Sayed-Ahmed, *Nasser and America*, p. 218; P. J. Vatikiotis, *Nasser and his Generation* (New York, NY: St Martin's Press, 1978), pp. 139–45.

16. US ambassador in Cairo to US Secretary of State, 1 March 1955, NA, RG 59, 674.84A/3-155.

17. A.L.M. Burns to the UN Secretary General, 2 June 1955, United Nations Archive, New York (UNA); Tal, *Tfisat haBitahon hashotef shel Yisrael: mekorotaya ve hitpathuta, 1949–56* [Israel's Day-to-Day Security Concept: Sources and Development] (Sde Boker: Merkaz lemoreshet Ben Gurion, 1998), pp. 190, 201–6, 229–30.

18. Tal, 'Israel's Road to the 1956 War', pp. 65–70; Ben-Gurion in a meeting with IDF high command, 5 July 1955, ISA, 5565/7.

19. Henry Byroade, Cairo Embassy, to Secretary of State, 5 April 1955, NA, RG 84, CE-GR, box 263; 23 June 1955, NA, 674.00/6-2355; Elie Podeh, *The Quest for Hegemony in the Arab World: The Struggle Over the Baghdad Pact* (Leiden: E.J. Brill, 1995), pp. 107–18, 126–32, 149–53, 172–95; translation of his speech is in R. Stevenson, Cairo to Foreign

Office, 29 March 1955, JE1015/12, FO 371/113578. See also the chapters by Rami Ginat and Yoram Meital in this collection.

20. NEACC – Israel Ground Weapons Strength, October 20, 1954, PRO, DEFE/7/228; Shimon Peres, *Kela David* [David's Sling] (Jerusalem: Weidenfeld & Nicolson, 1970), pp. 36–8; Bar-On, *Sha'arei Aza*, pp. 49–50.

21. On the British and US refusal to sell arms to Egypt, see DO (51) 20, 17 March 1951, PRO, CAB 131/11; Foreign Office to Washington, September 1952, PRO, DEFE 7/225; AEPC, P (52) 20, 19 December 1952, PRO, CAB 131/11; 'Military Jet Aircraft for the Middle East, C (54) 358', 23 November 1954, PRO, DEFE 7/229; on US terms for arms sale to Egypt, see To: NEA (Bureau of Near Eastern, South Asia and African Affairs), Mr Jernegan from NE (Near East), Mr Dorsey: 'Israel and Egyptian requests for arms', 25 June 1955, NA, RG 84, 84A.56/6-2555. See also Peter Hahn, *The United States, Great Britain and Egypt, 1945–1956: Strategy and Diplomacy in the Early Cold War* (Chapel Hill, NC: University of North Carolina Press, 1991), pp. 486–7.

22. Rami Ginat, *The Soviet Union and Egypt, 1945–1955*, (London: Frank Cass, 1993), pp. 111–12, 171–6, 188–9, 207–19; Mordechai Bar-On, *Etgar VeTigra* [Challenge and Quarrel] (Be'er Sheva: Ben-Gurion University Press, 1991), pp. 12–13.

23. Prime Minister's speech, 18 August 1952, *Divrei HaKnesset* [Knesset Record], XII:2985. On Israel's expectations of the revolutionary regime, see Meeting: Israel's ambassador to the US, A. Eban, with State Department officials, 31 July 1952, NA, RG 59, 774.00/7-3152; see also Sharett's response, 'On the Agenda', 31 July 1952, ISA, 2477/19; the Foreign Ministry to the Israeli embassy in Washington, 21 Aug. 1952, ibid.; US ambassador to Israel to the Secretary of State, 22 Aug. 1952, NA, RG 59, 674.84A/8-2252; Divon (Paris) to the Foreign Ministry, 7 Sept. 1952, ISA, 4373/15.

24. Ben-Gurion expressed these fears on several occasions on 27 Oct. 1949, see *Tsava u'Bitahon* [Army and Security] (Tel Aviv: Ma'arakhot, 1955), p. 138, and on 18 Oct. 1951, ibid., pp. 289–90. See also Sharett, *Yoman Ishi*, Vol. 4, p. 958, entry for 24 April 1955.

25. Ben-Gurion's speech to a meeting of the executive committee and the trade unions, 5 Jan. 1956 in Ben-Gurion, *Ma'arekhet Sinai*, pp. 54–5.

26. See Nasser's speech after the announcement of the Egyptian–Czech arms deal: From Cairo Embassy to Secretary of State, 3 October 1955, NA, RG 84, CE-GR, box 263; see also his talks with Byroade: From Cairo to the Secretary of State, 27 November 1955, NA, 674.84A/11-2755.

27. Joel Gordon, *Nasser's Blessed Movement: Egypt's Free Officers and the July Revolution*, (Oxford: Oxford University Press, 1991), pp. 177–9, 186; Sayed-Ahmed, *Nasser and America*, pp. 91–2; Vatikiotis, *Nasser and his Generation*, pp. 144–5.

28. Sharett, *Yoman Ishi*, Vol. 5, p. 1229.

29. General HQ/Operations Branch: 'The Omer plan', IDFA, 678/67/7; 'Operation Omer: order no. 1'. 1 Nov. 1955, IDFAL; General HQ/Operations Branch: 'Operation Dawn.' 30 Nov. 1955, IDFAL, 581/60/100; protocol of IDF General HQ meeting, 26 Dec. 1955, IDFAL, 847/62/30; Dayan, *Avnei Derekh*, pp. 155–6.

30. Telegram from the Department of State to the Embassy in Jordan, *FRUS* 1955–1957 XIV, pp. 540–1; Memorandum of conversation, 11 October 1955, Ibid., pp. 570–6; Sharett, *Yoman Ishi*, Vol. 5, entries for 19 October 1955, p. 1233, and 22 October 1955, p. 1239; Sharett meeting with Faure, ibid., entry for 25 October pp. 1248–50; entries for 23–27 October, 1955, pp. 1243–76; David Tal, 'American–Israeli Security Treaty: Sequel or Means to the Relief of Israeli–Arab Tensions, 1954–1955', *Middle Eastern Studies*, 4 (1995), pp. 842–4; Jacob Tsur, *Yoman Pariz* [An Ambassador's Diary in Paris] (Tel Aviv: Am Oved, 1968), entry for 25 October 1955, pp. 187–8.

31. Tsur, *Yoman Pariz*, p. 198, entry for 14 November 1955; pp. 200–2, entries for 18 and 29 November.

32. Bar-On, *Etgar VeTigra*, pp. 144–8; Tsur, *Yoman Pariz*, pp. 244–5, entry for 17 April 1956.
33. Bar-On, *Etgar VeTigrah*, pp. 146–9.
34. Dayan, *Avnei Derekh*, p. 200; Bar-On, *Etgar VeTigrah*, p. 148.
35. Dayan, *Avnei Derekh*, pp. 205–7, 210; Bar-On, *Etgar VeTigrah*, pp. 154–7.
36. On these attempts, see Tal, 'The American–Israeli Security Treaty'.
37. Protocol of meeting of Mapai Political Committee, 28 Dec. 1955, LPA, 26/56; Dayan, *Avnei Derekh*, pp. 174–5, 215–16; *Divrei HaKnesset*, Vol. XX, p. 2069, 19 June 1956. See also Ben-Gurion's speeches, in ibid., p. 2070, 19 June 1956, and to the Mapai Convention, 26 August 1956, in *Ma'arekhet Sinai*, pp. 147–52.
38. Sharett, *Yoman Ishi* Vol. 5, pp. 1385–6, entry for 3 April 1956.
39. Ben-Gurion's letter to Sharett, 26 March 1954, in Sharett, *Yoman Ishi 2*, p. 418; Ben-Gurion repeated this theme in his letter to Sharett on 16 April 1955, ibid., Vol. 4, pp. 937–8.
40. On Sharett's successful interdiction of Ben-Gurion's military ideas, see Sharett, *Yoman Ishi*, Vol. 3, pp. 874–5, entry for 29 March 1955; p. 894–9, entries for 3 and 4 April 1955; BGD, entry for 6 April 1955; and Sharett, *Yoman Ishi*, Vol. 5, p. 1375, entry for 18 March 1956; Sharett's letter to Ben-Gurion, ibid., pp. 1378–9.
41. Sharett, *Yoman Ishi*, Vol. 5, p. 1403, entry for 17 May 1956; pp. 1404–5, entry for 27 May 1956.
42. Sharett, *Yoman Ishi*, Vol. 5, p. 1411, entry for 1 June 1956; pp. 1412–14, entry for 3 June 1956; pp. 1455–8, entry for 18 June 1956.
43. BGD, entry for 29 July 1956; Dayan, *Avnei Derekh*, pp. 218–19.
44. BGD, 3 August 1956; Peres, *Kela David*, p. 155.

1

Suez: The Last Imperial War or an Imperial Hangover?

ARON SHAI

When Churchill once again found himself Prime Minister in October 1951, he brought with him to Downing Street an unusual combination of strengths and weaknesses. He was now the most remarkable war leader in Britain's history, a leader of legendary proportions. Nevertheless, as during the Second World War, he tended to overestimate both Britain's strength and its ability to shape US policies. From 1951 onwards, most of his time was in fact devoted to conducting a careful and determined rearguard action against the assault of time.[1] As a staunch conservative he was unable to accept the winds of change, especially so far as the empire was concerned. Even as late as 1943, when the future of Burma – still under Japanese occupation – was being debated, and its governor was looking ahead to the eventual self-government of the colony, Churchill wrote to the Secretary of State, Leo Amery, that the governor seemed to have been 'talking a lot of nonsense'. And when Amery replied to the effect that the governor's words had been entirely in keeping with British policy, Churchill reiterated that it was 'a most ill-timed utterance'.[2]

Indeed, while in the early 1950s Britain's resources shrank steadily and its electorate's demands for greater government spending on social welfare programmes continued to rise, the cost of a world role for Britain became increasingly difficult to sustain. The only question remaining was to what extent, by whom, and how rapidly this reality would be accepted and internalized. Raymond Callahan's thesis that Churchill's continuing presence as head of government served to mask the great inequality between the United States and Britain seems to be most penetrating. It can even be argued that Churchill's very retention of office managed to camouflage and hide the discrepancy between the objective reality and the vanity of the illusion of power. His continued presence, in fact, slowed down what might have been a much quicker and healthier British realization that times had changed, that the old world, the imperial world, no longer existed. The realization, when it did eventually come about during the Suez crisis, 18 months after Churchill's departure from office, had therefore to be painful and sudden.[3] Against this background, it may perhaps be argued that Churchill's final years as Prime Minister had negative consequences and were counter-productive as far as Britain's interests were concerned. Perhaps it might even be said that he should have taken his wife's advice and retired in 1945.

In 1955, in his last great speech on deterrence before the House of Commons which in fact addressed Britain's decision to construct its own hydrogen bomb, Churchill spoke about the world being divided between two creeds. 'We have...', he declared, 'the geographical division of the Mongol invasion in the thirteenth century, only more ruthless and more thorough.' He then went on and developed an argument for a strategy of deterrence. Indeed, it seems that the most dominant factor in British history in the postwar years was that very gap between the new emerging reality and the perception of that reality; the persistent conducting of a rearguard political and diplomatic operation which eventually, by 1956, metamorphosed into a pathetic, if not tragicomic, war as Britain found itself unable to wage a real imperial war as in days gone by.

Investigating British foreign policies in the 1940s and the 1950s, a case can be made that rather than embarking upon real imperial action, what Britain did, in fact, was to initiate a gesture derived from an imperial spasm, imperial momentum, or simply from an 'imperial hangover'.[4] The question to be asked is simply: Did Britain actually, rationally and intentionally, control its actions? Reference to an 'imperial hangover', alludes to developments connected with the imperial powers' relationship with the objects of imperialism, for instance, to Egypt and the Suez Canal which constituted significant parts of Britain's empire. The term may reinforce other terms like 'imperial spasm' or 'imperial momentum' which express attempts at restoring a unique bygone relationship. Indeed, while the Second World War served to hasten the rate of change in the objective, financial, military and diplomatic realities, old legacies and obsolete perceptions lagged behind these changes. It is this very dichotomy that characterized Britain's attempts, pathetic at times, to carry on playing a role it had been accustomed to for decades.

It should be remembered that on the whole, this state of affairs first became publicly discernible (perhaps surprisingly and unexpectedly) under the 1945 and 1950 Labour governments. It persisted under Churchill's and Eden's Conservative leadership. Indeed, it can be argued that Labour leaders were by no means less imperial in their basic practical attitude than their Tory counterparts. In his thorough research on Arab nationalism, the United States, and postwar imperialism, Wm. Roger Louis has already observed that under Bevin's leadership in the Foreign Office, the British prided themselves on a pragmatic approach to international and imperial problems, yet the phrase 'jugular vein of the Empire', when Suez was mentioned, still echoed and evoked a strong passion. When Bevin explained that British evacuation from the Suez base would be impossible because the Egyptians lacked the technical expertise to run it, he deeply and irreversibly insulted the Egyptians.[5]

Since discussions about the Canal Zone were taking place in the midst of the Korean War, British chiefs of staff found a congenial atmosphere in which not to yield on the issue of evacuation. Egypt, they argued, was the only country that fulfilled the strategic requirements of housing a base capable of supporting a major campaign in the Middle East.[6] Churchill, for his part, tried to block the 1954 agreement stipulating that British troops would withdraw over a period of 20 months, but that the facilities of the base were to remain available in the event of a threat to any Arab state or to Britain's NATO partner, Turkey. The so-called 'temporary occupation' of Egypt, which began in 1882, was to end 74 years later.[7] Yet, Churchill hoped that 'temporary occupation' would continue. Indeed, on both the Egyptian issue and the Sudan question an imperial spasm or 'hangover' was noticeable. These were not the only cases.

This chapter will suggest, on the basis of a thorough examination of other imperial cases, both formal and informal, in the decade under discussion, that far from being linear imperial decline was characterized by fluctuation, spasm and false momentum. Prior to the Suez crisis, students of the Palestine, Hong Kong and even the China questions witnessed the same erratic, spasmodic, dialectical and fluctuating motion. What was the historic, perhaps poetic, price paid for the political mistakes committed, for the hubris of holding on to an illusion of power, for constantly lagging behind reality? Elsewhere, I have attempted to demonstrate that at least in the East Asian context, the historic penalty imposed on Britain for misunderstanding and misrepresenting the new post-imperial reality, for permissively and lavishly wallowing in a state of 'imperial hangover', was 'imperial imprisonment' or 'hostage capitalism'.[8]

Prolonging a situation no longer compatible with the spirit of the times resulted in the somewhat surprising confiscation of the assets of the ex-colonial powers by the existing states, or alternatively, by new revolutionary regimes in existing states. Imperial representatives and metropolitan assets were at times even held hostage. While in China, particularly in Shanghai, the new communist government prevented managers of foreign firms (mainly British and French) from leaving the country for a few years until it was satisfied that wages and taxes had been duly paid and assets transferred to the state, it is suggested here that during the Suez crisis and in its aftermath, an instance of 'imperial imprisonment' may have occurred. It is by no means being argued that the cases of China and Egypt are inherently similar – far from it. Rather, I am suggesting that Britain's global position in the mid-1950s was feeble. Its investments and assets were threatened by emerging nationalist movements (Mao's China, Nasser's Egypt and others), and new answers had to be given to analogous challenges.

In order to understand fully the consequences of the 1956 war, developments and agreements of the late 1950s should be analysed and studied. Instead of obtaining safeguards for traffic through the canal, Britain and France lost the use of it for months and suffered oil shortages which reduced them to pleading with oil interests in the United States for a relaxation of restrictions on US oil production. Far from regaining full possession of the Canal Zone, Britain lost even its residual right (retained in 1954) to use the base there in times of war. In the economic sphere, the changing times and the irony of the situation were perhaps the most striking. Rather than enhancing their interests, British and French investments and assets in Egypt were in fact seized by the Egyptian government.

It may thus be argued, that in fact imperialism was reversed, and monies and assets, rather than being transferred at will from the periphery to the metropolitan core, remained securely held in perpetuity in revolutionary Egypt. Moreover, Nasser managed to sequester all British and French, not to mention Jewish, property.[9]

'The Suez crisis did not so much end as fade away', as Diane Kunz reminds us.[10] In April 1957, the Suez Canal, now totally under Egyptian control, was reopened to shipping. British authorities were soon to permit their ships to pay dues to Egyptian canal authorities in order to use the canal. No form of international control over the waterway was accepted by Nasser. British and Egyptian officials concurrently entered into negotiations over blocked Egyptian accounts and compensation for British property that had been sequestered.

In July 1958 the Suez Canal Company reached a settlement with the Egyptian government. The end result, as far as the imperial powers were concerned, was a far cry from the rhetoric of 1956.[11] In exchange for full legal possession of all Canal Company assets outside Egypt (amounting to about US$240 million), compensation for Egypt's nationalization (US$69 million) and the dues the Egyptians had collected between 1956 and 1958 (US$15 million), the company assumed the liabilities incurred by it abroad and renounced all rights to the canal. In short, for an amount of some US$324 million, the Egyptians managed not only to get rid of some unpleasant liabilities, but also to secure potentially prosperous business undertakings without really incurring either the odium or the financial burden of full and real compensation, if such a notion exists at all. They now controlled assets which had been built up over many decades of foreign investment and commercial activities. The imperial powers, for their part, were in fact compelled to abandon their assets ahead of time rather than carry on sinking more money and prestige without return. An agreement with the French was signed a month later.[12]

Nasser, instead of becoming a figure of shame, emerged as the Arab world's mightiest hero, having successfully defied two Great Powers, and liberated his country from the fetters of imperialism.[13]

Indeed, as Diane Kunz has demonstrated, economic diplomacy (an important emerging discipline in itself) is of the utmost importance to our understanding of international affairs, especially at crucial junctures.[14] While economic weapons proved to be ineffective against Egypt, which benefited both from a lack of economic pretensions and from alternative sources of financial sustenance, Britain and Israel were much more liable to economic pressure.

Britain struggled under blows from the United States (no support for sterling and no oil for Western Europe). Yet it remained economically vulnerable and this hardly matched its subjective self-image and the state of imperial hangover in which it remained enmeshed. Britain's vulnerability was a direct result of it having placed so much weight on the importance of sterling. Britain thus eventually agreed to withdraw from Egypt, trailing its French ally in its wake.[15] It should be noted, however, that the run on sterling the week following the landing of British and French paratroops near Port Said on 5 November 1956 was not as serious as Harold Macmillan, the Chancellor of the Exchequer, informed the cabinet – US$280 million. Nevertheless, there seems to have been a real financial crisis. From the moment the canal was nationalized the sterling exchange rate ceased to be credible and such credibility as had been gained was reduced decisively by the invasion.[16]

In practical terms 'imperialism imprisoned' meant that, just like the proverbial fox, the imperial powers were unable to leave the vineyard with their stomachs full since imperial spoils had to be duly returned. Indeed, something that empires with territorial ambition and imperial grandeur apparently find hard to learn is, as Sir Ivone Kirkpatrick put it, the ability to 'perish gracefully'.[17]

NOTES

1. R.A. Callahan, *Churchill: Retreat from Empire* (Wilmington, DE: Scholarly Resources, 1984) p. 258.
2. C. Thorne, *Allies of a Kind: The United States, Britain and the War against Japan,*

1941–1945, (London: Oxford University Press, 1978), p. 345.
3. Callahan, *Churchill*, pp. 258–65.
4. A. Shai, *Britain and China 1941–1947: Imperial Momentum* (London: Macmillan/St Antony's College, Oxford, 1984), pp. 2–3, 6–7.
5. Wm. R. Louis, *The British Empire in the Middle East, 1945–1951: Arab Nationalism, the United States, and Post-War Imperialism* (Oxford: Clarendon Press, 1984), pp. 718–35.
6. Ibid.
7. J. Darwin, *Britain and Decolonization: The Retreat from Empire in the Post-War World* (Basingstoke: Macmillan, 1988), p. 208.
8. A. Shai, *The Fate of British and French Firms in China, 1949–1954: Imperialism Imprisoned* (Basingstoke: Macmillan, 1996).
9. D. B. Kunz, *The Economic Diplomacy of the Suez Crisis* (Chapel Hill, NC: University of North Carolina Press, 1991), p. 187.
10. Ibid., p. 186.
11. Ibid., pp. 186, 277, n. 1.
12. Ibid., p. 277, n. 2.
13. G. F. Hudson, *The Hard and Bitter Peace: World Politics since 1945* (London: Pall Mall Press, 1967), p. 142.
14. Kunz, *Economic Diplomacy*. pp. 1–3.
15. Ibid.
16. A. Klug, 'Suez and Sterling: 1956', lecture delivered at the Hebrew University, 4 April 1997. For Macmillan's report to the cabinet see, Keith Kyle, *Suez* (London: Weidenfeld & Nicolson, 1991), p. 335.
17. Kunz, *Economic Diplomacy*. p. 4.

2

Eisenhower and the Sinai Campaign of 1956: The First Major Crisis in US–Israeli Relations

ISAAC ALTERAS

Israel's attack on Egypt on 29 October 1956 precipitated a crisis of major proportions in US–Israeli relations, the first of its kind since the creation of the Jewish state. With President Dwight D. Eisenhower leading the way and his Secretary of State, John Foster Dulles, carrying out the president's instructions, the administration embarked on an intensive and relentless diplomatic offensive in the Security Council and the General Assembly of the United Nations aimed at bringing about an immediate cessation of the fighting and the prompt withdrawal of Israeli troops from conquered Egyptian territory. Subsequently, and most surprisingly, the United States threatened to consent to the imposition by the United Nations of economic and military sanctions if Israel refused to withdraw unconditionally from the Sinai, the Gaza Strip and Sharm al-Shaykh. Needless to say such policies if carried out would have seriously under-mined Israel's economic viability and eventually its existence as a state.[1]

This negative attitude, if not outright hostility towards Israel must be seen in the context of US (Western) military, economic and political interests in the Middle East and as part and parcel of a global strategy aimed at containing Soviet attempts to penetrate this very important part of the world. To Eisenhower and Dulles, the Arab Middle East was a region of great strategic, political and economic importance to the free world because of its petroleum resources which were vital to the security and well-being of the West. In Dulles's words, 'the North Atlantic Treaty forces in Europe and the Mediterranean fly on Mideast oil'.[2] And a US National Security report warned the president that 'should the Soviets gain a Middle East position from which they could restrict this oil supply, Western Europeans' will to resist communist collaboration would be greatly weakened.'[3] The region was also viewed as important for its global setting, because it contained essential locations for strategic military bases in any world conflict against the Soviet Union. In addition, the presence of the holy places of the Christian, Jewish and Muslim world exerted religious and cultural influences affecting people everywhere.[4]

In their attempts to block Soviet influence in the Middle East, Eisenhower and Dulles soon realized that the Arab–Israeli conflict had given the Soviet Union its greatest opportunity to exploit Arab grievances against Israel and gain a foothold in the area. How could Arab cooperation against the Soviet Union be won if Arab eyes were focused on the 'loss' of Palestine and the 'menace' of 'an expansionist' Israel? What is more, the Arabs viewed the United States as closely associated with this problem. In this sense, a regional conflict became tied inextricably to the global balance of power between East and West.[5]

The solution to this problem, so Eisenhower and Dulles had hoped, would be a US policy of even-handedness, or what they liked to call 'friendly impartiality' in the Arab–Israeli conflict, replacing Truman's policy of a 'special relationship' with Israel. Accordingly, US policy would no longer be influenced by internal considerations (i.e. the Jewish vote), and both Israel and the Arab states would be treated equally, without any preference for the former over the latter as was the case during the Truman administration.[6] In practical terms, 'friendly impartiality' meant that the United States would disassociate itself publicly from various Israeli policies and actions and even condemn them in order to avoid antagonizing the Arabs. Thus the United States in July 1953, censured the transfer of Israel's Foreign Ministry from Tel Aviv to Jerusalem. In October of the same year, it condemned and used economic assistance as a 'stick' to halt Israel's water project in the demilitarized zone with Syria. The United States strongly denounced Israeli retaliatory raids against Arab infiltrators (*fedayeen*), as in the case of Qibya and Gaza. Eisenhower and Dulles also refused Israel's entreaties for a security pact or arms deliveries in the aftermath of the Egyptian–Czechoslovakian arms deal of September 1955. All these actions by the Eisenhower administration caused strains in the relationship between the two countries. In a sense, the Sinai campaign against Egypt further aggravated an already strained relationship, with the United States moving as quickly as possible not only to disassociate itself completely from the Israeli action but to adopt an uncompromising line towards Israel in order to convince the Arabs beyond any doubt as to where the United States stood, thereby preventing Soviet gains from the crisis.[7]

Israel's attack on Egypt caught the administration by surprise, since it expected an attack on Jordan rather than Egypt.[8] Israel's disinformation campaign which tried to disguise its true intentions by pointing to the security threat to Israel posed by the entry of Iraqi troops into Jordan, had worked, but at a heavy price: a deterioration in relations with its most important friend, something Israeli leaders failed to consider let alone anticipate.[9] After receiving reports from the US ambassador to Israel, Edward Lawson, about full-scale Israeli mobilization, on 27 October, Eisenhower cabled Ben-Gurion: 'So far as I am informed, there has been no entry of Iraqi troops into Jordan. I must frankly express my plea that there be no forcible initiative on the part of your government which could endanger the peace and the growing friendship between [our] two countries.'[10]

A day later another cable reached Ben-Gurion in which the president, still believing that an attack on Jordan was imminent, urged the Israeli Prime Minister that 'no forcible initiative be taken by Israel which would endanger the peace in the Middle East', and provide the Soviet Union with an opportunity to help the Arabs to the detriment of Western strategic, political and economic interests.

Yet, the threat of possible Soviet domination of the Middle East in the wake of the Israeli invasion of Egypt no matter how worrisome to US policy-makers, in my judgement, cannot explain fully the zeal and anger manifested towards Israel. I submit that there was an additional major factor, a personal one, that contributed to Eisenhower's fury. Geopolitical considerations notwithstanding, the Israeli attack on Egypt was to the president a personal affront.

According to Eisenhower's biographer, Stephen Ambrose, the president was badly surprised and he hated to be surprised 'even though experience taught him to expect surprises'. In this case it was far worse. The president felt deceived and double-crossed.[11] Until now he had believed that Ben-Gurion's pledges against a pre-emptive war were genuine. But no longer. Already in July 1953, Eisenhower had offered his assessment of the Israeli premier to Eli Ginsberg, a professor of economics at Columbia University in New York. The president admired the Prime Minister for the dedication, skill and energy with which he pursued his goal but also worried about him 'because he was an extremist who might go the whole way even to war to achieve his goals'.[12] Now in October 1956, the president's early assessment of Ben-Gurion as an 'extremist' had just been confirmed. In his view the Israelis were going to war in order to expand their territory. They wanted more land, 'but to survive they need peace with the Arabs'.[13] Moreover, through its action, Israel was doing a great service to the Soviet Union by diverting world attention from resistance to Soviet repression in Poland and Hungary. The president felt deceived. His personal prestige was at stake. He ordered Dulles to cable Ben-Gurion immediately. 'Foster, you tell them, goddam it, we are going to apply sanctions, we are going to the UN, we are going to do everything to stop this thing.'[14]

Still another element that influenced Eisenhower's negative attitude was the timing of Israel's invasion of the Sinai – eight days before the US presidential elections. He strongly suspected that Ben-Gurion had deliberately timed the attack close to election day in the belief that domestic political considerations would prevent him from taking an anti-Israel stand for fear of losing Jewish votes. That unjustified suspicion only added to his rage. In a conversation with his son, Eisenhower complained, 'well, it looks as if we are in trouble. If the Israelis keep going...I may have to use force to stop them...Then, I'd lose the election. There would go New York, New Jersey, Pennsylvania, Connecticut at least.' Regardless of the political cost, Eisenhower concluded, he would have to bring a halt to what he called 'Israeli aggression' for otherwise he could not live with his conscience.[15]

In a letter to his boyhood friend 'Swede' Hazlett, the subject of domestic politics and Israel's military campaign was again on Eisenhower's mind:

> The administration had realized that Ben-Gurion might try to take advantage of the pre-campaign period to launch a war because of the importance that so many politicians in the past have attached to our Jewish vote. I gave strict orders to the State Department that they should inform Israel that we'd handle our affairs exactly as though we didn't have a Jew in America. The welfare – the best interests of our country were to be the sole criteria on which we operated.[16]

In his rage, Eisenhower overestimated the importance of the Jewish vote in his bid for re-election. Rabbi Abba Hillel Silver, former chairman of the American Zionist Emergency Council and one of the most prominent Jewish leaders in the United States, had already told the president in April 1956, that his re-election was assured, even without a single Jewish vote.

The news of the Israeli attack reached the president while he was *en route* by plane to Florida in the course of the presidential election campaign. He flew back immediately to Washington where he summoned an emergency meeting at the White House. Present were Secretary of State John Foster Dulles, Secretary of Defence Charles Wilson, head of the CIA, Allen W. Dulles, Chairman of the Joint Chiefs of Staff, Arthur W. Radford, and other officials of the State Department and the Pentagon. The president lashed out angrily at Ben-Gurion for his deception. His tirade set the tone for the tense and angry atmosphere permeating the White House meeting. Aggravating the situation were incoming reports describing a build-up of Anglo-French invasion forces around Cyprus. Allen Dulles had for some time strongly suspected a connection between the Israeli attack and the Anglo-French intervention against Nasser.[17] The president interjected: 'We should let the British know at once our position...that nothing justifies double-crossing us. If the British back the Israelis they may find us in the opposition. I don't fancy helping the Egyptians, but I feel our word must be made good, the Tripartite Declaration must be carried out.'[18] The president stressed that the May 1950 Tripartite Declaration and subsequent statements committed the United States to come to the aid of the victim of aggression on either side of the conflict. The United States would redeem its pledge on behalf of Egypt. 'We must make good on our word.' In addition he instructed the secretary of state to bring the issue immediately before the United Nations Security Council (UNSC), 'We plan to get to the UN the first thing in the morning when the doors open, before the Soviet Union gets there.'[19]

For Eisenhower and Dulles, the UN would become the arena where political pressure would be brought to bear to restore the *status quo ante-bellum*, i.e. a cessation of the fighting and the withdrawal of Israeli troops from the Sinai. If necessary, US economic sanctions or the threat thereof would be applied 'so that aggression would not succeed in achieving its aims.' Eisenhower and Dulles had hoped that Britain and France would join the United States in that endeavour. After all, these NATO allies were signatories of the Tripartite Declaration pledging to take measures inside and outside the UN against any power seeking to alter the present borders between Israel and the Arab states by force. To Eisenhower's surprise, neither the British nor the French were in any hurry to cooperate. For a moment, Dulles viewed the reluctance of the two Western European countries to join the United States in calling on Israel to cease military operations as a 'blessing in disguise.' The United States, he told the president would be better off 'going it alone' than with 'our partners who are colonial powers.' Dulles had been greatly worried for two or three years now 'over our identification with powers pursuing colonial policies not compatible with our own.'[20]

While discussing with Dulles the strategy to be followed in the Security Council, the president was handed an urgent message from the British Prime Minister, Anthony Eden. After reading it, the president summarized its contents to Dulles. 'Eden says the attitude of Egypt over the past years has relieved the signatories of the Tripartite Declaration of any obligation.'[21] Unlike Dulles who saw the British position indirectly benefiting the United States, Eisenhower was deeply disappointed. Neither the president nor Dulles was as yet able to detect the true motives behind the British and French policies, namely, their collusion with Israel against Nasser.

Disappointment with the NATO allies would soon turn into outright fury and hostility. In accordance with the secret agreements reached at

Sèvres on 30 October, Britain and France issued a 12-hour ultimatum demanding that both the Israelis and the Egyptians withdraw ten miles from the Suez Canal so that they could intervene to secure the area. To require the Egyptians to withdraw from their own territory, and not require the Israelis to withdraw completely from Egypt ended all public pretence of the non-existence of any collusion. A furious Eisenhower again felt double-crossed – first by the Israelis and now by the United State's two NATO allies; that to him amounted to a betrayal of the special Atlantic relationship.

When Dulles broke the news to the president over the telephone, Eisenhower exploded in anger. In the words of the prominent *New York Times* columnist James Reston, 'the White House crackled with barracks room language the like of which had not been heard since the days of General Grant'. Dulles called the ultimatums 'about as crude and brutal as anything he has ever seen … it's utterly unacceptable'. An exasperated Eisenhower commented, 'they haven't consulted us on anything'. The Egyptians, he feared, would most likely turn to the Russians.[22]

The ultimatums were issued while the Security Council was debating the US-sponsored resolution for an immediate cease-fire and the withdrawal of Israeli troops from Egyptian territory. The draft resolution also implored member states to withhold all military, economic and financial aid from Israel until it had complied with the resolution. In light of the new developments, the US added a paragraph calling on all powers to desist from using or threatening to use force against other countries, thereby hoping to prevent an Anglo-French move in the canal area. The British and the French vetoed the resolution, an action that further intensified Eisenhower's and Dulles's anger and indignation.[23]

Ben-Gurion and the Israeli Foreign Minister Golda Meir assumed that the Anglo-French veto in the Security Council would halt any further anti-Israeli moves by the United States. They were sorely mistaken. The failure of the Security Council to take any action did not at all diminish Eisenhower's determination. He and Dulles decided to transfer the problem to the General Assembly under the terms of the UN for Peace resolution employed by the United States in 1950 during the Korean War.

Eisenhower's ire led to a most unusual situation in relations between the United States and Israel. For approximately 48 hours following the start of the war, White House and State Department officials shunned any contact with official Israeli representatives in Washington and Jerusalem. Instead, the administration used prominent Jewish personalities in the United States, such Rabbi Hillel Silver, Dr Arthur Burns, Dr Eli Ginsberg, attorney Philip S. Ehrlich and businessman James D. Zellerbach, as channels of communication with Abba Eban and Ben-Gurion, thus signalling to Jerusalem that the US Jewish community was actually supporting the administration. In fact Rabbi Silver had already told Eban that Israel's action was a grave error of judgement.[24]

With British and French forces poised to attack Egypt, the crisis assumed wider proportions. The president decided to address the nation on radio and television on the night of 31 October. Before that the White House Chief of Staff Sherman Adams asked Rabbi Silver to convey a message to Ben-Gurion: the president in his upcoming speech would refrain from any condemnation of Israel provided Ben-Gurion would make a public statement announcing that Israel would withdraw from conquered territory having accomplished its main goal, i.e. 'the destruction of the *fedayeen* bases'. Should such a statement be forthcoming, Adams promised, the president 'would reciprocate by including in his broadcast speech a statement of deep appreciation of friendship towards Israel'. Silver delivered the message to Eban, who conveyed it by telephone to Ben-Gurion who replied, 'the enemy is listening and I cannot possibly tell you if we will withdraw or not'.[25] Later that day Ben-Gurion's reply reached Eban who in turn relayed it to Silver, who transmitted it to Adams. Ben-Gurion's message was far from what Eisenhower expected. Israel, the Prime Minister indicated, had no territorial ambitions, and would be prepared to withdraw its forces provided 'Nasser would sign a peace treaty, including clear assurances to abstain from hostile acts against Israel'. That should include 'the dispersion of the *fedayeen* units, the abolition of the economic boycott, the stoppage of the blockade in the Red Sea and the Suez Canal and the abstention from any military alliance against Israel'. Ben-Gurion also emphasized the importance of the US–Israeli friendship as 'one of the most cherished assets of the Israeli government and people'.[26]

Even though Ben-Gurion's reply was far from satisfactory, Eisenhower's speech seemed quite conciliatory towards the NATO allies and Israel, referring to the three nations as 'allies' and 'friends' and implying a willingness to restore good relations once the fighting ended and Israel withdrew from Egyptian territory. The president also informed the people of the United States that with the stalemate in the Security Council, the UN General Assembly (UNGA) despite its lack of any veto power, would now become the forum where world opinion 'can be brought to bear in our quest for a just end to this tormenting problem', the raging war in the Middle East.[27]

While the tone of Eisenhower's public address was restrained towards Israel, in private his anger had not diminished. In fact, the president had been harsher than Dulles. During a National Security Council meeting held on the morning of 1 November, Eisenhower insisted that 'it would be a complete mistake for this country to continue with any kind of aid to Israel which was an aggressor'. When

Dulles enumerated the withholding of certain types of governmental aid, Eisenhower interjected that 'the sanctions outlined seemed a little mild'. Dulles promised to extend them after the General Assembly had condemned Israel for its aggression.[28]

In a meeting with Dulles on 1 November, the first since the outbreak of hostilities, Eban, buoyed by Israel's military successes, tried to change US policy into one that might lead to Nasser's collapse and peace in the Middle East. Dulles listened carefully to Eban's remarks and then, showing some personal misgivings about US policies, replied:

> Look, I'm terribly torn. No one could be happier than I am that Nasser had been beaten. Since Spring I have only had good cause to detest him...Yet can we accept a good end when it is achieved by means that violate the Charter of the UN....If we did that the UN would collapse. So I am forced to turn back to support international law and the Charter. I have to work on the basis that the long-term interests of the US and the world are superior to these considerations of self-benefit. Another thing...if the invaders do not evacuate and go back to the armistice frontier Secretary-General Hammarskjöld will resign.[29]

Dulles presented the same moral argument in his speech before the General Assembly,

> And while, Mr President, I would be the last to say that there can never be circumstances where resort to force may not be employed – and certainly there can be resort to force for defence purposes under Article 51 – it seems to us that...the violent attack by three of our members upon a fourth cannot be treated as other than a grave error, inconsistent with the principles and purposes of the Charter and one which if persisted in, would gravely undermine our Charter and undermine this organization.[30]

In short, for Eisenhower and Dulles, all that mattered now was peace, the integrity of the UN, the rule of law and the principle that aggression would not succeed. Justice must prevail with the United States leading the way. In a sense, moral principles had now merged with strategic interests as the driving force behind US policy. Moreover, for public relations purposes, the staunch commitment to broad principles of justice and international law superseded the question of the balance of power between East and West.[31]

Abba Eban, in a most impressive address, that was heard and seen by millions on Israeli radio and television, defended Israel's action on the basis of Article 51 of the UN Charter which he declared, 'accorded any nation the inherent right of self-defence'. Eban's speech notwithstanding, at dawn on 2 November, by an overwhelming vote of 64 to 5 (Britain, France, Israel, Australia and New Zealand) and 6 abstentions, the General Assembly approved a US-drafted resolution for an 'immediate cease-fire and withdrawal of all occupying forces from Egyptian territory as soon as possible'. Twenty-four hours later, Dulles was hospitalized with severe abdominal pain. For about a week thereafter, the president would be assisted chiefly by acting Secretary of State Herbert Hoover Jr and Henry Cabot Lodge Jr, the US representative at the UN. In essence, Eisenhower was now alone at the helm, determined as ever to intensify the pressure on Israel as well as on Britain and France.

With war raging in the Middle East and Soviet tanks crushing the Hungarian Revolution, an atmosphere of doom – a fear that the world was teetering on the brink of disaster – descended on the deliberations at the UN. In that crisis-laden atmosphere the UNGA voted overwhelmingly for a resolution inspired by the US but submitted by the Canadian Foreign Minister, Lester Pearson. It called for the establishment of a UN Emergency Force (UNEF) to be stationed between Israeli and Egyptian troops for the restoration of freedom of transit in the Suez Canal as soon as possible. Such a force would obviate the need for a British and French invasion purportedly 'to separate the combatants along the Suez Canal'. The General Assembly also renewed its demand that Britain, France and Israel immediately 'declare their acceptance of a cease-fire'.[32]

Ben-Gurion at his home in Tel Aviv, emboldened by Israel's military performance, found the UN debate totally irrelevant. When alarmed officials informed him about the barrage of anti-Israeli speeches delivered there, Ben-Gurion calmed them. 'Why are you so worried?' he asked. 'So long as they are sitting in New York and we are in the Sinai, the situation is not so bad!' That confident mood, however, would soon change to one of great anxiety.[33]

The Soviet Union had just crushed the Hungarian Revolution. The Soviet leadership was now free to tackle the Middle East. On 5 November, Soviet Prime Minister, Nikolai Bulganin dispatched sharply worded letters to the leaders of Britain, France and Israel. Bulganin's letter to Ben-Gurion was brutal, scornful and threatening. It expressed 'unqualified condemnation of the criminal acts of the aggressors' and called on Israel to stop operations and withdraw from Egyptian territory at once, adding: 'The government of Israel is criminally and irresponsibly playing with the fate of peace and the fate of its own people which cannot but leave its impression on the future of Israel and which puts a question mark against the very existence of Israel as a state.' And then this threat: 'The Soviet government is at this moment taking steps to put an end to this war and to restrain the aggressors.'[34]

On 2 November, Eban sent Ben-Gurion a cable describing the Pentagon's fear of possible Soviet intervention. Isser Harel, head of the Israeli intelligence service, Mossad, advised Ben-Gurion that the US would not come to Israel's defence should the Soviet Union take military action against Israel.[35] Coupled with Bulganin's threatening letter, came reports of massive shipments of Soviet weapons to Syria accompanied by 'volunteers'.[36]

The Soviet threat, and the fact that British and French forces had already withdrawn from Egypt, gave Eisenhower additional ammunition to intensify the pressure on Israel to withdraw immediately and unconditionally.

Yet, in spite of all these pressures, Ben-Gurion, at least for the moment, responded with resilience and even defiance. On 7 November, from the rostrum of the Knesset, he declared: 'The Sinai campaign was the greatest and most glorious in the annals of our people.' It restored, he said, 'King Solomon's patrimony from the island of Yotvat (Tiran) in the south to the foothills of Lebanon in the north.' He also made an oblique reference to Israel's intention to annex the Sinai Peninsula. 'Our army', he said, 'did not infringe on Egyptian territory...Our operations were restricted to the Sinai Peninsula alone.' Repeating his response to Eisenhower's message of 31 October, Ben-Gurion also declared:

The armistice agreement with Egypt is dead and buried and cannot be restored to life...we are ready to enter into negotiations for a stable peace, cooperation and good neighbourly relations with Egypt on condition that there are direct negotiations...On no account will Israel agree to the stationing of a foreign force, no matter how it is called in its territory or in any area occupied by it.[37]

This uncompromising triumph in the wake of Israel's great military victory would be short-lived. The speech marked the beginning of a four-month-long uphill diplomatic struggle, culminating in Israel's withdrawal from Egyptian territory under conditions far less favourable than those enumerated in Ben-Gurion's victory speech.

To Eisenhower, Ben-Gurion's speech was 'terrible' news. In an urgent message to the Israeli leader on 8 November, the president minced no words in describing his displeasure:

Any such decision by the Israeli government would seriously undermine the urgent efforts being made by the UN to restore peace in the Middle East and could not but bring about the condemnation of Israel as a violator of the principles as well as the directives of the UN...it is in this context that I urge you to comply with the resolutions of the UN General Assembly dealing with the current crisis and make your decision known immediately.[38]

The same day, acting Secretary of State Herbert Hoover Jr, in a harsh and uncompromising tone, told Reuven Shiloah, minister plenipotentiary at the Israeli embassy in Washington, that Israel's attitude would inevitably lead to most serious measures, 'such as the termination of all governmental and private aid, UN sanctions and eventual expulsion from the international organization.'[39]

From Nahum Goldmann, Ben-Gurion received a gloomy message expressing the view of the American Jewish community:

With regard to Israel's refusal to move from Sinai or even to transfer its positions to an international force...I must tell you that it will be impossible to mobilize an American–Jewish front to support this position. If there will be an open dispute between Israel and the US Government on this point...and if this should lead to cessation of the United Jewish Appeal and Bonds, I foresee great difficulties in renewing these enterprises, even if the American authorities would again give their agreement...What is needed is a step that will prevent an open split with Eisenhower.[40]

Ben-Gurion for the first time took these warnings very seriously. He asked Eban to arrange a secret meeting with Eisenhower in order to explain Israel's position. But Eisenhower would consider such a meeting only after 'the Israelis dropped out of Egyptian territory'. In his punitive mood, the president was not about to award Ben-Gurion with the prestige of a summit meeting. In a telephone conversation with Rabbi Silver on the subject Eisenhower wondered 'whether Ben-Gurion's reputation for balance and rationality was really well founded'.[41]

The warnings from the US, coupled with the Soviet threats of military intervention, eroded Ben-Gurion's earlier resolve. On 8 November, he wrote to Eisenhower: 'We have never planned to annex the Sinai Desert. In view of the UN resolutions regarding the withdrawal of foreign troops from Egypt and the creation of an international force we will, upon the conclusion of satisfactory arrangements with the UN, be willing to withdraw our forces.'[42] A day later the Israeli cabinet accepted the principle of withdrawal.

Although the withdrawal was scheduled to start on 2 December without any preconditions, the overall strategy adopted by Ben-Gurion was to 'withdraw in instalments, quickly enough to avoid a political showdown with the UN and the US, but not so quickly as to bring Israeli forces out of the Sinai and Gaza before achieving Israel's minimal demands'. Those demands included a two-fold US guarantee that would effectively keep the Straits of Tiran open for Israeli navigation and ensure that the Gaza Strip was not returned to Egyptian control.[43]

While Eisenhower had earlier appreciated Israel's agreement of withdrawal in principle, he was not at all mollified by Israel's conditions. In a sharply worded letter to Ben-Gurion on 3 February, he reminded the Israeli premier that three months had passed since Israel promised to withdraw its forces. 'Israel's withdrawal to the general armistice line has not yet been completed.' Israel, he continued, should proceed with its withdrawal without further delay. And then came a warning of the possible imposition of sanctions should Israel refuse to comply with UN resolutions. 'Such continued ignoring of the judgement of nations as expressed in the UN resolutions would almost surely lead to the invoking of further United Nations procedures which could seriously disturb the relations between Israel and other member nations including the United States.'[44]

In a follow-up to the president's warning, Dulles on 5 February, told a press conference that the US would give serious considerations to the UN call for sanctions. Dulles did not oppose the Israeli demand for guarantees. He believed, however, that they should be given only after total Israeli withdrawal to the armistice line. Moreover, he stated that those guarantees should be granted by the UN and not by the United States. At the UN, Hammarskjöld refused to meet any Israeli demands for security guarantees. He maintained that the *status quo* principle did not allow any Israeli presence in Gaza, civilian or military. And although the issue regarding the Straits of Tiran was quite different, according to the secretary-general, the Israeli military action should have no impact on the solution of the problem.

While unable to change official US policy, Israel fared a lot better in the arena of public relations in the United States. During the month of January and beyond, an Israeli public relations campaign succeeded in mobilizing public support for US guarantees of freedom of navigation in the Straits of Tiran. Newspaper editorials which had previously condemned the Israeli invasion of the Sinai and supported the US administration's policy, now opposed Eisenhower's demand for unconditional Israeli withdrawal from the Straits of Tiran – an action that in all likelihood would lead to the restoration of the Egyptian blockade. Now the issue was no longer 'territorial aggrandizement' on Israel's part, but a moral question of basic security needs, as well as a question of fairness.

The threat of sanctions against Israel led to an avalanche of criticism against the administration's policy. The chorus of protests led by members of Congress from both parties and leading public figures, condemned the policy of sanctions as unbalanced and unfair. Now

Jewish groups which had previously been torn between loyalty to Israel and support of the administration, began organizing congressional opposition to sanctions. Leading the charge was none other than William F. Knowland, the Republican senator from California and Senate minority leader. On 5 February, in a statement to the press, he criticized the 'double standard' of the UN in applying sanctions against a small country while side-stepping the question of sanctions against the Soviet Union which had so brutally crushed the Hungarian Revolution. Alexander Wiley, Republican senator from Wisconsin and a ranking Republican on the Foreign Relations Committee, declared that sanctions against Israel would not be fair, justified or even an effective answer to the Middle East dispute. Israel, he said, was entitled to reasonable guarantees that its citizens would not be attacked and that its freedom of navigation in international waters would be safeguarded. The Democrats, for some time now, had opposed the administration's policies. Vocal support for Israel's stance was expressed by such figures as Eleanor Roosevelt, Harry S. Truman and most importantly, by Lyndon B. Johnson, Senate majority leader.

Eisenhower and Dulles could not ignore the criticism emanating from Congress, because the issue was not only moral but political. Congressional displeasure would now affect the administration's general Middle Eastern policy. The question of sanctions had become intertwined with a general programme – the Eisenhower Doctrine for the Middle East which the administration submitted for Senate approval on 5 January 1957. The Democrats threatened to vote against it if the administration insisted on pursuing a policy of sanctions.

Eisenhower and Dulles believed that Israel must withdraw without preconditions in accordance with UN resolutions in order to maintain the prestige and respectability of the international organization, as well as to protect US interests in the Arab world. The longer Israeli troops remained in the Sinai, the more influence the Soviet Union would gain in the Arab world, by blaming the United States for not exerting sufficient pressure on Israel to withdraw. Additionally, the Administration believed, Nasser would in all likelihood obstruct the clearance of the Suez Canal until Israeli troops withdrew from Egyptian territory, consequently depriving Western Europe of oil from the Persian Gulf. Eisenhower and Dulles were facing a difficult dilemma. On the one hand, given Israeli intransigence, preventing a deadlock would require acquiescing to a UN resolution calling for economic and military sanctions on Israel. On the other hand, they became aware that sanctions were domestically unpopular and would face stiff opposition in Congress. The Eisenhower doctrine for which they had lobbied so hard would be doomed to failure unless the administration took a morally favourable attitude towards Israel.

These conflicting pressures led Dulles, with presidential approval, to break the deadlock by conceding partially to Israel's demands for US guarantees outside the context of the UN, something Dulles vowed previously not to do. The outcome was the 11 February 1957 *aide-mémoire* delivered to Eban and Shiloah at the State Department. The document explained the US position on the question of the Straits of Tiran and the Gaza Strip. With respect to the former, the text stated that the 'United States believes that the Gulf of Aqaba constitutes international waters and that no nation has the right forcibly to prevent free and innocent passage and access thereto.' The US, Dulles continued, 'is prepared to exercise the right of free passage of vessels of US registry and join with others to secure general recognition of this right'. Those assurances would be given by the US to Israel on the understanding that Israel would first agree to withdraw its troops in accordance with UN resolution of 2 February 1957.[45]

As to Gaza, Dulles acknowledged that the area had been a source of armed infiltration by *fedayeen* into Israel. However, the Secretary of State maintained that neither the UN nor the US had a right to require Egypt to modify the armistice agreement of 1949, which 'gives Egypt the right and responsibility of occupation'. According to Dulles, 'Israeli withdrawal from Gaza should be prompt and unconditional leaving the future of the area to be worked out through the efforts of the UN.' Finally, according to the *aide-mémoire*, the UNEF would be stationed in both Sharm al-Shaykh and Gaza following Israeli withdrawal.[46]

Dulles eagerly awaited the Israeli reply. At the UN, the Afro-Asian bloc was about to introduce yet another resolution, this time calling for sanctions. But sanctions would be ineffective and would not be voted upon unless the US were to approve them. Consequently, Henry Cabot Lodge kept postponing the vote, hoping that a US–Israeli agreement would obviate the need for it.

Eban saw in the *aide-mémoire* a very important breakthrough. But Ben-Gurion was far less enthusiastic. In its present form, he told Eban, it could not be accepted by Israel, sanctions notwithstanding. He rightly pointed out that the *aide-mémoire* was vague, ambiguous and did not go far enough in recognizing Israel's right to self-defence in the event of Israel's navigation being blocked or the Gaza Strip once again becoming a terrorist base against it. Eban's attempts at getting more 'effective' guarantees from Dulles led an exasperated Eisenhower to instruct his secretary of state to 'make clear to Eban that we're trying to be helpful and if they don't want it we'll have to go along and see what the UN does'.[47]

On 15 February, Dulles and Lodge flew to Thomasville, Georgia, to brief the president and Secretary of the Treasury, George Humphrey, on the Middle East crisis. Dulles was in an angry mood. Ben-Gurion, he told the president, would not agree to withdraw Israeli troops unless Israeli retained civil administration and police power in Gaza. Israel also demanded from the US a guaranteed right of self-defence should Egypt reinstate the blockade. The US, he continued, 'had gone just as far as was possible to try to make it easy and acceptable to the Israelis to withdraw'. Any further guarantee

> would almost surely jeopardize the entire Western influence in the Middle East and make it almost certain that virtually all of the Middle Eastern countries would feel that US policy towards the area was in the last analysis controlled by Jewish influence in the US.[48]

The Arabs would surely turn to the Soviet Union. Eisenhower decided to step up the pressure. Lodge urged immediate action for he could no longer delay a UN vote calling for sanctions. Various options were discussed. The president approved US support for a UN resolution calling on member states to suspend not only governmental assistance to Israel (which the US had already enforced) but also private assistance. Humphrey, after consulting treasury officials, reported that Israel received about US$40 million a year in private tax deductible gifts and about US$60 million worth of Israeli bonds sold each year in the United States. The president thought that the threat to stop the flow of that money should be enough to force Israel to compliance. He urged Humphrey to 'get in touch with one or two leading Jewish personalities who ought to be sympathetic to our position and help to organize some Jewish sentiment.'[49]

But Eisenhower and Dulles, to their dismay, would soon learn that there was no sentiment, Jewish or otherwise, for sanctions, and that of course weakened US leverage on Israel. On 12 February Dulles received a letter from Lyndon Johnson objecting to sanctions. Dulles was very concerned about the possibility of a Congressional resolution to that effect. If that happened, he told Lodge, 'we are going to be in very serious trouble and indeed may lose our authority to impose sanctions...we did not want the Israelis to know we are weak on this thing at all'. The secretary of state complained to Lodge about the 'terrific control the Jews have over the news media and the barrage which the Jews have built on Congressmen'.[50] Adding to the secretary of state's indignation was Senator Knowland's inquiry as to whether the president was still considering sanctions against Israel. Dulles replied: 'Unless the Israelis go we will probably go along with sanctions.' Knowland retorted:

I have gone along as far as I can go and this will mean a parting of the ways...sanctions are pretty serious. I would like to know the timing... I want to send in my resignation as a UN delegate before the delegation votes on sanctions.

An angry and frustrated Dulles pleaded with him to reconsider: 'We cannot have all our policies made in Jerusalem... if we can't get the Israelis out of Egypt the Russians will get them out and in the process we will lose the Middle East.' Knowland was not convinced.[51]

Adding to the administrations' woes was a secret memo from the Special National Intelligence Estimate (SNIE) which questioned the efficacy of sanctions in achieving the desired political results, i.e. Israeli withdrawal. Even with the active implementation of sanctions by the US, the report warned, NATO countries might be reluctant to carry out such a policy. Canada had already indicated it would not cooperate. Germany stated it would not suspend reparation payments and France not only would not take part in such a policy but would actually increase shipments to Israel. The SNIE report concluded, that while sanctions would be harmful, Israel could sustain the pressure for three to twelve months.[52]

With the option of sanctions in deep difficulty, Dulles decided to hammer out an agreement with Eban before the ambassador's return to Jerusalem for consultations with Ben-Gurion. This time, Dulles with Eisenhower's approval, went well beyond the 11 February *aide-mémoire*. The United States, he stated, viewed the Straits of Tiran as an international waterway. Any attack on Israeli ships would be viewed by the US as an attack on Israel proper, thus giving Israel the right to act in self-defence in accordance with Article 51 of the UN Charter. Additional US promises would include a letter from the president to Ben-Gurion stating US responsibilities if the principle of freedom of navigation was violated, as well as US support for Israel to build an alternative to the Suez Canal, i.e. a pipeline linking the Red Sea with the Mediterranean. As to the Gaza Strip, Dulles agreed on demilitarization, the entry of UNEF (its authority and length of stay to be discussed later) and the non-return of the Egyptian army to Gaza.[53]

In order to make Ben-Gurion more amenable to the US position, Eisenhower kept the pressure of sanctions alive even though he knew that the Achilles' heel in the threat of sanctions was the total lack of support in Congress for such action. But the pressure from the UN was mounting. On 22 February six Muslim countries, trying to force the United States into making a decision, introduced a sanctions resolution calling on all states to deny Israel 'all military, economic and financial assistance or facilities'. A spokesman for the group threatened that the Arabs would turn to the Soviet Union if their demands were not satisfied.

All these activities coincided with Eban's attempts to convince Ben-Gurion and the Israeli cabinet to be more forthcoming. Eban returned to Washington with new instructions relating to the future of the Gaza Strip. Ben-Gurion no longer insisted on any Israeli presence there, military or civilian. Israel's interest in Gaza, he told Eban, was security against *fedayeen* attacks and that could be assured by the non-return of Egyptian forces to the area in any form. Any Israeli presence there, he confided to Eban, would mean that Israel would have to absorb 250,000 refugees or rule over them and face world condemnation. But the more likely explanation for Ben-Gurion's change of heart is that he never intended to maintain Israeli rule in Gaza. His previous insistence on an Israeli presence in Gaza was aimed at improving Israel's negotiating position on the question of the Straits of Tiran and the Gulf of Aqaba, the waterway linking Israel with Africa and Asia and the route of vital oil supplies from Iran to the Israeli port of Eilat.[54] Ben-Gurion's about-face on Gaza, now opened the possibility for a resolution of the crisis.

Subsequently, Dulles gave Eban all the assurances sought by Israel in regard to the Straits of Tiran. On Gaza, Dulles was unequivocal – something that Israeli leaders chose to overlook, and that would create a crisis later on. Couching his words in diplomatic nuances, he told Eban, that while the US understood Israel's position that no Egyptian military or civil administration should return to Gaza, legally speaking, Egypt, according to the Armistice Agreement of 1949, had rights that neither the US nor the UN had the authority to abrogate. Dulles only suggested the possibility that Egypt might be convinced not to exercise its rights in practice, an issue Israel should take up with Hammarskjöld.[55]

Dulles wanted Hammarskjöld to give the Israelis 'reasonable' assurances that Egypt would not return to Gaza. But Hammarskjöld, never a friend of Israel, would not. He told Eban that 'he could not promise the non-return of the Egyptians to Gaza'. According to the secretary-general, the Egyptian government agreed that the take-over would be 'exclusively by the UNEF in the first instance'. There was no agreement of how long the 'first instance' would last. Dulles hoped that the Egyptians could be persuaded to stay out of the area permanently and allow the UNEF to be deployed between the armed forces of Egypt and Israel, thereby preventing incursions and raids on either side. The Egyptians for their part, while allowing a UNEF role in Gaza never promised their non-return to the Strip. To Israel's chagrin, neither Hammarskjöld nor Dulles pressed them on that point.[56]

Finally, the impasse was broken with the proposals suggested by the French leaders Guy Mollet and Christian Pineau who were in Washington on a state visit. Israel would announce from the rostrum of the UN its readiness to withdraw in accordance with UN resolutions based on certain 'assumptions' or 'understandings'. The ambiguities in those 'assumptions' and 'understandings' were quite obvious to Ben-Gurion. But as he told Dayan on 28 February, 'we must accept the French proposal because of our complete isolation and the possibility that France also would move away from us and that will place us in great jeopardy because we will not receive arms for defence'.[57]

On 1 March, Golda Meir, from the UN rostrum, declared Israel's withdrawal from Gaza and Sharm al-Shaykh on the basis of the 'assumptions' and 'expectations' that upon Israel's withdrawal the UNEF would be deployed in Gaza and that the take-over of Gaza from the military and civilian control of Israel would be exclusively by the UNEF.

She also declared Israel's expectations that the Gulf of Aqaba and the Straits of Tiran would be open to free navigation for all nations. Any reinstatement of the blockade would entitle Israel to act in self-defence in accordance with Article 51 of the UN Charter. Finally, Golda Meir stated that her government expected that any proposal to remove the UNEF from Sharm al-Shaykh would first be referred to the Advisory Committee of the General Assembly to ensure that no precipitate changes were made that could have the effect of increasing the chances for blockade or belligerency.[58]

But now, Israel was double-crossed by US representative Henry Cabot Lodge who, under pressure from Hammarskjöld and the Afro-Asian bloc in the UN, deviated from the Dulles–Pineau–Eban agreement. Succeeding Golda Meir on the rostrum, he failed to confirm the prearranged agreement declaring Israel's 'assumptions' and 'expectations' as 'legitimate', but instead substituted a half-hearted phrase calling Israel's conditions for withdrawal 'not unreasonable'. What is more, he went out of his way to emphasize the importance of the 1949 armistice agreements which gave Egypt the legal right to control Gaza.

Israel's anger was not assuaged by a personal letter from Eisenhower expressing his gratitude at Israel's decision to withdraw behind the armistice lines, which became irreversible in the present circumstances, despite the quick return of Egyptian military and civil authority in Gaza. Dulles, for his part regretted very much that not all US 'hopes and expectations' were realized. He cautioned Israel to abstain from any action without first notifying the US, and alluded to the fact that Israeli retaliation would not be justified, since Egypt had not yet engaged in any acts of aggression against Israel. Ben-Gurion agreed reluctantly with Dulles's assessment. So far Nasser's action was not worth a military confrontation.[59]

True, Israel had to withdraw under conditions far less desirable than those put forth by Ben-Gurion on 7 November 1956 but Israel did achieve the objectives it had set out for itself on 29 October 1956. Moreover, it did not endure the political humiliation suffered by Britain and France as a result of their ignominious swift withdrawal.

As for the United States, contrary to previous prevailing opinion, Eisenhower, and not Dulles, was in charge of US policy throughout the crisis. The president was even harsher towards Israel than his secretary of state, which in my judgement was not due solely to geopolitical considerations but also to Eisenhower's anger at being deceived by the United States' allies and Ben-Gurion.

All in all, Eisenhower failed to achieve his erstwhile goal of pushing Israel back to the 1949 frontiers without security guarantees on the premise that 'aggressors' should not set conditions for their withdrawal. His guarantee concerning the Straits of Tiran served Israel well ten years later when Nasser reinstated the blockade and precipitated another war. And, despite Eisenhower's contention that domestic political pressures would have no impact on his foreign policy decisions, the facts proved otherwise. If it were not for Congressional opposition to sanctions, generated in large part by US Jewry, Israel would have been forced to withdraw without guarantees. Ben-Gurion's tenacity, Eban's diplomatic skills, backed by a united US Jewish community, had finally produced a resolution to the crisis. The most difficult period in US–Israeli relations had come to an end with relations strengthened and Israeli security relatively enhanced.

NOTES

This paper is based in part on my book *Eisenhower and Israel: United States–Israeli Relations, 1953–1960* (Gainesville, FL: University Press of Florida, 1993).

1. Abraham Ben Zvi, *The United States and Israel: The Limits of the Special Relationship* (New York, NY: Columbia University Press, 1933), pp. 68–9.
2. State Department replies to written questions submitted by Senator J. William Fulbright; see Congress Senate Committee on Foreign Relations and Committee on Armed Services, hearings: The President's Proposal on the Middle East, p. 171.
3. Whitman File, National Security Council Series, NSC 5428, Box 12, Progress Report, 17 May 1956, 'US Policy towards the Middle East' (Eisenhower Library, Abeline, KS).
4. Alteras, *Eisenhower and Israel*, pp. 30, 55.
5. Ben Zvi, *The United States and Israel*, p. 30.
6. Alteras, *Eisenhower and Israel*, p. 77.
7. Steven L. Spiegel, *The Other Arab–Israeli Conflict: Making America's Middle East Policy from Truman to Reagan* (Chicago, IL: University of Chicago Press, 1985), p. 71; William Stivers, 'Eisenhower and the Middle East', in R.A. Melanson and D. Mayers (eds), *Reevaluating Eisenhower: American Foreign Policy in the 1950s* (Chicago, IL: University of Illinois Press, 1987), p. 193. As Dulles told his brother, CIA Director Allen Dulles, in a phone conversation on 17 February 1957, 'if we could not get the Israelis out, Russia will take over the area, by aid to the Arabs in the resumption of war'. Dulles Papers, Box 6, Mudd Manuscript Library, Princeton University, Princeton, NJ.
8. There is evidence that at least some officials within the US administration might have been aware or suspicious of a possible Israeli attack on Egypt. On 24 October, the Federal Bureau of Investigation (FBI) reported that Israel was considering preparations

for military action against Nasser. Another report alleged that 'France may be planning actions in conjunction with Israel against Egypt.' On 26 October Dulles cabled London requesting any information on possible Anglo-French 'complicity' with the Israelis. The Watch Committee set up by the CIA to monitor developments in the Middle East, in analysing the motives behind Israel's full-scale mobilization, did consider the possibility of an Israeli attack against Egypt under the pretext of retaliation for recent border incidents. The US military attaché in Tel Aviv speculated that the French might be working with the Israelis and that an Israeli move against the Straits was a 'good bet.' See Matthew F. Holland, *America and Egypt from Roosevelt to Eisenhower* (Westport, CT: Praeger, 1996), p. 118. On the other hand, James Angleton, the CIA counter-intelligence director who maintained close contacts with Mossad which had, apparently duped him, kept reassuring his superiors that there would be no Israeli attack. See Ian Black and Benny Morris, *Israel's Secret Wars: A History of Israel's Intelligence Services* (New York, NY: Grove Weidenfeld, 1991), p. 132.

9. For more information on the question relating to the entrance of Iraqi troops into Jordan, see Benny Morris, *Israel's Border Wars* (Oxford: Clarendon Press, 1993), p. 411; Black and Morris, *Israel's Secret Wars*, pp. 131–2.

10. Whitman File, Diary Series, 27 Oct. 1956; Israel State Archives (ISA) 2448/6, 27 Oct. 1956, (Prime Minister's Office, Jerusalem).

11. Stephen E. Ambrose, *Eisenhower*, Vol. II (New York, NY: Simon & Schuster, 1990), p. 54.

12. Eli Ginsberg, *My Brother's Keeper* (New Brunswick, NJ: Transaction Books, 1989), p. 78.

13. Emmet J. Hughes, *The Ordeal of Power: A Political Memoir of the Eisenhower Years* (New York, NY: Atheneum, 1963), p. 212.

14. Dwight D. Eisenhower, *The White House Years: Waging Peace 1956–1961* (Garden City, NY: Doubleday, 1963), p. 73; Donald Neff, *Warriors at Suez: Eisenhower Takes America into the Middle East* (New York, NY: Simon & Schuster, 1981), p. 365.

15. Ambrose, *Eisenhower*, p. 353.

16. Whitman File, Diary Series, Box 20, 2 Nov. 1956.

17. *Foreign Relations of the United States* (*FRUS*), Vol. 16, Oct. 26, 1956, p. 790; Herman Finer, *Dulles Over Suez: The Theory and Practice of His Diplomacy* (Chicago, IL: Quadrangle, 1964), p. 365.

18. Eisenhower, *The White House Years*, p. 73.

19. Neff, *Warriors at Suez*, p. 365.

20. Alteras, *Eisenhower and Israel*, p. 225.

21. Whitman File, Diary Series, Box 19, Memorandum of Conference with the President, 30 Oct. 1956.

22. All quotes from Whitman File, Diary Series, telephone call, Dulles to Eisenhower, 2:17 pm, 30 Oct. 1956. For a comprehensive study of the Suez War, see Keith Kyle, *Suez* (New York, NY: St Martin's Press, 1991).

23. Alteras, *Eisenhower and Israel*, p. 229.

24. Haggai Eshed, *Mossad shel ish Ehad: Reuven Shiloah Av' Ha-Modyin Ha-Israeli* [One Man's Mossad: Reuven Shiloah, Father of the Israeli Intelligence Service] (Tel-Aviv: Edonim, 1988), pp. 219–21; Ginsberg, *My Brother's Keeper*, p. 80; Abba Eban, *Personal Witness: Israel through My Eyes* (New York, NY: Putnam's, 1992), p. 224.

25. Abba Eban, *An Autobiography* (New York, NY: Random House, 1977), p. 117.

26. Ibid., p. 218.

27. *The New York Times*, 1 Nov. 1956.

28. Ambrose, *Eisenhower*, p. 364; Diane Kunz, *The Economic Diplomacy of the Suez Crisis* (Chapel Hill, NC: University of North Carolina Press, 1991), pp. 166–7; Alteras, *Eisenhower and Israel*, p. 233. Among the economic sanctions in place were the postponement of a scheduled trip to Israel by a team from the Export–Import Bank which would delay if not cancel a badly needed US$75 million loan to Israel. Also held up were negotiations concerning the utilization of grant-in-aid and the Food Surplus Agreement, as well as several technical assistance programmes.

29. *FRUS*, Vol. 16, 1 Nov. 1956, pp. 925–7; Eban, *An Autobiography*, pp. 219–20; Finer,

Dulles over Suez, p. 392.
30. *The New York Times*, 2 Nov. 1956.
31. Ben Zvi, *The United States and Israel*, p. 519.
32. Alteras, *Eisenhower and Israel*, p. 238.
33. Moshe Dayan, *Story of My Life* (New York, NY: Morrow, 1967), p. 249.
34. Finer, p. 419. For the full text of the letters between Ben-Gurion and Bulganin, see, Moshe Zak, *Arbayim Shnot Du-Siah im Moskva* [Forty Years of Dialogue with Moscow] (Tel-Aviv: Ma'ariv Guild, 1989), pp. 181–2.
35. Ibid., p. 180.
36. *FRUS*, Vol. 16, 1956, p. 1014.
37. Michael Brecher, *Decisions in Israel's Foreign Policy*, (New Haven, CT: Yale University Press, 1967), p. 282; Ben Zvi, *The United States and Israel*, p. 63.
38. ISA, 2448/13, 8 Nov. 1956.
39. Alteras, *Eisenhower and Israel*, p. 77.
40. Brecher, *Decisions in Israel's Foreign Policy*, p. 287.
41. Eban, *An Autobiography*, p. 231.
42. ISA, 2456/4/B, 8 Nov. 1956.
43. Ben Zvi, *The United States and Israel*, p. 67; Alteras, *Eisenhower and Israel*, pp. 252–3.
44. ISA, 2448/6, 3 Feb. 1957.
45. Alteras, *Eisenhower and Israel*, p. 262.
46. ISA, 2448/6, 11 Feb. 1957; *FRUS.*, Vol. 17, 11 Feb. 1957, pp. 132–4.
47. Dulles Papers, telephone call series, Box 6, 15 Feb. 1957.
48. Alteras, *Eisenhower and Israel*, p. 264.
49. Ambrose, *Eisenhower*, pp. 286–7.
50. Dulles Papers, telephone call series, Box 6, 12 Feb. 1957.
51. Ibid.
52. *FRUS*, Vol.17, 19 Feb. 1957, pp. 208–11.
53. ISA, 2448/16, 19 Feb. 1957.
54. Gideon Rafael, *Destination Peace: Three Decades of Israeli Foreign Policy* (New York, NY: Stein and Day, 1981), p. 64.
55. ISA, 2448/6, 24 Feb. 1957.
56. Eedson M. Burns, *Between Arab and Israeli* (Toronto: Clark, Irwin, 1963), p. 269; Kyle, *Suez*, pp. 540–41.
57. Ben-Gurion, *Diary*, 27 Feb. 1957.
58. For the complete text of Golda Meir's speech, see UN General Assembly, Official Records, 11th Session, 666th meeting, pp. 1275–6.
59. ISA, 2456/4, 14 March 1957.

3

France and the Crisis of Suez: An Appraisal, Forty Years On

PAUL GAUJAC

In 1984, 30 years after the Suez campaign, the Information and Public Relations Office of the French armed forces asked me to put together for the public, a volume covering the military events of 1956. At the outset, I was surprised by the small number of documented texts published in France. As for the archives, these turned out to be deficient, sometimes non-existent, and the witnesses practically silent.

The reasons for this soon became obvious: first, the secrecy that accompanied the preparation and the execution of the Suez campaign, and second, the discontent and bitterness provoked in the entire country by the affront endured under the pressure of the Great Powers and the UN.

Nevertheless, I was able to carry out the project devoted mainly to the military aspects of the French–British operations, based upon documents which had been withheld from public view by the army, navy and air force centres of military history of the French army at Vincennes. For the first time these documents were put at the disposal of a researcher.[1] Upon publication in September 1986, I expected remarks or criticisms but received none.

DISCONTENT SURROUNDING THE SUEZ CAMPAIGN

The impression of discontent felt in 1959–60 by those I met in Algeria who had been bound for Cyprus and Egypt, and then in 1984–85 during the research[2] commissioned by the armed forces, was confirmed during lectures or signing sessions after the book's publication. Time had passed, we had left Algeria, but for the French army and the French people, the campaign in Egypt remained a synonym for missed opportunities and failure imposed by the international community. The success of the aid to Israel went undisclosed because of the need for secrecy, while the bitterness of being stopped on the road to Cairo and of being replaced by 'perfumed' UN soldiers, remained.

One would think that by the fortieth anniversary of the Suez campaign such erroneous impressions would have been obsolete. But there have been only a few disclosures, such as some interviews with witnesses by the provincial press, a series of articles on French fighters in Israel,[3] and the involvement of merchant ships in the clandestine transport of military equipment.[4] In 1996 the magazine *Historia*[5] devoted a special issue to 'The Failure of Suez', which included some interesting testimonies. However, it examined only two theses and did not refer directly to 'French–Israeli collusion'. According to the first, the failure of Suez lay in depriving the military of an attainable victory over a country which abetted the Algerian uprising. The second argued that it had been a mistake to link Egypt and Algeria, and that the French should never have become involved in a military confrontation.

To everyone's surprise, the Information and Public Relations Office of the French air force produced a 20-page illustrated magazine for the fortieth anniversary, which was extremely bold and well-documented. Carried out in cooperation with the Historical Service of the air force, it presented a number of extremely interesting testimonies in which collaboration with the Israelis was, for the first time, openly acknowledged.[6] One of the testimonies confirmed the secrecy surrounding the action, which had been fiercely maintained until that moment:

> The decision to maintain secrecy for a very long time was the government's. Thus when medals were awarded, it was stressed that the citations would not appear in the Official Bulletin. Things went so far, that we were confined to our base for several weeks after our return. We were asked to destroy all the archives regarding this action. Needless to say, all the orders which the Israelis sent us daily, the day-to-day progression of the war, all those documents were destroyed as well.[7]

The most important event marking the anniversary of Suez was the organization of a round table in Paris in October 1996, during which British, Israeli, US and French participants and historians could finally engage in a dialogue and freely give details and disclosures about their roles at the time of the events, as well as the discoveries they had made by checking the archives that were gradually being opened to researchers.[8]

Nevertheless, restricted as they were to specialized magazines and to meetings of historians, such revelations reached neither the public nor the mass media, and so the discontent caused by this unfortunate expedition continues to exist. Public opinion continues to maintain a facile and unrealistic perception of a single 'war' which began with the 'events' of Algeria. In fact, there was not only one war, but rather several wars nested one within the other like Russian dolls: the official and unofficial diplomatic war, the war between the British and the French, the war with NATO and the United States, the French–Israeli war, the special services war, the generals' war, and many more. Three of those wars – the French–British, the French–Israeli and the so-called Franco-French war – deserve to be analysed carefully here, at least according to French viewpoints and their political–military aspects.

THE FRENCH–BRITISH *MISENTENTE CORDIALE*

The major mistake of the French was to put themselves deliberately under British leadership. There were several reasons for this choice which was made at the very beginning by the French defence attaché in London: the relative strength of the armed forces (50,000 British versus 30,000 French), the use of Cyprus, the fact that Egypt was within the traditional sphere of British influence, and the special relations with the United States which guaranteed its neutrality during the operation.

But the decision, taken primarily for military reasons, had the direct consequence of putting the main political weight onto London and of placing the French under British command where liaisons and consequently signal codes were concerned. Such a situation, in a coalition war, is always unfortunate if communication is less than perfect and if aims are different or opposing.

The French had thus to accept the system of collegial command kept by the British in spite of their absorption into NATO, where the leader giving orders to his staff was the rule. Such a system[9] was not adapted to the habits and the constitution of the French, and in this particular situation, it was not suitable. According to the French air force, in its report after the action:

> the collegial system of the English spreads responsibilities and dilutes them, and although it cancels serious mistakes it does give rise to mediocrity. Our system is loyal to the concept of one single leader who decides alone; this may be the source of serious miscalculation, it is true, but it is often the best method to exploit successfully and quickly the advantages found in unforeseen circumstances.[10]

The integration occurred, nevertheless, without difficulties, since

French officers at all levels were picked according to their familiarity with the English language and the British forces. General Keightley's[11] deputy, Admiral Pierre Barjot, who had been commanding the Mediterranean Fleet for a year, served in the Free French Forces during the Second World War. General Stockwell's deputy,[12] General Beaufre,[13] who spoke English fluently, was posted in Washington and later became a lecturer at the Staff College in Camberley, England. As for the airman, General Brohon, he had been in the Royal Air Force Bomber Command and taken courses at the former staff school.

With the delegates selected, the endless staff discussions began. Besides the collegial system, the French were confronted with British slowness. This slowness was legendary – a US general in NATO said at the time to a group of French officers: 'The English always take twice as long to make any kind of move.' This did not suit the French, who, ever since the end of the conflict with the Germans, had been fighting in Algeria, whereas the British army, apart from those of its troops committed against Cypriot partisans, was enjoying a peaceful era.

Some French, of course, tried to overcome those drawbacks. First, upon the request of Admiral Barjot, they attempted to establish direct communication between Paris and Cyprus in order to maintain a certain independence of movement. Then they established a special area – out of limits for the British – where people operating in Israel or preparing a special operation in Egypt could work without being disturbed. Finally, they intervened in the planning of the operation, with relative success: they prevailed in the matter of shortening the time limit for the start of amphibious operations before Egyptian forces were reinforced, but lost out on the issue of linking paratroopers to the 'strategic' level, i.e. the allied commander-in-chief level where direct contact was maintained with governments.[14]

A major shortcoming persisted, which was highlighted by Beaufre in his report on the Egyptian operation:

The establishment of two superimposed echelons of command to deal with the same operation was troublesome. The 'theatre' level (meaning Keightley), organically non-operational, tended from the very beginning to see itself as the joint national command which did not exist, and at a certain point it even demanded direct command of airborne operations (which was requested by French parachutists). The (naval, land and air) task forces echelon, handling all problems of execution, tended to try participating in the general concept. Once more, the old rule that an upper echelon is justified only in cases where it covers several subordinate commands, which was not the case here, had proven true.

The superimposition of those two echelons turned out to be especially damaging after the Israeli victories in the desert and at the time of the imposed cease-fire – two circumstances which demanded urgent and rapid decision making.[15]

Below the brigade level, things seemed to run more smoothly, due possibly to the demands of combat. However, some of the troops noted, in private conversations, incidents in Cyprus regarding sallies into Nicosia, but mainly the fact that some idle French paratroopers stayed in the mountains with the Cyprus underground, a situation which was obviously not to the liking of the British authorities. It also seems that some equipment was 'recovered' from British depots, with or without British consent.

However, beyond the problems of living together and of misunderstanding among officers, which was made worse by differences of approach, the fact remains that each side looked after its own national interests. Obviously, the temporary allies were not fighting the same war. The British, on one hand, were trying to prevent another country from conquering a critical point of passage. The French, on the other hand, in addition to their unequivocal and vigorous assistance to Israel against the Egyptian threat, saw here mainly an opportunity to erase Egypt as an active supporter of Algerian rebels and to take advantage of their victory over Cairo to wipe out the rebellion once and for all. For these reasons the French commander-in-chief in Algeria agreed to pay the price requested: two general reserve divisions – one airborne and one mechanized – for a period of six months.[16]

The position towards Israel was just as ambiguous. Indeed there was no question of collaborating openly with the Israelis, because any kind of common military operation was rejected a priori by the British for two reasons: first, there was still strong resentment within the British army from the Mandate period (General Stockwell had commanded the 16th Airborne Brigade in Palestine in 1946–48); and second the Britsh army did not trust the Israel Defence Forces (IDF) in a traditional war. The reason the French accepted British leadership from the very beginning was out of a desire to overcome British hesitation and drag them into the adventure.

But the French decision to accept British leadership would also have negative consequences for the entire concept of the military expedition: first, due to the geographic distance between various headquarters, which remained in their positions for reasons of secrecy and comfort. The top army brass had to travel between Cyprus, Malta, Libya, Toulon, Algiers and Paris, but it was in London – for purely political reasons – that the planning and the decision-making processes were organized.[17] Consequently, feeling excessively bound to the British signal system,

Barjot had a strictly national communication network set up from Cyprus.

Second, the British feared a repetition of the 1915 disaster at Gallipoli,[18] and demanded a complex operation of combined land, air and sea forces. Then, when there was talk of advancing the airborne operation out of Cyprus in order for it to anticipate the seaborne operation out of Malta – they rejected it outright because of the inadequate Cyprus ports. This time it was no second Arnhem at Port Said![19] As a matter of fact, the operation adopted seemed more like a long-term invasion of Egypt than a quick take-over of the canal.[20]

Lastly, at the command level, General Keightley primarily followed the instructions of his own government, which set different aims from those of the French government. These differences led to a vacillating dance that lasted three months, during which several operational projects were initiated:

- on 15 August, the *Musketeer* plan – landing at Alexandria on 17 September and going up to Cairo;
- on 2 September – postponement of the landing to 25 September;
- on 20 September – a renewed version of the *Musketeer* plan, with the canal as the new target; landing planned for 8 October following a phase, imposed by the British, called 'aerial–psychological';
- on 6 October – winter plan, with conditions that practically put an end to any kind of action;
- on 19 October – winter plan discarded and a new version of *Musketeer* adopted, called *Musketeer Revise*.

As Beaufre wrote in his report:

Everything was political in the Egyptian operation, and French politics were very different from British politics due to the Arab countries and Israel. It was thus essential for us to maintain our freedom of action. It is further possible that the British tendency towards complete integration had as its purpose the complete control of our operations.[21]

THE 'COLLUSION' BETWEEN FRANCE AND ISRAEL

Relations between British and French leaders were complicated mainly by the fact that the French were by then playing a complex and secret game with the Israelis. The first links were formed between officers of both countries in 1952, when Israel decided to purchase part of its military equipment from France. The years that followed witnessed the first Israeli endeavours to neutralize the Quai d'Orsay with its pro-Arab diplomats, by seeking the support of Hotel Matignon and the French army. The latter fully agreed to such cooperation, first because the horrors of the Second World War were still very much alive in their memories, and second – after the eruption of the 1954 Algerian rebellion – because of their common enemies: namely the Arabs and the Soviet Union which assisted them. The veterans of the Free French Forces[22] played a major role in bringing the two countries closer. General Dayan's official visit to Paris in August 1954 further strengthened relations and hastened the delivery of military supplies. At the end of that year an initial agreement was signed between Shimon Peres, director-general of the Israel Defence Ministry, and Diomed Catroux, secretary of state for the French air force, for the purchase of Ouragan and Mystère jet fighters.[23]

A year later, several changes of government notwithstanding, the Israelis obtained delivery of the new aircraft, thanks mainly to the unequivocal support of the defence ministers and Generals Koenig and Billotte.[24] Guy Mollet assumed power in 1956,[25] and the talks were supported by the delivery of ever larger quantities of materièl: Mystère IIC and then Mystère IVA fighters and AMX-13 tanks, in order to counter-balance Soviet and Czech supplies to Egypt. With the arrival of equipment from the Eastern bloc, the correlation of forces, according to the Israelis, stood at a ratio of four to one in favour of Egypt.[26] French officials and politicians did not ignore the pragmatic and mutual interest. But for most French, saving Israel was equivalent to compensation for the German invasion of the Rhineland in 1936 or for the German retreat from Munich in 1938 when Adolf Hitler became powerful and threatened tiny Czechoslovakia.

After August 1956, relations between France and Israel became closer and more secret. The US government had refused to intervene with military means against Colonel Gamal 'Abd al-Nasser who had taken over the control of the Suez Canal. Consequently, the British were willing to consider an expedition against Egypt only after long and thorough preparation. Tired of US opposition and British objections, the French turned progressively towards the Israelis, in order jointly to launch an operation on the canal. But the hostility of the Quai d'Orsay and the refusal of the British to engage in any type of cooperation with Israel dictated a highly covert series of meetings and conversations. On 20 September Defence Minister Maurice Bourgès-Maunoury's[27] cabinet chief Abel Thomas and adviser Colonel Louis Mangin travelled to Tel Aviv. They offered the protection and support of air and naval forces for an eventual Israeli operation which might be accompanied by direct intervention and by a Franco-British landing in Egypt towards the beginning of November.

After a stop in Bizerte for security reasons, General Dayan returned to Paris on 1 October and was received, at the defence minister's request, by General Ely,[28] defence chief of staff, who met him in strictest secrecy at the private home of Louis Mangin. The meeting lasted two hours, in the presence of General Challe and Colonel Simon from the defence staff,[29] who were about to leave for Israel. Dayan tried unsuccessfully to learn the true state of French–British military preparations, and he negotiated a new aid package, including approximately 100 tanks and a large quantity of vehicles. However no final commitment was made, since the French envoys were leaving that same evening.

On 5 October the envoys returned from Israel highly impressed with the outstanding organization and training of the Israeli forces.[30] According to the Israelis, their offensive capacity was strong enough to enable them to reach the bank of the canal alone and to remain there. The delegation's report, which was delivered on 7 October to Bourgès-Maunoury, confirmed the aid requested by Tel Aviv as follows:

- an urgent supply of designated equipment;
- a detachment of air formations able to attack Egyptian aviation;
- the presence of naval units in Israeli ports;
- a landing operation which could create a diversion if the Israelis attacked Sinai.

On 8 October Admiral Barjot received instructions from the minister asking him to study the possibility of an action by the French forces to support Israel, without British participation, or within the first phase of the operation already planned by the allied Chiefs of Staff. Concerning the former option, General Ely wrote in his memoirs: 'The minister [i.e. Bourgès-Maunoury] is aware of the seriousness of a decision which would imply our intervention with Israel without the intervention of the British, but he is also very worried by the consequences upon the troops' morale of the absence of any intervention.'[31]

It is true that the French army was at the time already deeply implicated in the affair. Several bases were operating in Cyprus and the transit camp was ready for the arrival of the troops, who had been training for many months in Algeria and were ready to leave for the island of Aphrodite.

General Ely, for his part, continued to oppose any intervention which was not, from its inception, made in cooperation with the British.[32] Guy Mollet agreed with that viewpoint, but support for Israel in the face of Egyptian threats appeared to him to be a political necessity. Therefore he ordered continuing supplies to Cyprus via Brindisi, escorted by military staff in civilian clothes.

On 10 October Admiral Barjot defined the contours of the combined operation with Israel.[33] It presupposed the positive neutrality of the British, which was essential for using the bases in Cyprus, and of the United States. The Israeli attack, supported by French fighter-bombers and guarded on the coast by French warships, was to be followed by a French raid on Egyptian air forces. The landing at Port Said and Port Fuad would occur only three or four days after the beginning of the Israeli attack, when their forces would be near the canal and they could support the offensive jump off towards El Kantara. Three paratroop regiments would land on the shore: one parachuted, one disembarked and one helicopter-borne from an aircraft carrier. After securing the beachhead, two motorized regiments and helicopters would push in the direction of El Kantara with tanks. Then, with Ismailiya seized by the fourth parachute infantry regiment, the landed forces would advance towards Cairo, with or without the backup of the mechanized division.

On 10 October General Challe also travelled to New York in order to update the minister of foreign affairs, who was participating in a meeting of the UN Security Council, on the developments. On 14 October he was received by British Prime Minister Anthony Eden. Eden was apprised of the state of mind of the Israelis, who were 'determined not to give in and were firm in their decision to defend themselves by taking the offensive, if need be, at the slightest provocation from the Egyptians'. Challe then suggested the following plan: allow the Israelis to attack Egypt, and then let Franco-British forces intervene in the Suez Canal Zone to restore peace by an operation which would appear to bring order to the area.

Strangely enough, Eden did not seem astonished to hear of an Israeli enterprise which had been discussed previously by the French and Israeli authorities. On the contrary, he seemed most interested by the proposal of a combined intervention, and Challe admitted to feeling very 'surprised'. He thought it probable that the discussions between the French and Israelis had not gone unnoticed by the watchful British or US intelligence services.[34] General Ely wondered, for his part, whether the British themselves had not had secret contacts with the Israelis.[35]

On 16 October Guy Mollet succeeded in convincing Eden, who had, arrived secretly in Paris, to follow the Israeli lead and take action before the weather broke in the Eastern Mediterranean and before the presidential elections in the United States. The British accepted the French plan on condition that the Israelis attacked on 1 November and reached the canal on 5 or 6 November; an allied intervention would then be clearly justified in order to protect the waterway threatened by the fighting, after an ultimatum delivered to the two warring sides. And despite the wish to abstain from any 'collusion' with the Israelis and to maintain the façade of independent action, the British agreed finally, with reservations, to the principle of a written commitment to their new allies.

On 22 October, when the episode of the *Athos* – a ship loaded with arms coming from Egypt and intercepted by the French navy off Oran – unsettled all chanceries, Ben-Gurion arrived incognito in Paris and went to Sèvres where secret discussions were held over several days. Ben-Gurion found the words to win over Guy Mollet. He defended the cause of Israel, which faced the threat of being encircled by powerful Arab states. Deeply touched, the president of the council confirmed the direct support which had tacitly been promised by Bourgès-Maunoury: air and sea protection of the coastline and towns, and support of the columns advancing towards the canal by transport airplanes based in Cyprus. French fighter squadrons would arrive on the scene on 27–28 October, immediately after general mobilization in Israel, and the warships would survey the shores starting 29 October.[36]

The plan was adopted by the British after some arguments and alterations, and on 24 October the Tripartite Agreement was achieved, with the signature of a 'declaration of intentions' initialled by the three heads of government. The arrangement constructed with and around Israel had finally obtained the agreement of the British. Without them, the campaign against Egypt would have been buried.

THE FRANCO-FRENCH WAR

Relations were tense not only among British and French decision-makers. Within the French camp itself a 'war among leaders' was said to be brewing.[37]

Having just emerged from a conflict against the Germans, the French army had entered a war in Indo-China which was followed immediately by what was modestly called 'action to maintain order in Algeria' or 'the events in Algeria'. The withdrawal from Indo-China had a profound emotional effect and radicalized the struggle underway in North Africa. The divisions between those soldiers fighting for the empire and those fighting against communism blurred as *fellagha* bands in North Africa and Warsaw Pact divisions in central Europe were increasingly viewed as a single enemy in various guises. The conflicts were integrated further when part of the conventional troops – four armoured or motorized divisions previously under NATO command in France and Germany – were assigned to pacification and counter-guerilla operations. However, differences of temperament and hierarchy meant that sensitivities remained which emerged at the slightest provocation, frequently in connection with Cyprus.

It so happened that history grouped together some sharply contrasting personalities. Barjot, who was known as much for his unorthodoxy as for his efficiency, shocked the traditional British but also annoyed the French with his taste for publicity and his whims. Beaufre, on his part, irritated the French with his British sympathies and his staff college qualifications. As for Admiral Lancelot,[38] who was efficient and much loved in naval circles, he was well known in the Royal Navy for having nearly sunk the battleship HMS *Resolution* off Dakar in 1941 and for his full-fledged success as naval attaché in Washington.

In addition to the eight allied military leaders,[39] one must add on the French side, the commander of airborne operations (Operation Aeroportée – OAP), with no counterpart in the British hierarchy. His task was to study the conditions for the commitment of the airborne forces, to direct their actions and to supply them until contact was made with the amphibious forces. Arriving from Paris, it was General Gilles who carried out those functions. At the head of the airborne division was General Massu assisted by two generals (Beaufre and Gilles), who was also being kept very busy by his strong-willed regiment commanders who were highly jealous of their prerogatives.[40] Although he was from the colonial infantry, he had not fought in Indo-China as a paratrooper.[41]

Although Gilles got along very well with the group of officers of the 10th parachute division (DP), the special services and the transport pilots, 'he didn't have good chemistry with Beaufre'. The paratroopers themselves preferred the casualness and the practical nature of their British leader, Stockwell, who was one of them, to Beaufre – the guarded and brilliant commander of Force A.[42] The British said that 'Beaufre is good in the office, Stockwell is good in the field.' The two, although complementary in character, formed a disastrous team. Stockwell, stubborn as a mule, would consistently reject any decisions taken by Beaufre, however impeccably well presented they were.

Consequently, and against basic logic, the OAP commander was not acknowledged by the British, and his staff did not appear as part of the command organization. However, this detail did not prevent the French from planning and carrying out actions according to their own methods formulated in Indo-China. Thus, the troop carrier wing, the fighter-bomber squadrons and the parachute battalions were all operating under a joint command, in spite of the conflicts with the British command and central system.[43]

Another reason for conflict among the French was the relations of the military command in Cyprus with groups working in Israel, which were enveloped in a shroud of secrecy and conspiracy. In any event, the secret of the operation was well kept. This was no easy task, given that the paratroopers all knew each other and the transport crews and riggers were participating simultaneously in two operations – one out of Cyprus and one out of Israel – which were militarily complementary but politically antagonistic.[44]

Summing up the liaison tasks with the IDF headed by Colonel Simon, one should note above all the protection of Israeli air and sea space, the parachute drop at the Mitla Pass, supplying of columns in the desert, paralysis of the 'Russian tank brigade', and all those actions carried out thanks to inter-allied resources, but without the knowledge or the agreement of the British authorities in Cyprus.

Also in Cyprus was the team known as 'information-action-protection' or RAP 700, formed by representatives of several special services attached to the commander-in-chief of the French forces in the East and to Force A. At its disposal was a group of 420 parachutists of the 11th Shock Brigade[45] to carry out special missions such as clandestine sallies on targets of a political nature or to ensure the protection of French interests or sallies on tactical targets on behalf of the allied intervention force.

But RAP 700, confined to Akrotiri, had very little transport equipment. Completely isolated from the various groups of staff which were mounting the operation, it had no knowledge of the plans drawn, possessed no significant documentation on assigned targets and, clung instinctively, to Gilles's staff. Out of 14 actions requested by the commanders, none could be carried out, either because they were unrealistic, or because the necessary means, and in particular the time allotted for preparation, were insufficient.[46]

Only when a mission was carried out for General Gilles at D-5 did the head of Service Action (the action branch of the SDECE) receive information about the area of invasion and the landing date. The latter suggested that 100 men from the 11th Shock Brigade and the two planes of the special flight be alerted the evening prior to the drop of the 2nd RPC (Colonial Parachute Regiment), in order to intercept the Egyptian retreat from Gaza. As time passed and no decision was taken, General Gilles then assigned them directly to the task of capturing the water processing plant originally designated for the regimental commando unit.

Having carried this out, the riflemen of 11th Shock accompanied Centurion tanks sent in as an advance guard towards Ismailiya. But they would not reach El Kantara; they were stopped at 2 A.M. by a cease-fire which had already been announced on the BBC.

CONCLUSION

Never will that cease-fire – followed by the evacuation of Port Fuad imposed by the United States and the UN – be forgotten by the French, who believed they had been betrayed by their NATO allies. The consequences of this unfortunate expedition, both on the international and the national levels, were just as distressing.

The 'estrangement' of France from both the United States and Britain was real, and the Atlantic Alliance was shaken. As for Nasser, not only was he not expelled from Egypt but he came out of the conflict strengthened, and aid to Algerian rebels continued to increase.

For France, besides successfully defusing the threat to Israel which was an important factor in its decision to enter the war and weighed heavily upon its relations with Britain, the operation was a complete disaster. France had lost its closest allies and its influence in the Near East, and found itself isolated diplomatically and weakened politically at a time when the Algerian crisis demanded to be resolved.

Not only would the Algerian problem not be solved, but it would become an international matter, and support for the rebels would increase and become more diversified: the Soviet bloc would help the rebels militarily, and the Third World countries would do so on the diplomatic and psychological levels. The Bandung Conference and the Suez crisis set the stage for the second phase of decolonization, mainly in Africa, after which France was condemned repeatedly by the UN for its actions in Algeria.

At the same time Britain and the United States applied pressure on the French government to accept their good offices for a solution to the Algerian conflict, which threatened the integrity of the Atlantic Alliance. The possibility of negotiations led on 13 May 1958 to a rebellion by the military who were highly resentful, especially after having been restrained in Indo-China, Morocco and Tunisia, of a government which showed weakness during the campaign against Egypt and the fight against terrorists in the city of Algiers.

Commentators observed that 'the defeat in Suez heralded the May 1958 putsch in Algiers'.[47] The Suez crisis increased the government's uneasy position and underlined the separation between military leaders in Algiers and politicians in Paris. When the parachutists fled to Cyprus, they were convinced that the government was backing them. But when they were obliged to stop 'on the road to Cairo', and then re-embark to Algeria, they knew that this government was like others before and that there was no other way but to change the form of government. This would be confirmed when the men of the 10th DP had to relieve policemen during the Battle of Algiers and were confronted by official weakness concerning the terrorists and their European supporters. For most of the officers at that time, this regime was definitely unreliable.

The Algerian rebellion gave General Charles de Gaulle the opportunity to return to power and, soon afterwards, in September 1958, he asked President Eisenhower to substitute the strictly US command of NATO with a tripartite one. Then he ordered a continuation of the nuclear testing programme despite British and US reservations. He opposed the American project of the union of strategic forces and finally, in 1966–67, he withdrew French troops from the integrated military organization of NATO.

Forty years later, one is still astonished by the futility for France, of this campaign, about which many issues still remain open for investigation. Shrouded in mystery from its very beginning, the *expedition d'Egypte* remains so despite some 'revealing' documents with intriguing titles.[48]

Topics which might interest future researchers include: the performance of the French Special Services and their relations with the diverse lobbies at the Quai d'Orsay, the precise role played by the United States and specially by NATO's Supreme Allied Commander in Europe (SACEUR) and the US Central Intelligence Agency (CIA), the actions of the Arab and Soviet secret service agencies in France, the assistance given to the Israeli armed forces, and the efforts made by France to guarantee support to the mission and to adapt the military and logistic resources to this new situation.[49]

But their task will not be an easy one, as is often the case in France. For reasons of secrecy at the time of the events, all operational documents were destroyed and even their mention in memoirs was omitted. Consequently, military archives are practically devoid of any information. Among private papers, those of General Ely for example, it is possible to find everything except documents concerning the Suez crisis. Material relating to intelligence, if it does exist, can be made available only under certain conditions.[50] As for the witnesses, they still seem to be bound by the oath of secrecy 40 years on, and thus can impart only very little information. But all these reasons should not discourage further investigation.

NOTES

1. Paul Gaujac, *Suez 1956* (Paris and Limoges: Lavauzelle, 1986).
2. The gist is given in the last chapter of *Suez 1956*: 'Suez, Thirty Years Later.' It contains two sections meaningfully titled 'Silence and Revelations' and 'Myths and Reality.'
3. 'Les Dassault Ouragan en Israel', *Le Fana de l'Aviation* 298 (September 1994) and 'Les Mystères IVA en Israel', *Le Fana de l'Aviation* 311 (October 1995).
4. A series of 38 articles (1996: Oct. 25, Nov. 15, 22, 29, Dec. 6, 13, 20; 1998: Jan. 3, 10, 17, 20, 24, 31, Feb. 7, 14, 21, 28, March 7, 14, 21, 28, April 4, 11, 18, 25, May 2, 9, 16, 23, Dec. 5, 12, 19; 1998: July 31, Aug. 7, Sept. 3, 10, 17, 24, Oct. 1, with no author under the heading 'Memoire de l'histoire' in the weekly *Le Marin*.
5. *Historia*, 598 (October 1996).
6. *Air Actualités*, 493 (June 1996), Service d'Information et de Relations Publiques des Armées (SIRPA) Air, Paris. Gone are the days when, as was the case for *Suez 1956*, it was forbidden to publish colour photographs of pursuit planes with a Star of David

manned by French pilots and taking off from Israeli bases.

7. Testimony given by General Vaujour, then a captain leading the Fighter Squadron 1/1 Corse, in *Air Actualités*, 493 (June 1996), p. 36.

8. Symposium, 16–18 October 1996 at the Ecole Militaire by Maurice Vaisse, director of the Centre of Defence History. The proceedings were published by the CEHD as *La France et Operation de Suez de 1956* (Paris: Addim, 1997).

9. According to the collegial system, every decision is taken in concert with the chiefs of the three services after several meetings.

10. Report of General Brohon, commander of Groupement mixte No. 1, in SHAA, Vincennes.

11. General Sir Charles Keightley, allied commander-in-chief for Amilcar, was commander-in-chief of the British Middle East Land Forces at Episcopi (Cyprus) from 1953. He was awarded the French Legion of Honour in 1943 in Tunisia.

12. Lieutenant General Sir Hugh Stockwell, Land Task Force Commander, was previously Corps Commander in Germany.

13. Major-General Beaufre was at SHAPE (Supreme Headquarters Allied Powers in Europe) before taking command of the 2nd Motorized Infantry Division in Eastern Algeria.

14. Report on the airborne action at Port Said – Port Fuad on 5 November 1956 (No. 702/EMOAP/3, dated 18 November 1956). (EMOAP is Etat-Major des Operations Aeroportées, a special unit built around General Gilles' staff from Paris. Its archives are within those of Beaufre's Force A.)

15. Report on the Egyptian operation – Force A, Vol. 2, *The Launching*, and Vol. 3, *The Conquest of Port-Said and Port-Fouad* (Paris: AIA, 1957).

16. The 10th Division Parachutiste, with four of its five regiments, and 7th Division Mécanique Rapide, both from the so-called 'intervention' reserve in the vicinity of Algiers.

17. Report on the Egyptian operation – Force A, Vol. 1: *The Preparation* (Paris: AIA, 1957).

18. During the Dardanelles campaign (June 1915–January 1916), the Allied forces were contained on the shore of the Gallipoli peninsula and failed to capture Constantinople. Their only way out was to evacuate after 250,000 casualties.

19. In September 1944, 10,000 British paratroopers where dropped 'one bridge too far' and failed to seize the one in Arnhem, suffering 7,600 losses.

20. See n. 14.

21. See n. 17.

22. The Forces Francaises Libres, led from 1940 to 1943 by General de Gaulle.

23. *Le Fana de l'Aviation*, 311 (October 1995).

24. General Marie-Pierre Koenig was chief of the Free French Forces at Bir Hakim in 1942, commander of the French Forces of the Interior during the second battle of France in 1944, commander-in-chief of the French-occupied zone in southern Germany in 1945, and minister of defence and the armed forces, June–August 1954 and February–October 1955. General Pierre Billotte was chief of De Gaulle's staff in London in 1941, armoured brigade commander during the liberation of Paris and defence minister from October 1955 to February 1956.

25. Guy Mollet was président du conseil (Prime Minister) from February 1956 to June 1957.

26. See n. 20, and G-2 Force A files, SHAT, Vincennes.

27. Bourges-Maunoury, defence minister from February 1956 to June 1957, was a leader of the French underground during the Second World War. In 1955, as minister of interior he was in charge of the struggle against the Algerian rebels: his sentiment towards Israel was probably not the only motivation for France's support, but during his term in the Ministry of Defence, Algerian affairs were primarily the responsibility of the secretary of state for the army, leaving him time to deal with other matters.

28. General Paul Ely, served during WWII with the ORA (Army underground organization). He was chief of staff of the armed forces from August 1953 to June 1954 and from March 1956 to May 1958.

29. That is, the Armed Forces General Staff, at the ministry level. Air Force General Maurice Challe was the organizer of an intelligence circuit in occupied France in 1943–44. Colonel Jean Simon served with the French Foreign Legion from the very beginning of the Free French movement.

30. Maurice Challe, *Notre révolte* (Paris: Presse de la Cité 1968) p. 27.

31. Suez – on 13 May. General Ely, *Mémoires*, Vol. 2: *Suez et le 13 Mai* (Paris: Editions Mondiales, 1979).

32. We do not know if there was any debate between Ely and Barjot at the time of the planning. What can be said is that Ely, at the political and strategic level, clearly recalled the experience of the Indo-Chinese (France alone) and Korean (France within the UN) Wars and was anxious to find partners to launch the Suez expedition. Barjot, a sailor, concentrated on the operative level: his major concern was the intermediate harbours between the target and his fleet bases in Toulon and Bizerte or Algiers.

33. Namely personal and secret instructions defining the guidelines of Hypothesis I (I for Israel), see Report on the Egyptian Operation, Force A. Vol 1, *The Preparation*.

34. Challe, *Notre révolte*.

35. Ely, *Mémoires*.

36. One might be surprised by Mollet's reaction to Ben-Gurion's appeal and his altruism, but all witnesses agree on his generous nature and the strange mood of secrecy and heroism which reigned at the time in Paris among those involved in the plot, and which was reminiscent of their covert war against the German police a decade before.

37. This section is based primarily upon evidence gathered throughout the years by the author and upon his own personal experience.

38. Rear-Admiral Lancelot, commander of the French naval intervention force, was deputy to the naval task force commander.

39. Allied commander-in-chief, naval, land and air task force commanders with their respective French deputies.

40. At the 10th DP there was a '*tour d'alerte*' (state of readiness) taken by each parachute regiment. Owing to that spell of service, the 2nd Colonial was dropped in Egypt and the 1st Foreign Legion regiment landed at Port Fuad, taking the place of the 3rd Colonial which normally should have come in second position, but whose colonel was injured.

41. Brigadier-General Jean Gilles, a Senegalese battalion commander during the Campaign of Liberation (of Paris), was with the airborne forces in Indo-China and parachuted with them at Dien Bien Phu; his mission in Paris was inspector of airborne troops. Brigadier-General Jacques Massu followed Leclerc and his Free French Forces from Chad to Tunisia, and then his armoured division from Normandy to Indo-China.

42. The Allied expeditionary force in Egypt was code-named 'Amilcar' (Force A); in French it was written 'Hamilcar'. Thus, there was misunderstanding between the allies from the outset.

43. See no. 14.

44. Airborne base diary (Journal des Marches et Operations de la Boap, SHAT) and After Action Report of the 10th Parachute Division (DP) on Operation 700 bis (IOE DP, SHAT).

45. A special unit based in France and Algeria, which carried out missions like those performed today by the British SAS.

46. Reports of operations by the head of RAP 700.

47. *Historia*, 598 (October 1996), p. 1.

48. Merry Bromberger, *Les secrets de l'expédition d'Egypte* (Paris: Les Quatre Fils Aymon, 1957); Bernard La Foresse, *Le bilan de l'équipée d'Egypte, ce que les frères Bromberger n'ont pas pu dire.* (Paris: Editions Etheel, 1957); Andre Beaufre, *L'expédition de Suez ou la vérité sur les sept jours qui auraient peut-être épargné une guerre au monde* (Paris: Grosset, 1967); Jacques Massu, *Vérité sur Suez* (Paris: Plon, 1978); and Thomas Abel *Comment Israël fut sauvé: Les secrets de l'expédition de Suez* (Paris: A. Michel, 1978).

49. The French navy is the only service which, until now has drawn logistic lessons from Operation 700 (Report No. 781 EMG/4/SEC of 4 June 1957 – Service Historique de la Marine, Vincennes). Less involved in the events at the time, the navy was also the only service to look critically at them, or to try to describe their development in 'Reflexions sur les opérations de Suez 1956' by Admiral Barjot in the *Revue de la Défense nationale* (December 1966) or in *La crise de Suez, November 1956–April 1957* by Philippe Masson, published by the Service historique de la Marine in 1966.

50. Sixty years for some files, later for others, with the agreement of the intelligence services.

4

The Soviet Union and the Suez Crisis

LAURENT RUCKER

After seven years of unstable peace, war came once more to the Middle East in October 1956. The major turning point of the Suez crisis tolled the knell of the French and British empires, marked the rise of US power in the region, established Israel's military superiority over its neighbours, and provided the Soviet Union with an almost unhoped-for opportunity to become a central player in that part of the world.

Limited access to the archives and the publication of a number of memoirs by former Soviet officials have in the meanwhile made it possible to read the Soviet attitude more accurately. We are now able to shed new light on the way that this crisis developed from the Soviet viewpoint.

How did the Soviet leaders react to the different events which punctuated this crisis? Were they affected by them, or did they try to shape them? Did they have a strategy or was their policy improvised? What information did they have? What perspective did they apply? Was it based on ideological criteria, or did it follow power-politics considerations? Is it possible to identify the decision-making process during crisis periods? What were the constraints – internal, external, regional and international – which Khrushchev and the other members of the Soviet leadership had to take into account? Was the Suez crisis a tool in the power-struggle confrontations at the top of the Soviet party/state? Was it used in order to enable the Soviet Union to crush the Hungarian uprising?

To begin to answer to these questions, the following assumptions will serve as a guideline:

1) Despite what was often an improvised policy and limited political and military investment, the Soviet Union gained maximum benefit from this crisis. It allowed the Soviet Union to achieve the goal it had

been pursuing since 1945, i.e. to become a key player in the Near East and to weaken the 'imperialist powers', France and Britain.
2) The Suez crisis constituted a stake in the struggle for power in the Soviet Union and was used as a tool by both Khrushchev and his adversaries.

TRIGGERING OF THE CRISIS

A number of factors brought about the Suez crisis, both immediate (the US withdrawal from the Aswan Dam project, competition for leadership in the Arab world, tension between Egypt and Israel) and more structural ones (the decline of colonial empires, instability in the region since the creation of the state of Israel, the competition between Egypt and Iraq, the upsurge in Arab nationalism). Taking just the immediate factors, the roots of the Suez crisis lie not so much in the *rapprochement* between Cairo and Moscow which, from September 1955 onwards, took the form of Soviet arms deliveries to Egypt, as in the failure of Operation Alpha, which the United States and Britain had been trying to implement from the end of 1954 to resolve the Israeli–Arab conflict.[1]

Until March 1956, the United States and Britain did not adopt a coercive policy in respect of Cairo, despite its *rapprochement* with Moscow. They were afraid that too much pressure on the Egyptian government might produce the opposite effect. Egypt might strengthen its alliance with the Soviet Union. The two Western powers, and in particular the United States, preferred a policy which would allow them to pursue both their strategic goals (strengthening the Northern Tier pact) and their political goals (weakening Egyptian nationalism), as part of their policy of containment of the Soviet Union. Participating in financing the construction of the Aswan Dam was viewed as part of this policy, which was designed to bring Nasser back into the Western fold. But in March 1956, after the failure of the Alpha Project, the United States decided to adopt a new policy – dubbed the Omega Project – with regard to Nasser. According to John Foster Dulles, the US Secretary of State, this policy, which among other things involved suspending US aid to Egypt, financing Iraqi anti-Nasser propaganda and supporting Arab countries which distrusted the Egyptian leader, was intended to 'let Colonel Nasser realize that he cannot cooperate as he is doing with the Soviet Union and at the same time enjoy most-favoured-nation treatment from the United States'. Nevertheless, Dulles added, there was a need to avoid any open break which would force Nasser irrevocably into Soviet satellite status and one had to leave him a bridge back to good relations with the West if he so desired.[2]

However, Nasser's intransigence during the negotiations over financing the Aswan Dam, combined with the US Congress's opposition to this project and Egypt's recognition of Communist China in April 1956,[3] led to a crisis. In May, Dulles and British Foreign Secretary Selwyn Lloyd decided to harden their policy in respect of the Egyptian leader. It was at this time that the decision was taken to withdraw the offer to finance the Aswan Dam, but it was agreed to keep it secret. The two diplomats preferred to engage in delaying tactics rather than a direct confrontation, as explained by Evelyn Shuckburgh, under-secretary at the British Foreign Office in charge of the Middle East, in a note to the British ambassadors.[4] At the end of June, during a US National Security Council meeting, US officials agreed to announce the withdrawal of the United States from financing the Aswan Dam. The Soviet offers, made by Shepilov during his visit to Cairo at the beginning of June, had provided them with an opportunity they had previously only dared dream of.[5] The United States, as Secretary of State Dulles said at the meeting, need not be concerned about Soviet financing of the Aswan Dam because 'the long-term results might be very good'. Foster Dulles thought that the construction of the dam would require the Egyptian population to make such sacrifices that there would be a backlash against the country providing the financing: 'Building the dam would prove a terrible headache to any nation that undertook it.' His brother, Allen Dulles, head of the CIA, was also convinced that the United States could benefit from any Soviet participation in financing the dam: 'We can make a lot of use of it in propaganda within the satellite bloc. You don't get bread because you are being squeezed to build a dam.'[6]

On 19 July 1956 Foster Dulles told the Egyptian ambassador in Washington that the United States was withdrawing its offer, which was followed four days later by the withdrawal of the World Bank's offer of credit. On 26 July, in a speech in Alexandria, Nasser announced the nationalization of the Suez Canal Company.

Was the Soviet Union aware of Nasser's decision even before he announced it? Even if the former KGB agent in Cairo, Vadim Kirpichenko, states that this possibility had been envisaged by the Soviet intelligence services,[7] Nasser's gesture certainly seemed to have surprised the Kremlin leaders, given the time they took to react officially to the nationalization of the Suez Canal. Even the Yugoslav leaders, albeit close to Nasser, were not aware of the decision, as attested by the exchange between Soviet Deputy Foreign Affairs Minister Vladimir Semenov[8] and the Yugoslav ambassador in Moscow.[9] It took over five days for the Soviet Union to react in the form of a comment by Khrushchev and nearly two weeks for an official statement to be issued.

The day after nationalization, Shepilov received the Egyptian ambassador in Moscow. During these talks, the Soviet minister emphasized the legitimacy of Egypt's historical claim over the canal and said that it did not appear to him that the Egyptian government's action was a breach of international law; but, he said, it should be ascertained whether there were grounds which would allow the Western powers to challenge its legal basis. Shepilov did not, however, give a specific commitment as to how the Soviet Union would express its support for Egypt.[10]

On 28 July, MID (Ministerstvo Innostrannykh Del – the Soviet Ministry of Foreign Affairs) submitted to the Central Committee of the Communist Party of the Soviet Union (CPSU) a series of measures for supporting Egypt and to show, through articles to be published in the Soviet press and a declaration by MID, the legitimacy of Nasser's decision. The text was also intended as a warning to the Western powers who might be tempted 'to make use of Israel for purposes of provocation'.[11] However, these measures remained limited in scope. On 31 July, in a speech in Moscow, Khrushchev declared that in nationalizing the Suez Canal, Egypt had simply exercised its sovereign right, that it had undertaken to respect the freedom of shipping in the canal and that the Soviet Union considered that 'the policy of pressure on Egypt is wrong', adding that 'the Suez Canal issue can and must be resolved peacefully'.[12]

On 2 August, France, Great Britain and the United States published a declaration in London proposing a conference to be held in the British capital on 16 August in order to find a way out of the conflict. This conference was a US initiative. While France and Britain were tending towards a military solution, the United States tried to dissuade them. During talks between British Prime Minister, Anthony Eden and Dulles in London on 1 August, Dulles tried to convince Eden that armed intervention would have disastrous consequences for France and Britain, and that it would simply strengthen the influence and prestige of Egypt and the Soviet Union in the Arab world. US public opinion, Dulles argued, was not prepared to support France and Britain in a military adventure which could be described as being motivated by imperialist and colonialist ambitions.[13] The warnings of the US secretary of state fell on deaf ears.

FROM CRISIS TO WAR

The London Conference
The Soviet Union was invited to the London Conference as a signatory of the Constantinople Convention of 1888, which laid down the principles for using the Suez Canal. In all, 24 countries, including Egypt but not Israel, received invitations to London.[14]

At first, the Soviet Union considered not going to London. On 4 August Shepilov sent the Presidium (Politburo) a copy of a draft telegram for the Soviet ambassador in Cairo. In the telegram Shepilov asked the ambassador to inform Nasser that the Soviet Union endorsed the Egyptian decision not to take part in the London conference and to indicate to the Egyptian leader that the Soviet government was thinking of acting similarly. The reason given was that 'the list of participants is composed in a clearly tendentious fashion in order to ensure the passing of decisions prepared in advance, favourable to the colonial powers and to the detriment of the interests of Egypt and peace-loving peoples'. The Soviet Union was in favour of the proposal, presented to the Soviet ambassador by Nasser on 3 August, to submit the matter to the United Nations Security Council (UNSC).[15] The Presidium rejected this option, deciding that the Soviet Union would attend the conference and asking Shepilov to draw up the list of delegates and to prepare a set of draft instructions.[16]

On 9 August the Soviet government published a declaration on the Suez issue. This text was the first official stand since the beginning of the crisis (Khrushchev's speech on 31 July having been unofficial). The Soviet Union reiterated its support for the Egyptian decision, which it called 'an entirely legal act deriving from Egypt's sovereign rights', denounced 'the measures taken by the English and French government's, calling them 'completely unacceptable', and a 'challenge to the cause of peace', and announced that it would attend the London conference, while criticizing the conditions and principles underlying its organization. The Soviet government also expressed reservations about the list of countries invited to attend. All the Soviet satellites, including Hungary, Czechoslovakia and Yugoslavia, had been excluded even though, according to Soviet officials, as successor states of the Austro-Hungarian Empire they should have been entitled to a voice in the matter, like the Arab countries, which were successor states of the Ottoman Empire. It should, however, be noted that the Soviet government carefully refrained from mentioning Israel which was also excluded. The Soviet Union also condemned the exclusion of other communist states (China, Bulgaria and Poland). Although it had agreed to take part in the conference, the Soviet Union argued that the conference had no decision-making powers whatsoever: 'The conference cannot, whether through composition or character and aims, be considered as authorized to take any decisions whatsoever on the Suez Canal.' Similarly, the Soviet government felt it was in no way accountable for any decisions taken in London: 'Soviet participation in the conference shall in no way impose on the Soviet Union any limitations or commitments resulting from principles formulated by the three Western powers in their joint statement of 2 August or which might harm Egypt's sovereign rights and dignity.' The only virtue which the Soviet Union officially recognized in the conference was that it 'may make it possible to find means to resolve the problems relating to freedom of shipping in the Suez Canal'.[17]

Why did the Soviet Union agree to take part in a conference organized by the Western powers and intended to promote their interests? In fact, beyond the Suez Canal problem, the Soviet leaders tried to take advantage of the opportunity – with which the West provided them – to become as crucial a player on the Near East scene as the United States, France and Britain.

The instructions reflect the political goals pursued by the Soviet Union, which can be divided along three lines; first, to support Egypt while showing that the Soviet Union was seeking a balanced solution to the crisis. The delegation was to defend Egypt's refusal to take part in this conference 'whose composition was constituted in a tendentious fashion without consulting the Egyptian government and in violation of the 1888 Convention'. The conference organizers had also laid down 'aims and goals which are incompatible with the national dignity and sovereign rights of Egypt'.[18] As an independent state, Egypt had an indefeasible right to nationalize the Suez Canal Company. The Soviet delegation was to hinder the plan, worked out by France, the United States and Britain, providing for the internationalization of the Suez Canal. It was to oppose 'this plan with its platform for settling the Suez question' by proposing a revision or replacement of the 1888 convention which would guarantee both Egypt's sovereignty over the canal and freedom of shipping.[19] At the same time, the Soviet delegation should not find itself in a situation in which its 'declarations and its proposals could be interpreted as if the Soviet Union unconditionally supported one party's actions and ignored the interests of the other party, in particular those of England and France',[20] particularly since the Soviet Union had common interests with the Western powers on the other aspects of the Suez problem, namely freedom of shipping in the canal.

Second, to reinforce the Soviet Union's position in the Near East and in the Third World. For the first time since the end of the first Arab–Israeli war in 1949, the Soviet Union had an opportunity not to let the Western powers monopolize the Middle East. Thus the delegation was to use meetings with the representatives of the Western powers in order to show that 'the Soviet Union, as a great power whose frontiers adjoin the Near and Middle East region, is directly concerned not only by the questions concerning shipping in the Suez Canal, but also by those involving the overall situation in the Near and Middle East'.[21] The Soviet leaders wanted to take advantage of this crisis in order to weaken the Western powers and develop their policy of *rapprochement* with the decolonized countries. 'Any peaceful resolution of the dispute over the Suez Canal which would address the main claims of Egypt's sovereignty, would have major significance not only for the Near and Middle East area but would represent a major blow to the plans of the imperialist powers in Africa and Asia.'[22] To this end, the Soviet delegation was asked to reach agreement with the Indian and Indonesian delegations. In this way, Moscow tried to forge an alliance with the three main players of the Bandung Conference: Nasser, Nehru and Sukarno.

Finally, and notwithstanding these goals, the Soviet Union did not wish to see the conflict between Egypt, France and Britain degenerate into warfare. This concern was not merely a propaganda tactic designed for public opinion. It was stressed several times in the instructions: 'The delegation must, as far as possible, use the conference in order to reduce international tension[23]...If, during the conference, the Western powers threatened the use of force, this threat must be calmly but firmly removed by referring to the dangerous consequences of such actions.'[24]

These political instructions were accompanied by technical ones about organizing the delegation's work in London.[25] The list of delegates which comprised 73 individuals, mainly officials from MID and the Ministry of Defence, the KGB, journalists and technical personnel, was sent on 8 August to members of the Presidium as well as to the Central Committee Secretariat.[26]

The Soviet delegation strictly followed the instructions laid down for it. The proposal for the canal to be under the control of an international council, which was presented by the United States, was adopted by 18 of the 22 countries present. The Soviet Union, together with India, Indonesia and Ceylon, voted against the proposal. Thus the alliance with these states which the Soviet delegation was instructed to pursue, was indeed achieved. On his return to Moscow. Shepilov presented a report to the Presidium, and prepared a draft Central Committee resolution on the results of the London conference. In this draft resolution, corrected by Suslov,[27] Shepilov emphasized that the nationalization of the Suez Canal was 'a new and powerful blow to the colonialist positions which will impart momentum to the development of the fight by the peoples of the countries of the East against the unequal agreements imposed on them in the political and economic spheres';[28] that the Suez crisis reflected a heightening of the internal contradictions of imperialism, that the Soviet Union was right to participate in this conference because it 'had become a major world power. No problem in the Near and Middle East or any global problem in general can be settled without taking account of its opinion';[29] and finally that the creation of a common front in the speeches of the Soviet Union, India, Indonesia and Ceylon had been an important political outcome of the London conference. According to Shepilov this unity made it possible to remove the danger of Western military intervention without, however, ruling it out completely. Hence measures had to be taken in order 'to lessen international tension, unmask the antipopular plans of the aggressive circles of England, France and the United States, and strengthen the resistance of Egypt and the other Arab countries'.

This first phase of the Suez crisis was also marked by the complete dismissal of the Israeli factor in Soviet policy. While the Soviet Union deplored the absence of several countries from the London Conference, it gave no support whatever to the Israeli request to take part. However, the Jewish state was one of the main players to be concerned by the issue of shipping in the canal since this problem had been a reason for permanent tension between Israel and Egypt since 1948. The Soviet policy towards Israel can mainly be explained by the desire to limit the problem of Suez to the framework of a conflict between Egypt and the West – potentially favourable to the Soviet Union – without other factors clouding the issue and complicating the situation.

The Soviet Union and Israel had a shared interest: to obtain guarantees for freedom of shipping in the canal. But Moscow did not wish officially to support this Israeli demand, because this would weaken its position with regard to Egypt and the Arab world. Thus when Golda Meir, at that time Israel's foreign minister, stated to the Soviet ambassador to Israel that the results of the London Conference were very negative for Israel because it had not been invited and its claims had not been examined, Abramov replied that the question of freedom of shipping in the canal was one of the problems of the Arab–Israeli conflict that could only be resolved by the achievement of peace.[30] In other words, Israeli claims were postponed indefinitely. The Soviet Union, involved in a policy of supporting Egypt, was again enmeshed in a bi-polar arrangement which, unlike the United States, prevented it from mediating between warring parties.

While the London Conference was an unqualified success in the eyes of the Soviets, it did nothing to solve the problem triggered by the nationalization of the Suez Canal Company. When Nasser rejected the London Conference proposals, this left France, Britain and Israel with elbow room they required to prepare their military operation. What strategy would the Soviet Union adopt until the unleashing of the three-pronged attack at the end of October? Was it aware of the plans of France, Britain and Israel?

Tension Mounts
After the London Conference, the Soviet Union attempted to thwart the task given to Australian Prime Minister Robert Menzies, who was to go to Cairo in order to initiate negotiations with Nasser on the basis of the resolution passed by the 18 states in London. On 28 August, the USSR's ambassador in Cairo presented Nasser with a declaration by the Soviet

government, reasserting that a resolution of the Suez problem 'must be based on respect for Egypt's sovereign rights, the sole master, owner and manager of the canal while guaranteeing freedom of shipping on the canal at all times to all those countries which use it'.[31] The Menzies mission was a failure.

During the weeks after the London Conference, the Soviet Union did not budge from the line it had laid down at the beginning of August. On 11 September Bulganin sent letters to the French and British Prime Ministers, highlighting the potential negative consequences of armed intervention and pointing out that the Soviet Union fully recognized the rights and interests of France and Great Britain. On 15 September the Soviet government published a declaration in response to the French–British–US proposal to establish an association of Suez Canal users which would manage the canal.[32] Opposing this plan, the Soviet Union supported instead an Egyptian proposal, drawn up on 10 September[33] to convene a conference with the signatory states of the 1888 Convention to consider its revision. In the 15 September declaration, the Soviet Union warned the Western powers against using force, while declaring its commitment to freedom of shipping in the canal and recognizing the importance of the canal for France and Britain. Above all, however, the Soviet Union emphasized its Great Power status, as a result of which it could not

keep out of the Suez question and refrain from showing its concern over the situation which has come about at the present time as a result of the actions of the Western powers. This can be readily understood because any violation of the peace in the region of the Near and Middle East would affect the security interests of the Soviet State.[34]

The plan to establish an association of canal users was to be explored during a second conference in London from 19–23 September, but to no avail. It had been conceived by the United States, not so much in order to come up with a solution to the Suez crisis as to delay military intervention by France and Great Britain.[35]

After the failure of this project, France and Britain took the Suez problem to the UNSC. Despite the potential obstacle of a Soviet veto, they thought that they would be able to prove to world public opinion how intransigent Nasser had been, thereby acquiring legitimacy for the planned military intervention.[36] A few days before the Council session began, MID's information committee analysed the reasons behind the Franco-British move at the UN. Ivan Tugarinov, deputy head of MID's Information Committee envisaged three hypotheses: First that France and Britain were aware that they were running the risk of a Soviet veto, but wanted to take advantage of it to show that the UN was incapable of solving the problem; second that by resorting to the Security Council, they intended to force the hand of the United States so that it would go along with Franco-British plans (and adopt a more conciliatory attitude to Egypt); and finally that Paris and London wanted to reach a compromise with Egypt.[37] However, Tugarinov did not indicate preference for any one of these hypotheses.

During the discussions in the Security Council, Shepilov defined the Soviet position along two lines: initiating negotiations in order to discuss with Egypt conditions for shipping in the canal, and refusing any international control structure over it. According to Muhammad Haykal, Shepilov urged the Egyptians to reject any compromise on the second point:

> Shepilov stated adamantly that Egypt could not accept any compromise whatsoever over its sovereignty or ownership of the Canal, and Fawzi [Egyptian Minister of Foreign Affairs] understood that if it came to it, the Soviets could use their right of veto to oppose the wishes of the majority of the Council members...Shepilov thought that the Americans would differ from the British and the French on the means only, and not on the goals. Everybody agreed that the Suez Canal should be internationalized. Hence, without making any concessions over principles, Egypt's goal should be to persuade the Western powers to play a role in running the Canal, while ensuring that it remained effectively under Egyptian control.[38]

While refusing any compromise whatsoever on this point, in his 8 October speech to the Security Council, Shepilov proposed the setting up of a committee, consisting of Egypt, Britain, India, France, the United States and the Soviet Union, to draft a new convention designed to guarantee the freedom of shipping on the canal and to replace the 1888 Convention.[39] The presence of the Soviet Union and India on this committee would put Egypt in a far more advantageous position. Although the Security Council did not accept this proposal, the discussions resulted in a compromise. France and Britain presented a two-part resolution: the first part laid down the six principles which were intended both to guarantee freedom of shipping in the canal and to respect Egypt's sovereignty.[40] The Soviet Union voted in favour of this first part of the resolution, which was adopted unanimously by the Council. However, Moscow vetoed the second part of the resolution, which provided for Egypt to cooperate with the Canal Users' Association 'in order to ensure the proper functioning of the Canal'. Shepilov declared himself satisfied with the results obtained following these days of Security Council talks.[41] This satisfaction was shared by Eisenhower, who stated, 'It looks like here is a very great crisis that is behind us.'[42]

During the next few days, the diplomats displayed the same optimism. For example, during talks with Egypt's ambassador in Moscow, Zaitsev, the head of the Near East department, declared that 'the danger of a military intervention by the Western powers' had 'lessened considerably but', he added cautiously, 'it is still premature to speak of its total elimination'.[43] These declarations are rather surprising in view of the fact that at that very moment, France, Great Britain and Israel were finalizing their military preparations.

What did the Soviet leaders know of the British–French–Israeli military plans? According to the MID documents available to us, Soviet diplomats ruled out the hypothesis of the use of force by France and Britain after the nationalization of the Suez Canal. Thus, in a report dated 10 August, the MID's information committee estimated that military sanctions against Egypt were unlikely for three main reasons: 1) The Arab world's support for Nasser and the risk that a blockade of the canal would lead to the stoppage of oil transport through it, resulting in a considerable degree of paralysis of the French and British economies. 2) The United States, the Federal Republic of Germany, Italy and other NATO members were opposed to military sanctions against Egypt. 3) Leading British circles feared that Britain's participation with France in anti-Egyptian measures would be extremely detrimental to its position in Asia.[44] We have seen that, after the first London Conference, Shepilov thought that the threat of military intervention had passed. At the beginning of October, Iurii Andropov, at that time Soviet ambassador in Budapest, sent a report concluding, on the basis of information collected by 'Hungarian colleagues' among Western embassies in Budapest, that a war could not possibly break out in the near future.[45] The Soviet leaders also received reassuring information from high-ranking members of the British Labour Party visiting Moscow. On 14 August, MID's information committee sent a note to Khrushchev reporting a conversation between Guy Burgess, the former British diplomat and Soviet agent who had fled to Moscow in 1951, and Tom Driberg, a journalist who was a member of the Labour Party's Executive Committee.[46] According to Driberg, the threats of Britain and France were nothing but bluff, and would not be implemented. This note was read by Khrushchev.[47]

Burgess and Driberg met again two months later to discuss the Labour Party's situation. In a note reporting on this meeting, addressed to Khrushchev, Bulganin and Shepilov, Burgess expressed his view that Driberg was being over-optimistic.[48] On 19 October, Burgess met another leading figure from the left wing of the Labour Party, Koni Zilliacus,[49] who stated that the British government had no idea how to extricate itself from the Suez crisis. Under Eden, the cabinet was undertaking a policy of threat and bluff, because it knew that there would be no war between East and West over the Middle East.[50] The text of this conversation was also sent to Khrushchev, who had met Zilliacus a few days earlier. On 11 September one of the Arab leaders of the Israeli Communist Party, Tawfik Tubi, stated to the Soviet ambassador in Tel Aviv 'that Israel would not itself engage in armed conflict with the Arabs...Israel might join a military operation by the Western powers. But currently there is no information indicating that the Western powers will undertake a war. They understand that an armed conflict could lose them the entire Near East.'[51]

All these elements indicate that the Soviet leaders had received information which could have led them to believe that France and Britain would not act on their threats of military reprisals. However, they also received information which might have led them to draw the opposite conclusion. This information came from the KGB, the MID's information committee and the Soviet embassy in Tel Aviv.

According to Vadim Kirpichenko, who was at that time a KGB agent in Cairo, the KGB *rezident*, Vikentii Pavlovich Sobolev, had announced the day after the canal was nationalized that war was inevitable. 'The head of the foreign intelligence department in Moscow', said Kirpichenko, 'instructed the Cairo *rezidentura* to provide more information and waited for our forecasts about the possible launching of a war.'[52] The documents from the KGB *rezidentura* in Cairo are still inaccessible, but Soviet leaders certainly received daily reports from the KGB on the Suez affair. The content of the communications between Western embassies in Moscow and their capitals was known to the KGB and circulated to members of the Presidium. On 13 August the KGB warned Soviet leaders that the Western powers and Israel were preparing an operation whose implementation had been planned following the end of the London Conference.[53] We do not know whether this information relates to Operation *Musketeer*, which was adopted by France and Britain on 11 August and which scheduled a large-scale Franco-British landing for 15 September. However, at that moment Israel was not yet officially associated with the military preparations. Indeed, it is still difficult to determine exactly when Israel's participation was first envisaged, since accounts are contradictory.

On 15 September, after the announcement of establishment of the Canal Users' Association,[54] the MID's information committee sent a note to Zaitsev, with copies to all Presidium members, which highlighted the dangers of military sanctions against Egypt, on the basis primarily of declarations made by Eisenhower and Dulles. On 11 September, during a press conference, the US president replied to a journalist who had asked him whether the United States would support France and Britain if they were to use force against Egypt, by saying:

I don't know exactly what you mean by 'backing them.' As you know, this country will not go to war ever while I am occupying my present post, unless the Congress is called into session and Congress declares such a war. Now if, after all peaceful means are exhausted, there is some kind of aggression on the part of Egypt against a peaceful use of the canal, you might say that we would recognize that Britain and France would have no other recourse than to continue to use it even if they had to be more forceful than merely to sailing through it.

But, Eisenhower added: 'We established the UN to abolish aggression and I am not going to be a party to aggression if it is humanly possible.'[55]

In his note, Tugarinov failed to reproduce the last part of Eisenhower's declaration, and misinterpreted it: he saw it as a sign that the Western powers might use military sanctions against Egypt.[56] In fact, the United States opposed the use of force. British leaders were not too thrilled by the US president's words,[57] and were even more displeased by what Secretary of State Dulles said two days later: 'We have no intention of forcing a way through by gunfire.'[58] But no word about this 'interimperialist contradiction' can be found in Tugarinov's note. At the end of September Tugarinov wrote two notes on the position of the political forces in Britain[59] and France[60] concerning the Suez question. He indicated that, even if in the two countries the forces opposed to a policy of military sanctions were gaining ground, they were nevertheless still in the minority. However, he emphasized that the British government was in a difficult position, because 'the influence of the forces in favour of a peaceful solution of the Suez crisis is growing',[61] while in France 'opposition to the Western powers' policy on the Suez question is still weak and very inconsistent in Socialist and bourgeois circles'.[62] On 1 October, the KGB sent a note to the Presidium about the possibility of military action against Egypt and the measures taken to this end by the French intelligence services.[63] At the same time, the Presidium decided to send two KGB agents to Cairo in order to protect Nasser.[64] Up to the end of October, the Soviet leaders continued to receive information from the KGB, but we do not know whether they were aware of the French–British–Israeli plan adopted in Sèvres, near Paris, on 24 October.[65]

The Soviet embassy in Tel Aviv was also one of the sources which drew the attention of the Kremlin leaders to Israeli military preparations. On 20 September Gromyko sent a note to the Central Committee, reporting the information of the Soviet ambassador to Israel according to which:

the Israeli government has recently intensified the implementation of military measures within the country. Large amounts of heavy and light arms are arriving in Israel, and the reservists are drilling intensively. It is therefore clear that the Western powers intend to use Israel in any armed conflict with Egypt.[66]

Gromyko proposed to the Central Committee to issue a serious warning to Israel's ambassador in Moscow 'in order to dilute the militarist mindset of the leading circles in Israel and to make it more complicated for Israel to be used by the Western powers as a military force against Egypt'.[67] One month later, the secretary-general of the Israeli Communist Party, Shmuel Mikunis, stated to the Soviet ambassador in Tel Aviv 'that Israel was preparing a new military provocation against Egypt' and that, according to information provided by a journalist from *Kol Ha'am* – the ICP's official organ – who was also a reservist in the Israeli army, a large quantity of military equipment was being transported to the Egyptian border.[68] Two days later, the Soviet ambassador in Tel Aviv, Abramov sent a report to Shepilov emphasizing that while the Soviet Union's warnings to Israel had made a major impression and led to a 'lively reaction', they 'had not influenced the Israeli government's policy'.[69]

On the eve of the launching of the tripartite operations, the Soviet leaders had at their disposal a fairly wide range of information and analyses. However, it would not seem, on the basis of documents currently available, that they had detailed knowledge of the preparations for the British–French–Israeli attack, and in particular the Protocols of Sèvres, any more than US leaders.[70] On the other hand, the United States was aware of the mobilization of the Israeli army, but until the eve of the war US intelligence services were unable to determine whether the IDF's target would be Jordan or Egypt.[71] Furthermore, Ben-Gurion – familiar with the divisions within Eisenhower's administration about how to react in the case of a military operation against Nasser – thought that the United States would not intervene to stop it.[72] As we have seen, Israeli military manoeuvres did not escape the attention of Soviet diplomats and agents. However, the Kremlin leaders did not make any statements warning Israel or the Western powers in the days prior to the start of operations. They did not take any preventive measures to protect Soviet personnel in Cairo, who according to Vadim Kirpichenko's account were evacuated in a panic.[73] This was confirmed by the minutes of the meeting of Soviet ambassadors posted to capitals in the Near and Middle East which was held in Moscow a year after the Suez crisis. At the meeting Soviet diplomats posted in Cairo were blamed for giving way to panic and asking the Soviet government to send warships to defend them and take their families to safety.[74]

Not only does the Soviet Union appear to have been extremely passive on the eve of the war; it also took several days to react to the launching of hostilities.

THE KREMLIN GAMES

Threat or Bluff?

How did the Soviet Union react to the launching of the Israeli–French–British war against Egypt? Did it sense the differences between the United States and its allies? Were Soviet threats of reprisals against Paris, London and Tel Aviv serious, or were they just a bluff? How did the Soviet Union manage the contradiction between its regional constraints – its obligations to its Egyptian ally – and its international constraints – preventing the conflict from leading to a direct confrontation with the United States?

On the night of 29–30 October, in accordance with the plan agreed at Sèvres, the Israeli army launched Operation Kadesh, engaging its troops in the Sinai Peninsula. They had the secret support of the French air force and navy, and made rapid progress. On the afternoon of 30 October, the Sinai was cut in two by the Israeli army, and the Mitla Pass was conquered the next day. That day two identical ultimatums were delivered to Egypt and Israel by Anthony Eden in the House of Commons and Guy Mollet in France's National Assembly which ordered the two countries' armies to cease fighting immediately, withdraw their troops to a distance of 15 kilometres from the Suez Canal, and the Egyptian government to agree to the temporary occupation by Franco-British forces of Port Said, Ismailiya and Suez in order to guarantee freedom of shipping in the canal. The Prime Ministers announced that if, within 12 hours, one of the two parties had not complied with these demands, they would use force in order to obtain their implementation.[75] The next day, after Egypt had rejected the ultimatum, Franco-British aircraft launched an offensive. Moscow took several days before reacting to the events taking place in Egypt.

At the time that the war in Egypt broke out, the Syrian President, Shukri al-Kuwatly, was on an official visit to Moscow. He asked the Kremlin leaders to help Egypt 'with the great Red Army which had defeated Hitler'. Khrushchev replied that 'the USSR [does not have] the means to help Egypt militarily, but that it [will] mobilize world public opinion'.[76] That same day, 31 October, the Soviet government published a declaration condemning the Israeli attack and the Franco-British ultimatum. However, there was nothing in the text to dissuade France, Britain or Israel from continuing to apply the Sèvres protocols. Moscow simply asked the UNSC to take immediate measures in order to stop the aggression of France, Britain and Israel against Egypt.[77] But it was the United States, not the Soviet Union, which took the initiative. It presented a resolution which was adopted by the UNGA on 2 November, calling on all parties to accept an immediate cease-fire and withdraw their troops behind the armistice demarcation lines, and recommending that all member states refrain from bringing equipment into the area of hostilities. Up to 5 November, the Soviet Union simply sent protest notes to France and Britain. Meanwhile, Egyptian leaders were becoming increasingly concerned at Soviet passivity. A delegation sent by Nasser to the Soviet embassy in Cairo stated that if the Soviet Union did not intervene, the regime would be unable to hold out for longer than 24 hours. The information was conveyed to Moscow.[78] The next day, 5 November, the last phase of Operation *Musketeer* was launched with French commandos parachuting into Port Fuad and their British counterparts into Port Said, while the Israeli army captured Sharm al-Shaykh, a strategic site for the control of shipping in the Straits of Tiran and access to the Israeli port of Eilat. The next day, amphibian troops landed at Port Fuad and Port Said.

Having crushed the Hungarian uprising on 4 November,[79] the Soviet Union decided to launch a major diplomatic offensive. On 5 November, Bulganin, president of the Soviet Union's Council of Ministers, sent four letters to his opposite numbers, Ben-Gurion, Eden, Mollet and US President Eisenhower.

In his letter to the Israeli Prime Minister, Bulganin adopted a very hard line in respect to the Jewish state:

The whole of peace-loving humanity condemns with indignation the criminal action of the aggressors who have tried to undermine the territorial integrity, sovereignty and independence of the Egyptian state. Entirely ignoring this fact, the Israeli government, acting as a tool of imperialist external forces, is continuing its crazed adventure, challenging all the people of the East who are fighting against colonialism and for their freedom and independence. This behaviour on the part of the Israeli government clearly shows the value that should be attached to all of Israel's false protestations of love for peace, and its desire to coexist in peace with the neighbouring Arab states. Through these protests, the Israeli government is criminally and irresponsibly jeopardizing the fate of peace, the fate of its people. It is sowing among the peoples of the East a hatred for the State of Israel – a hatred which will inevitably impact on Israel's future and will call into question Israel's very existence as a state.[80]

The Soviet Prime Minister concluded by declaring that Moscow was recalling its ambassador to Israel. For the first time since 1948, the Soviet leaders were calling into question Israel's existence. The formulation was, it is true, sufficiently ambiguous for the Soviet Union to avoid charges of wanting to destroy Israel. However, it worried

Israeli leaders and would appear to have played some role in Israel's decision to accept the cease-fire, even if the pressures that Eisenhower brought to bear on Israel played a greater role in that decision.[81] The violent nature of the message to the Jewish state also constituted a sign to Egypt, to which Moscow had to provide pledges since it had decided not to intervene militarily. However, in order to comply with its obligations towards Egypt, the Soviet Union had to return to a situation in which Israel fell into the category of the enemy.

The Soviet Union did more than berate Israel. Bulganin also issued threats to France and Britain: 'What situation would France be in if it were subjected to an act of aggression by other states which had terrible modern instruments of destruction?...The Soviet government is fully resolved to use force in order to crush the aggressors and re-establish peace in the East.'[82] The message to Anthony Eden was more specific:

In what situation would Great Britain find itself if it were attacked by more powerful states, armed with all types of modern weapons of destruction. And what if these countries could, instead of sending naval or air forces to the shores of Britain, use other means – for instance – missiles. If missiles were used against Great Britain or France, you would certainly call this conduct an act of barbarism.[83]

The explicit reference to 'missiles' certainly relates to the fact that, unlike France,[84] Britain was a nuclear power. At the same time, of course, this reduced the scope of the threat: Britain could respond to a nuclear attack. This decision to issue a nuclear warning was taken by Khrushchev and confirmed a year later by Gromyko, during the plenum session of the Soviet Central Committee in June 1957.[85]

Nobody in Britain or France really took the Soviet nuclear threat seriously. Eden considered his country to be protected by its possession of nuclear weapons. Mollet tried to find out from the US ambassador to Paris, Douglas Dillon, what the United States would do if France, which was not yet a nuclear power, were attacked by Soviet missiles. Dillon replied that he was convinced that the United States would stand by France, but he added that the White House would not make any official declaration to this effect just a few hours prior to the US presidential election.[86] In point of fact, Britain and France were more concerned by the US attitude than by Soviet threats.

Bulganin also sent President Eisenhower a letter in which he suggested to the United States that there should be military cooperation between the 'two great powers possessing the hydrogen bomb' in order to stop the aggression against Egypt.[87] Eisenhower rejected the Soviet proposal and did not appear really to believe Soviet threats, despite the concerns of the US ambassador in Moscow, Charles Bohlen, who thought that the Soviet Union would not be able to refrain from acting if fighting continued in Egypt. However, the U-2 flights over Syria did not reveal any Soviet military presence which could be transferred to the Egyptian theatre of war.[88]

Why did the Soviet Union suggest joint action to the United States? This was an initiative that clearly surprised all players. Through Soviet diplomatic action, combining threats – against France, Britain and Israel – with conciliation in its proposal to act jointly with the United States, the Soviet Union tried to avoid the contradiction between its regional and international constraints.

On the regional level, the threats were designed to show Egypt and the Arab world that the Soviet Union was a reliable ally which was taking action to help a partner in difficulty. This demonstration was all the more necessary since the United States, having dissociated itself from France, Britain and Israel, might in the eyes of the Arab world appear to be a potentially better ally than the Soviet Union. It is in this light that the Soviet Union's nuclear intimidation can be read.

On the international level, Moscow had to deal with two requirements: on the one hand, it had to affirm its Great Power status to the United States, in particular in the Near East, and on the other hand it had to adhere to the line of peaceful coexistence which meant ensuring that the conflict did not degenerate into an open confrontation with the United States. Hence threats against France, Britain and Israel, combined with the proposal to the United States for joint action, offered the best possible combination in light of all the constraints affecting it.

Were the Soviet threats serious? This is a question that has been asked constantly since the end of the Suez crisis. A number of elements would seem to indicate that they were symbolic rather than real, and improvised rather than planned. Dmitrii Shepilov states that the threats were a bluff and that he himself, during his conversations with the French and British ambassadors outside the Security Council sessions, used Khrushchev's unpredictable character to back his claims.[89] Taking into account Soviet passiveness up to 5 November and the evidence provided by Syrian President al-Kuwatly, it would appear that Moscow did not have a clear idea about how to behave. At that time the Soviet Union did not have any military resources for rapid intervention in the Near East, and the threat of sending Soviet volunteers to fight side by side with the Egyptians was made on 10 November,[90] in other words several days after France and Britain had agreed to the cease-fire, and at a point when fighting had stopped and the volunteers would, in any case, have been useless. After the crisis, the Egyptian ambassador in Moscow asked Soviet Deputy Minister of Foreign Affairs Zorin why the

Soviet Union had issued this declaration after the fighting had stopped. 'It seemed to us', replied Zorin,

> that in the prevailing situation it was very important to undertake this step in order, on the one hand, to bring additional moral pressure to bear on the aggressors and, on the other hand, to show that the Soviet Union and the other peace-loving countries were not interested in a deterioration of the international situation.[91]

Thus Zorin acknowledged that this threat of sending Soviet volunteers to Egypt was purely tactical.

Similarly, the Soviet leaders stated that their action had forced France and Britain to put a stop to their undertaking, but in fact, this factor was far less significant than the United States' political and economic pressures on its allies.[92] On 3 December, France and Britain announced the withdrawal of their troops, which concluded on 22 December, while Israel kept its armed forces in Gaza and Sharm al-Shaykh until March 1957.

Before drawing up an appraisal of Soviet policy during the Suez crisis, there are several questions which we should try to answer: How did the Suez crisis influence the Soviet attitude in the Hungarian crisis? Were Moscow's threats against France, Britain and Israel linked to the crushing of the Hungarian Revolution? Who inspired Soviet policy during the Suez crisis? Was there unanimity within the Soviet leadership? Was policy influenced by a power struggle between Khrushchev and his adversaries?

Suez and Budapest

To answer the first question it is necessary to know whether the British–French–Israeli operation was launched when the Soviet Union was paralyzed by the situation in Budapest. The reply to this question is in the negative, insofar as the Sèvres protocols were signed at the same time as the first Soviet intervention in Hungary on 24 October 1956, something which the negotiators in Sèvres could not have foreseen.

The second relevant question involves determining whether the Soviet Union benefited from the launching of the tripartite operation in order to launch its second military operation against Hungary on 4 November. The documents which have been found in the Soviet archives provide us with information which somewhat modifies this interpretation. The notes taken during this period at the Presidium meetings by Vladimir Malin, head of the General Department (*Obshchii Otdel*) of the CSPU,[93] show that like the Western powers, the Soviet leaders were primarily afraid of becoming embroiled in the Suez conflict. During a Presidium meeting on 28 October, in other words before military operations were launched, Khrushchev referred to the Western powers' situation in Suez when he argued for a swift resolution of the Budapest crisis: 'The English and the French are in a real mess in Egypt. We should not get caught in the same company.'[94]

Subsequently, on 31 October, in other words after the start of the Israeli military offensive in Sinai and the first bombings of Egypt by Franco-British aviation, Khrushchev declared that the attack on Nasser's regime was the first stage in an offensive in which Budapest would be the second stage if Moscow did not react:

> We must re-examine our declaration and not withdraw our troops from Hungary and Budapest. We must take the initiative by re-establishing order in Hungary. If we leave Hungary, this will give a boost to the Americans, the English and the French – the imperialists. They will take this for weakness on our part, and they will launch a major offensive. In that way we would be laying bare the weakness of our positions. If we do that, our party won't accept it. The imperialists will then add Hungary to Egypt. We have no alternative.[95]

From these comments it can be seen that the war in Egypt probably expedited the decision to intervene in Budapest, even if it was highly likely that the decision would have been taken in any case. The comments also provide us with two vital pieces of information. At that point, Khrushchev thought that France, Britain and the United States were waging a concerted operation against Egypt – it should be noted that he did not mention Israel – and believed that the defeat of his Egyptian ally was inevitable. This element could in part explain the Soviet passiveness until 5 November. Moscow did not want to mobilize its forces for a lost cause while interests which were essential in another war – in Hungary – were at stake. The apparent Soviet passiveness can also be explained by the mobilization of the chief Kremlin leaders over the situation in Hungary. Khrushchev and Malenkov went to Brest-Litovsk on 31 October for a meeting with a Polish delegation headed by Gomulka. On 1 November they returned to Moscow and the same day left for Bucharest in Romania for talks with the Romanian, Czechoslovak and Bulgarian leaders. On 2 November they went to Brioni in Yugoslavia to talk to Tito. The next day, they returned to Moscow[96] and took part in a meeting of the Presidium. Hence practically all of Khrushchev's attention was taken up by the Hungarian situation until 4 November.

Lastly, the hypothesis that the crushing of the Hungarian Revolution allowed the Soviet Union to recapture the initiative in the Near East is confirmed here by Malin's notes. On 4 November, after the beginning of the Soviet intervention in Hungary, the Presidium decided 'to play a more active role in helping Egypt. Think of measures (maybe a demonstration outside the embassy of Great Britain). More newspaper coverage.'[97] This does not indicate that the Presidium discussed or took a decision on sending Bulganin's letters of 5 November, nor on their contents – merely that the situation was, in the eyes of the Soviet leaders, being resolved in Hungary, so that they could now focus on their Egyptian ally.

DECISION-MAKING AND POWER STRUGGLES

After Stalin's death and the elimination of Beria, the power struggle at the top of the Soviet state became more 'peaceful'. Violence, as a principle tool for resolving conflicts, was abandoned. Nevertheless, conflicts did not disappear. In the period 1953–57 – between Stalin's death and the elimination of the 'anti-Party group' – the Soviet Union went through an almost continuous political crisis from which Khrushchev would emerge as the (provisional) winner in 1957, after defeating Beria, Malenkov,[98] Molotov and Kaganovich.[99]

Khrushchev's foreign-policy decisions can also be explained by internal constraints, the power struggle with his adversaries constituting one of the main components of these constraints. From 1955 onwards, Khrushchev made every effort to consolidate his power by making sure that he controlled foreign policy. This goal had almost been achieved when the Suez crisis erupted in July 1956. Khrushchev managed to remove Molotov from the position of minister of foreign affairs by replacing him with Shepilov in June 1956, and he formalized his new Soviet foreign policy line at the 20th CPSU Congress in February 1956. This new line was based on three pillars: peaceful coexistence, opening up to the Third World, and de-Stalinization. In October 1956, these three pillars threatened to collapse, with the simultaneous crises in Budapest and Suez. Khrushchev's decision to issue a nuclear threat to France and Britain while proposing joint action to the United States was as much designed to avoid the collapse of its Egyptian ally and affirm the Soviet Union's status as a Great Power capable of running world affairs on an equal footing with the United States as to saving his own policy and proving its validity to his main domestic supporters. A failure in Egypt would have considerably weakened his position – already undermined by the Hungarian attempt at dissidence – within the leadership apparatus.

We do not know if voices were raised opposing Khrushchev's initiative to threaten France, Britain and Israel. Given what we have learned from the documents in the Soviet archives about the Hungarian crisis, it is perfectly possible that a debate took place on the Suez issue. Indeed, the shorthand records of the June 1957 plenary session of the Central Committee show that Khrushchev's policy towards Egypt in 1956 generated lively opposition. The Suez crisis was one of the topics of confrontation between Khrushchev and his opponents, who were in the 'anti-Party group' united around Molotov, Malenkov and Kaganovich.

As far as foreign policy was concerned, the difference of opinion between Molotov and Khrushchev concerned the nature of the relationship between the Soviet Union and the United States. Molotov thought that the notion of peaceful coexistence implemented by Khrushchev, which gave priority to the dialogue with the United States, contravened the Leninist principle of exploiting contradictions in the imperialist camp:

> If we think that the Soviet Union and the United States can reach agreement and that this is the expression of the principle underlying our policy, then we are forgetting the fundamental Leninist position of using the 'cracks', the contradictions in the imperialist camp. We must not unite the capitalist and imperialist states round the United States, nor incite them into this position, and we must not present things as if the Soviet Union only had to reach agreement with the United States and all other states would play an insignificant role. No, comrades, now we have become a great power, a vigorous force, and our socialist camp is enjoying vast support in the West and the East. Under these conditions, we must concentrate on widening every crack, all the differences of opinion and the contradictions in the imperialist camp in order to weaken the international positions of the United States, which is the strongest of the imperialist powers. This is the reason why we support all contacts with the other non-Socialist states and we consider this to be very important. We maintain contacts with little Denmark, with Norway, Burma and Egypt. So exploiting contradictions in the camp of the capitalist states is of major significance. Only in this way, by bringing pressure to bear not only on America but also on the other states which are moving away [from the United States] or which are wavering in the capitalist camp, is it possible to weaken America which is fighting us.[100]

In response to these attacks by Molotov, Mikoian came to Khrushchev's defence:

> Previously, three imperialist powers used to get together without us and decide on all the issues of the Near East. And, when we sold arms to Egypt, we bared our teeth at our enemies and Nasser was a leader

who stood firm, and now they cannot decide on questions about the Near East without us. Is this not the outcome of applying the Leninist policy of exploiting imperialist contradictions? In this case, we are supporting the bourgeois nationalists against the imperialists.[101]

And Mikoian added:

Remember this: the uprising in Hungary, our troops occupied Budapest, the Anglo-French decided: the Russians are entangled in Hungary, let's strike Egypt, they cannot help it, they cannot fight on two fronts... We found the strength to keep our troops in Hungary and threaten the imperialists with using our [nuclear] rockets if they did not stop the war in Egypt... When it comes to using the contradictions of imperialism in the interests of Communist policy, there has never been such a broad application, such rich results as in recent years with Comrade Khrushchev's participation in our Central Committee.[102]

This exchange between Molotov and Mikoian shows that foreign policy generally, and the Suez affair in particular, constituted a subject of debate and one of the stakes in the power struggle between Khrushchev and his adversaries.

The heated exchange between Khrushchev's supporters and adversaries shows that, despite the growing importance of geopolitical factors in shaping Soviet foreign policy after Stalin's death, the ideological dimension remained pivotal in the Soviet leaders' representations of the outside world. Dividing the world into friend/enemy categories remained an essential element in their perception of the international scene. The principles of foreign policy as defined by Lenin still constituted the source of legitimacy for the party leaders' action. Their policy was evaluated in this light. Even if ideology was undeniably rendered an instrument in this power struggle, it continued to occupy an essential position because it shaped behaviour and, to a certain extent, determined positions. Whether it was used to rationalize a policy or inspired decisions, ideology was a constraint for Khrushchev, as it was for the other Soviet leaders.

The Suez crisis was referred to again seven years later during another episode in the power struggle. However, this time Khrushchev would be its victim and the Suez crisis would be used at his expense. During the Presidium meeting of 12 October 1964, and then two days later during the Central Committee plenary session called to topple Khrushchev, he was accused of having brought the Soviet Union to the brink of war three times in just a few years (Suez, Berlin, Cuba):

Remember the Suez crisis. We were that close to a major war! But what would have been the basis for making war? We did not even have a mutual aid agreement with Egypt; there was no request for aid. How, in practical terms, could we engage in war? At this time, our country had not yet recovered from the war against Hitler, the people did not want war, they were not expecting it. War would have been like a clap of thunder out of a clear sky and the Soviet people would not have thanked us for such a turn of events. It may be said that we did not seriously have any intention of making war. But then it is not politics, but political adventurism, blackmail, juggling irresponsibly with the country's fate, the party's fate, our great cause. Fortunately, everything worked out and Comrade Khrushchev presented this as the outcome of his genius.[103]

Khrushchev replied that he was the person who had initiated the Soviet Union's actions during the Suez crisis and that he was still proud of the policy pursued.

For the Soviet Union, the balance sheet of the Suez crisis was entirely positive. Without any large-scale investment, it managed to obtain a three-way result which strengthened its position on both the regional and the international stage. First, its main enemies, France and Britain, emerged from the crisis much weakened. Their failure at Suez marked the irreversible decline of their colonial empires; second, the crisis highlighted the contradiction of interests – what was known in Soviet language as inter-imperialist contradictions – within the Atlantic alliance in an area which might well have been considered essential to Western security, and finally, while the pressure which the United States brought to bear on its allies constituted the decisive factor in resolving the crisis, the Soviet Union did manage, as a result of its diplomatic signals, to derive major political benefit, acquiring prestige and power in the Third World, even if its standing in the West was seriously damaged by the repression in Hungary which, coming after the revelations of the 20th Congress, unleashed a profound crisis in the communist movement. In addition, the Suez crisis was a decisive stage in the 'globalization of the Soviet power'[104] which enabled it to impose itself as a Superpower in the same league as the United States.

But this positive balance sheet is far more the outcome of circumstances, the inconsistencies of Western policy and a military operation based on an unlikely scenario. Throughout this crisis, Soviet policy was improvised. On each occasion it was forced into responding late. The upbeat aspects of this policy were the result of Khrushchev's initiatives, and to a large extent it has not yet been decided whether they were discussed prior to their implementation or whether they were the outcome of Khrushchev's actions alone.

The Suez crisis set the political framework for Soviet–Egyptian ties for the next two decades. In a classical instance of balance of forces, the USSR supported Egypt in order to thwart the development of US influence in the Near and Middle East. Nevertheless, this support had limits which were clearly defined during the Suez crisis: the regional conflict must not lead to a direct confrontation with the United States, even if a defeat of Moscow's main ally were the price to pay for this result, as in 1967 and to a lesser extent in 1973. However, at least three reasons suggest why the ideological dimension of the Soviet Union's policy in the Near East should not be seen as an insignificant factor.

The first reason relates to the fact that the perception of the outside world which determined the Soviet leaders' approach continued to be based on a profound hostility to the capitalist world, grounded in categories of analysis established by Lenin, involving a world divided into two camps. The dynamics of Soviet foreign policy were based on a desire to compete with the enemy camp on all levels, even if according to the doctrine of peaceful coexistence, war between the two camps was not inevitable. Nevertheless, the conflict had not vanished and it was still essentially ideological in nature.

The second reason, which makes it vital to take account of the ideological dimension, relates to the fact that Egypt would act as a model and laboratory for all theoretical formulations of the ties between the Soviet Union and non-communist Third World countries.

Lastly, the existence of the alliance with Egypt damaged ties between the Soviet Union and Israel, preventing the Soviet Union from occupying a privileged position among all the parties of the Near East conflict. Israel was again returned to the category of 'enemy'. This inability, which over time would become a handicap, was rooted in the Soviet leaders' conflict-based political culture, which shaped their notion of international relationships.

NOTES

1. On Project Alpha, see Shimon Shamir, 'The Collapse of Project Alpha', in Wm. Roger Louis and Roger Owen (eds), *Suez 1956: The Crisis and Its Consequences* (Oxford: Clarendon Press, 1989), pp. 73–100; Neil Caplan, *Futile Diplomacy: Operation Alpha and the Failure of Anglo-American Coercive Diplomacy in the Arab–Israeli Conflict, 1954–1956* (London: Frank Cass, 1997); Peter Hahn, *The United States, Great Britain and Egypt, 1945–1956* (Chapel Hill, NC: University of North Carolina Press, 1991) pp.186–94; David Devereux, *The Formulation of the British Defence Policy Towards the Middle East, 1948–1956* (London: Macmillan, 1990), pp. 168–72.
2. Hahn, *The United States, Great Britain and Egypt*, p. 200.
3. According to Muhammad Haykal, Nasser's adviser, this decision was taken not to defy the West, but to bring pressure to bear on the Soviet Union because Nasser feared that the Soviet Union and Britain would reach an agreement over restricting arms deliveries to the Middle East; Mohamed Heikal, *L'affaire de Suez: Un regard égyptien* (Paris: Ramsay, 1986), p. 149.

4. PRO FO 371/118862, 28 May 1956. Document reproduced in Anthony Gorst and Lewis Johnman, *The Suez Crisis* (London & New York, NY: Routledge, 1997), p. 50.
5. At the moment there is no proof that this offer was ever made.
6. Hahn, *The United States*, p. 204.
7. 'We did not have any specific information about Nasser's intentions, but in our reports we always emphasized that such an action was always possible. Moreover, in Egypt both political and diplomatic circles discussed this. We also studied this question, which became even more acute after the English troops evacuated the Canal Zone in June 1956. Following this event, action by Nasser to reaffirm Egyptian sovereignty could of course be expected', Vadim Alekseevich Kirpitchenko, 'Les Soviétiques et la crise de Suez', in Ministère de la Défense, Centre d'études d'histoire de la défense, *La France et l'opération de Suez de 1956*, Actes d'une table ronde organisée sous la direction de Maurice Vaisse (Paris: Addim, 1997), p. 145.
8. In his memoirs, Semenov states that Moscow had no information about Egyptian intentions. See Wladimir S. Semjonow, *Von Stalin bis Gorbatschow: Ein halbes Jahrhundert in diplomatischer Mission 1939–1991* (Berlin: Nicolai, 1995), p. 317.
9. Arkhiv vneshnei politiki federatsii Rossii [Archives of the Foreign Policy of Russian Federation] (AVPRF), f. 087, op. 19, p. 38, d. 2, l. 46, 9 August 1956, confidential.
10. AVPRF, f. 087, op. 19, p. 38, d. 2, 11. 211, 27 July, 1956, confidential. A copy of this conversation was sent to members and candidate members of the Presidium of the CPSU, as well as to a number of MID officials.
11. AVPRF, f. 537, op. 1, p. 1, d. 4, l. 1, 28 July, 1956, confidential.
12. MID, *SSSR i arabskie strany 1917–1960. Dokumenty i materialy*, (Moscow: Gosudarstvennoe izdatel'stvo politicheskoi literatury, 1961), pp. 143–4.
13. *Foreign Relations of the United States (FRUS)*, 1955–57, Vol. XV (Washington DC: Government Printing Office, 1988), pp. 98–9.
14. Apart from Egypt, and the signatory states to the Constantinople Convention (Austria, France, Germany, Spain, Great Britain, Italy, Netherlands, the Soviet Union and Turkey), invitations were also issued to the United States, Australia, Ceylon, Denmark, Ethiopia, India, Indonesia, Iran, Japan, Norway, New Zealand, Pakistan, Portugal and Sweden.
15. AVPRF, f. 0537, op. 1, p. 1, d. 4, 11. 2–5, 4 August 1956, confidential.
16. AVPRF, f. 0537, op. 1, p. 1, d. 4, 11. 1–3, 7 August 1956, confidential.
17. MID, *SSSR i arabskie strany*, pp. 145–51.
18. AVPRF, f. 0537, op. 1, p. 1, d. 1, l. 76.
19. Ibid., l. 78, 88–9.
20. Ibid., l. 74.
21. Ibid., l. 85.
22. Ibid., l. 75.
23. Ibid., l. 74.
24. Ibid., l. 82.
25. AVPRF, f. 0537, op. 1, p. 1, d. 2, 11. 24–5, 15 August 1956, confidential, only copy.
26. AVPRF, f. 0537, op. 1, p. 1, d. 2, 11. 24–5, 8 August 1956, confidential, 11.1–3.
27. There are several successive versions of this draft: AVPRF, f. 0537, op. 1, p. 2, d. 13, 11. 2–4, 28 August 1956; Tsentr Khraneniia sovremennoi dokumentatsii [Centre for the preservation of contemporary documentation], (TsKhSD), f. 5, op. 30, d. 162, 11. 149–51, draft to Suslov, 29 August 1956 and TsKhSD, f. 5, op. 30, d. 162, 11. 152–4, draft to Suslov, Mikoian and Kaganovich, 30 August 1956.
28. TsKhSD, f. 5, op. 30, d. 162, l. 153.
29. Ibid.
30. AVPRF, f. 089, op. 9, p. 21, d. 3, l. 151, 24 August 1956, confidential.
31. *Notes et études documentaires*, No. 2249, La documentation française, p. 8.
32. See the texts in MID, *SSSR i arabskie strany*, pp. 190–208.
33. *Notes et études documentaires*, No. 2249, La documentation française, pp. 8–9.
34. MID, *SSSR i arabskie strany*, p. 207.
35. Keith Kyle, *Suez* (New York NY: St Martin's Press, 1991), pp. 227–55; Hahn, *The United States, Great Britain and Egypt*, pp. 217–23; Gorst and Johnman, *The Suez*

Crisis, pp. 77–81.
36. Denis Lefebvre, *L'affaire de Suez* (Paris: Bruno Leprince, 1996), p. 60; Kyle, *Suez*, pp. 272–7.
37. AVPRF, f. 087, op. 19, p. 39, d. 8, ll. 98–9, 3 October 1956, confidential.
38. Heikal, *L'affaire de Suez*, pp. 222–3. The French ambassador in Moscow, Maurice Dejean, attributed Nasser's intransigence during the negotiations which followed the London Conference in August to the attitude of the Soviet Union, which had incited it to adopt this position, Telegram of September 1956, reproduced in Ministère des Affaires étrangères, *Documents diplomatiques français* (Paris: Imprimerie nationale, 1956), Vol. III, p. 363.
39. MID, *SSSR i Arabskie strany*, p. 226.
40. The six principles were as follows: (1) transit through the canal shall be free and open without any overt or covert discrimination, either politically or technically; (2) Egypt's sovereignty shall be respected; (3) insulation from the politics of any one country; (4) dues to be decided between Egypt and users; (5) a fair proportion of the revenue to go to improving the canal; (6) if differences of opinion arise, matters outstanding between the Suez Canal Company and the Egyptian government shall be settled by an arbitration tribunal whose powers and purpose shall be clearly defined with appropriate provisions for payment of any sums due, *Articles et Documents*, No. 421, 18 October 1956.
41. Ibid., p. 229.
42. Kyle, *Suez*, p. 288.
43. AVPRF, f. 087, op. 19, p. 39, d. 3, l. 35, 22 October 1956, confidential.
44. AVPRF, f. 087, op. 19, p. 39, d. 8, l.56, 10 August 1956, strictly confidential. Report to Zaitsev, sent to all presidium members.
45. TsKhSD, f. 5, op. 28, d. 394, l. 257, quoted in V. Afiani, N. Ivanov, *Sovetskii Soiuz i Suetskii Krizis 1956*, unpublished, 1994., p. 8.
46. An MP for many years, Driberg had been an agent working for Czechoslovakia and the Soviet Union. He provided information about the private lives of the Labour Party leaders. See Christopher Andrew and Oleg Gordievsky, *Le KGB dans le monde, 1917–1900* (Paris: Fayard, 1990), p. 517.
47. TsKhSD, f. 5, op. 30, d. 162, l. 114, 14 August 1956, confidential.
48. TsKhSD, f. 5, op. 30, d. 163, l. 122, 26 October 1956, confidential. The conversation took place on 12 October, but the minutes were sent to Khrushchev several days later.
49. In the 1930s, Zilliacus had been one of the most zealous advocates of the Soviet Union joining the League of Nations. Sabine Dullin, 'Diplomates et diplomatie soviétiques en Europe (1930–1939)', doctoral thesis, University of Paris I, 1998,
50. TsKhSD, f. 5, op. 30, d. 163, l. 122, 26 October 1956, confidential.
51. TsKhSD, f. 5, op. 28, d. 445, l. 90, 11 September 1956, confidential. The notes from this talk were sent to the Central Committee by Deputy Foreign Affairs Minister, Vladimir Semenov.
52. Kirpitchenko, 'Les Soviétiques et la crise de Suez', p. 146; and *Iz arkhiva razvedchika*, (Moscow: Mezdunarodnye otnosheniia, 1993), pp. 37–44. The *rezidentura* was the name used for the KGB section of the embassy in any given city.
53. Afiani and Ivanov, *Sovetskii Soiuz i Suetskii Krizis 1956*, p. 13.
54. See above.
55. Kyle, *Suez*, pp. 243–4.
56. AVPRF, f. 087, op. 19, p. 39, d. 8, l. 33, 15 September 1956, strictly confidential.
57. Kyle, *Suez*, p. 244.
58. Anthony Eden, the British Prime Minister, admitted that agreeing to the establishment of the Canal Users' Association was the biggest mistake of his life. Louise Richardson, *When Allies Differ: Anglo-American Relations during the Suez and Falklands Crisis* (London: Macmillan, 1996), p. 51.
59. AVPRF, f. 087, op. 19, p. 39, d. 8, ll. 60–66, 25 September 1956, strictly confidential.
60. AVPRF, f. 087, op. 19, p. 39, d. 8, ll. 69–75, 29 September 1956, strictly confidential.
61. Ibid., l. 66.

62. Ibid., 11. 74–5.
63. Afiani and Ivanov, *Sovetskii Soiiuz i Suetskii Krizis*, p. 14.
64. Kirpichenko dates this episode to the end of July when the Egyptian intelligence services, having found out that the Western powers were preparing Nasser's physical elimination, asked him to organize the training of the Egyptian president's bodyguard: 'Moscow agreed without delay and, shortly after, the heads of the KGB security service arrived in Egypt.' Kirpichenko, 'Les Soviétiques et la crise de Suez', p. 146.
65. On the Sèvres protocols, see Avi Shlaim, in this volume; Kyle, *Suez*, 314–31; Lefebvre, *L'affaire de Suez*, pp. 81–98; Mordechai Bar-On, 'David Ben-Gurion and the Sèvres Collusions', in Louis and Owen, *Suez 1956*, pp. 145–60.
66. AVPRF, f. 022, op. 9, p. 135, d. 62, l.1, 20 September 1956, confidential.
67. Ibid.
68. AVPRF, f. 089, op. 9, p. 21, d. 3, l. 193, 20 October, 1956 strictly confidential.
69. AVPRF, f. 089, op. 9, p. 21, d. 1, ll. 9–10, 22 October 1956, strictly confidential.
70. According to Charles G. Cogan, 'the American government was not aware of this meeting in Sèvres; until the very end it did not know the precise scenario of this operation. This fact is proved by a long retrospective report, dated 5 December1956, drawn up by the State Department and approved by the CIA. This report had been commissioned by Foster Dulles who wanted, after the event, to know more about the 'collusion and deceit' of the British and French towards the United States.' See Charles G. Cogan, 'De la politique du mensonge à la farce de Suez: appréhension et réactions américaines', in Vaisse, *La France et l'opération de Suez*, p. 128 and Kyle, *Suez*, p. 343.
71. Cogan, 'De la politique du mensonage', p. 128.
72. Peter Hahn, 'The View from Jerusalem: Revelations about US Diplomacy from the Archives of Israel', *Diplomatic History*, 4 (1998), p. 523.
73. 'The Egyptians, to whom much had been said about ties of friendship and cooperation between Egypt and the Soviet Union, stopped our compatriots in the street and accused them of betrayal, constantly asking the same questions: "Where are your planes? Where are your tanks? Why are Soviet soldiers not coming to Egypt's assistance?" We remember these lessons for the future. In order to avoid acts of violence, the Egyptian authorities ordered our embassy to have its vehicles marked with Soviet colours. Since it was impossible to foresee how the situation would develop, we decided to send our families to Sudan, from where they could return to Moscow by road. But for a long time we had no news from them.' Kirpitchenko, 'Les Soviétiques et la crise de Suez', p. 144.
74. TsKhSD, f. 5, op. 50, p. 35, l. 161, 7–10 October 1957, quoted in Afiani and Ivanov, *Sovetskii Soiuz i Suetskii Krizis 1956*, p. 18.
75. See the text of declarations in *Articles et Documents*, No. 427, 3 November 1956, La documentation française.
76. Heikal, *L'affaire de Suez*, p. 262.
77. MID, *SSSR i arabskie strany*, p. 242.
78. Kirpitchenko, 'Les Soviétiques et la crise de Suez', p. 147.
79. On the link between Suez and Budapest, see below.
80. MID, *SSSR i arabskie strany*, p. 261.
81. Yosef Govrin, *Israeli–Soviet Relations, 1953–1967: From Confrontation to Disruption* (London: Frank Cass, 1998), p. 45; Yaacov Bar-Simon-Tov, *Israel, The Superpowers and the War in the Middle East* (New York, NY: Praeger, 1987), pp. 57–65.
82. MID, *SSSR i arabskie strany*, p. 260.
83. Ibid., p. 258.
84. The British exploded their first atomic bomb on 3 October 1952. Lucien Poirier, *Des stratégies nucléaires* (Brussels: Complexe, 1988), p. 92.
85. Session of 25 June 1957 of the plenum of the CPSU Central Committee (CC), *Istoricheskii Arkhiv*, No. 5, p. 27.
86. Kyle, *Suez*, pp. 458–9.
87. It should be remembered that the Soviet Union did not at that time have any long-

range bombers capable of delivering nuclear bombs to the United States, and was therefore in a strategically weaker position: Jean-Christophe Romer, 'Image de l'ennemi et perception de la menace en URSS (1945–1965)', *Cahiers de l' Institut d'Histoire du Temps Present*, 28 (1994), p. 147.

88. Cogan, 'De la politique du mensonge', p. 138.
89. Alexei Vassiliev, *Russian Policy in the Middle East: From Messianism to Pragmatism* (Reading: Ithaca Press, 1993), pp. 40–1.
90. MID, *SSSR i arabskie strany*, pp. 264–6.
91. AVPRF, f. 087, op. 19, p. 38, l. 106, 12 December 1956, confidential.
92. On the economic dimension, see Diane Kunz, *The Economic Diplomacy of the Suez Crisis* (Chapel Hill NC: University of North Carolina Press, 1991).
93. On these notes, see Mark Kramer, 'New Evidence on Soviet Decision-Making and the 1956 Polish and Hungarian Crisis', *Cold War International History Project Bulletin*, 8–9 (1996–97), p. 359.
94. TsKhSD, f. 3, op. 12, d. 1005, l. 61, quoted in Kramer, 'New Evidence on Soviet Decision-Making', p. 393.
95. TsKhSD, f. 3, op. 12, d. 1006, ll. 15–180b, Kramer, 'New Evidence of Soviet Decision-Making', p. 393.
96. Ibid., pp. 373–4.
97. TsKhSD, f. 3, op. 12, d. 1006, l. 34; Kramer, 'New Evidence of Soviet Decision-Making', p. 397. The telegraphic style of Malin's notes has been preserved.
98. On the elimination of Malenkov, see Mikhail Reiman, 'Reshenie ianvarskogo (1955g) plenuma TsK KPSS o G. M. Malenkove', *Voprosy istorii* 1 (1999), pp. 29–33.
99. V. P. Naumov, 'Bor'ba N.S. Khrushcheva za edinolitchnuiu vlast', *Novaia i Noveishaia Istoriia*, 2 (1996), pp. 10–31; James G. Richter, *Khrushchev's Double Bind: International Pressures and Domestic Coalition Politics* (Baltimore, MD and London: Johns Hopkins University Press, 1994); Vladislav Zubok and Constantine Pleshakov, *Inside the Kremlin's Cold War* (Cambridge, MA and London: Harvard University Press, 1996), pp. 174–274.
100. Molotov's speech at the plenum of the CPSU CC, 24 June 1957, *Istoricheskii arkhiv*, 4 (1993), p. 5.
101. Ibid., pp. 33–4.
102. Ibid., p. 36.
103. Report by the Presidium of the CC CPSU during the October plenary of the CC CPSU, 14 October 1964, *Istochnik*, 2 (1998), p. 112; see also the report by Aleksandr Shelepin, head of the KGB between 1958 and 1961 and a Presidium member between 1961 and 1964 in *Neizvestnaia Rossiia XX Vek*, (Moscow: Istoricheskoe Nasledie, 1992), Vol. 1, pp. 281–3.
104. Marie-Pierre Rey, 'Puissance régionale? Puissance mondiale? Le point de vue des décideurs soviétiques, 1953–1975', *Relations internationales* 92 (1997), p. 398.

5

Britain's Slow March to Suez

KEITH KYLE

For Britain in the Middle East, 1956 was a year of paradox. It began with the new pro-Zionist Labour leader Hugh Gaitskell, mounting an attack against Anthony Eden, the Conservative prime minister, for allowing British arms to be delivered to Egypt after it had received massive supplies from the Soviet bloc, and with Britain and France openly at daggers drawn over their policies in the Middle East. British service chiefs were planning for the uncomfortable possibility of war alone against Israel in defence of Jordan,[1] while joint British and US studies were going ahead for action against either Israel or Egypt, whichever should be the aggressor.[2]

The year 1955 had ended with Israel's Premier David Ben-Gurion speaking of Anthony Eden as though he were his least favourite British statesman. 'After the Arab nations, [Britain's] is for us the most hostile government in the world', Ben-Gurion had said. 'I feel that Eden wants to be rid of us.'[3] No one would have predicted that 1956 would end with what the Egyptians still call the Triple Aggression – military action by an undercover alliance of Britain, France and Israel against Egypt. This having been violently denounced as 'collusion' by Gaitskell and the British Labour Party, it was to be aborted by the combination (though, despite Federal German Chancellor Adenauer's assertions to the contrary,[4] not the collaboration) of the United States and the Soviet Union.

In the first days of January, a period associated with very little political news, Gaitskell, still fresh to his party's leadership, opened up a sustained barrage on the Eden government for supplying arms to the unpopular government of Egypt.[5] The polemical Egyptian editor and future president Anwar Sadat, asserted that the Zionists in Britain had exceeded all bounds by buying up an entire political party.[6] In fact the arms contract with Egypt was an old one, and the tanks involved were reconditioned. But Eden's personal standing nine months after succeeding Churchill and convincingly winning the ensuing election was oddly precarious. The Conservative press was turning against him, reproaching him with 'dithering'. Because he had a reputation for being pro-Arab and had been responsible for two politically controversial treaties with Gamal 'Abd al-Nasser's Egypt, the *Daily Telegraph*, which wanted a change in Tory leadership, spoke of his 'clumsy courtship of unfriendly and fickle Arab statesmen'. Another right-wing organ, the *Spectator*, which was then owned and edited by Sir Ian Gilmour, subsequently a campaigner for the Palestinian cause, was urging that Britain should arm Israel in response to the Soviet decision to supply Egypt with advanced weapons. This also was the policy recommended in the House of Commons by Gaitskell, who, as Sadat never failed to mention in his articles, had a Jewish wife.

In the spring of 1956 the British tabloids were conducting a media war against Nasser, who was portrayed habitually by cartoonists as a would-be pharaoh, while in both Britain and France, politicians and officials were becoming obsessive about the propaganda campaigns being waged by Cairo Radio against their colonial interests throughout the Middle East and North Africa. Unfortunately, Eden and Nasser were both thin-skinned about press criticism and both avidly consumed foreign press cuttings and radio monitoring reports. In April Libyan Prime Minister, Mustafa bin Halim found Nasser beside himself with fury about the British press. 'The very mention of Britain made him go purple in the face and start pacing round the room like a wild animal.' When his Libyan visitor mentioned the absence of press censorship in Britain, Nasser was only rude to him for his pains.[7]

While he had been foreign secretary, Eden by negotiating first the treaty liquidating the Anglo-Egyptian condominium over the Sudan and, second the treaty for the military evacuation of Britain's Suez Canal base, had invested much political capital in earning Nasser's goodwill. In the service of that policy he had antagonized an important section of his own party, the so-called Suez group headed by Charles Waterhouse and Julian Amery who accused him of appeasement such as he had practised towards Hitler while at the Foreign Office in 1936. In a personal letter to the Egyptian ruler that went through many drafts and was in the end never sent, Eden was to have reminded Nasser of the moment in Cairo when the latter 'took my hand in his and assured me that a new chapter had opened in our relations'. Yet from that moment on the Egyptian press had never ceased to treat Britain as 'the enemy' and to abuse it and its allies 'in and out of season with a vehemence worthy of the Kremlin'.[8]

Criticized from within the Conservative Party for seeming to be an apologist for Colonel Nasser, Eden fulminated against him in a private meeting of the 1922 Committee of Conservative backbenchers in March 1956, declaring that Britain had to suffer constant humiliations from Egypt for the sake of 'oil, oil, oil'. One of those present said that 'he spat the words out like cherry stones'.[9] Britain's industrial recovery since the war had been fuelled by oil from the Middle East that was not only cheap but could be paid for in sterling and that was delivered mainly through the Suez Canal. When the Soviet leaders, Khrushchev and Bulganin visited Britain in April 1956, Eden took the opportunity to warn them that without regular supplies of oil Britain would have mass unemployment and would slowly starve to death. He told them that he must be 'absolutely blunt about the oil because we would fight for it'.[10]

Many of the issues that were to arise after the seizure of the Suez Canal Company had been raised beforehand in the staff talks beginning in March between Britain and the United States to determine in practice how they would fulfil the obligations they and the French had entered into under the Tripartite Declaration of 1950, to intervene on behalf of whoever was the victim of aggression in the Middle East. (The French were excluded from detailed talks because the US State Department objected to their supposed propensity to leak.[11]) At first the British insisted that the military staffs address themselves urgently to the case of Israeli aggression and only formally to the possibility of trouble from Egypt.[12] On 16 March Eden suddenly switched signals and had Air Chief Marshal Sir William Dickson, chairman of the British Chiefs of Staff, send a telegram urging 'the probability that Egypt is now more likely to be the aggressor'. The explanation was the receipt of an urgent telegram from Sir Humphrey Trevelyan, the normally calm British ambassador in Cairo, to the effect that he had received a warning from 'a generally well-informed source' that Nasser had decided on hostilities with Israel in June, as soon as the last British troops were to have left Egyptian soil.[13]

Dickson thought that the response to Egyptian aggression should provide for 'a combined US/UK operation to seize Port Said and other key points on the Suez Canal . . . to paralyze Egyptian army operations in Sinai and to safeguard international use of the canal'. He insisted that US ground forces should play a major part in any action, which would require three or four divisions of allied troops. The US planners, however, were not having any of that. Their idea was to halt the aggression by action from the air alone against the aggressor's lines of communication. This, said the British, would do nothing to protect the Suez Canal.[14]

Supposing that Nasser were to close the canal, what would Britain do? John Foster Dulles, the US secretary of state asked Sir Roger Makins, the British ambassador. The answer from the Foreign Office was that it was doubtful whether Britain had any legal right to use force to keep the canal open. 'But', it went on, 'it may be necessary for all that.' And it added, so as to make the United States understand the significance of the oil supply, 'The possibility of holding Kuwait by force is under consideration.'[15] Kuwait was the latest Middle East Eldorado; its foreign policy was supposed still to rest in British hands; it was not a member of the United Nations. But even Kuwait's staunchness was being put to the test by Nasser's pan-Arab populism. The ruler had had to subscribe to the Pan-Arab fund established to pay for the Russian arms purchase though he whispered to the British agent that he had not contributed very much and that it was not contributed in his own name.[16]

In the course of these talks in Washington, the British first raised the question of Soviet 'volunteers', only five years after Chinese 'volunteers' had intervened dramatically in Korea. It was feared that should fighting break out Soviet, Czech and Polish instructors already in Egypt to train the Egyptians on the advanced Soviet weapons would be driving the tanks and flying the planes on behalf of Egypt. Therefore, military plans could not rely on low assessments of the Egyptians' skills. Owing to these talks in advance of the crisis, US officials had precise knowledge of British capabilities and plans.[17]

But when the Canal Company was seized on 26 July this did not seem to President Eisenhower the right occasion to go to war. He wanted to see Nasser 'downgraded' but he held that this should not be done in the glare of the Suez controversy.[18] Both Britain and France, however, were prepared to use force, as President Bush said in 1990, as a last resort. Until Nasser thrust them together over the Suez Canal the two countries' Middle Eastern policies had been sharply divergent. At the beginning of the year Eden had been infuriated by a memorandum leaked by officials of the Quai d'Orsay to *Le Monde* at a moment when France was between governments.[19] This denounced the wisdom and expediency of a policy such as Britain's which was tied so tightly to Iraq, through the Baghdad Pact. This pact had an exceptional array of enemies – Egypt, Israel, Saudi Arabia, France and the Soviet Union. The French considered it to be a factor for instability in the region and, even in Iraq, to be only as firm as General Nuri al-Sa'id's hold on power in Baghdad. When the French Socialist leader Guy Mollet was installed as prime minister at the end of January 1956 Eden, who fancied himself to be a francophile, invited him for a weekend at Chequers, his official country house, in the hope that the two of them could make a fresh start. They found themselves in agreement over the threat of Nasser (Mollet was the first to compare his methods with those of Hitler) and much else. Eden congratulated himself on his initiative, only to have that mood dissolve into fury when his French counterpart, in an interview after his return, repeated France's objections to the Baghdad Pact.[20]

The French were preoccupied by the rebellion against their rule in

Algeria, for which they largely blamed Nasser, who had in fact supplied a few arms and some military training together with the backing of Cairo Radio, but was not, as they thought, a prime mover. The nationalization of the Canal Company, whose individual shareholders, headquarters and corporate ethos were French although the largest single shareholder was the British government, seemed to offer the chance of dethroning Nasser with British help. Thereby, so it was thought, the rebellion in Algeria would be decapitated. Fearing wrongly that Eden would only be interested in the management of the Suez Canal, Mollet and his dynamic Defence Minister, Maurice Bourgès-Maunoury, sent over to London an admiral, followed by the Foreign Minister, Christian Pineau, to urge the British to pursue the overthrow of Nasser. To encourage them to do so the French offered from the start their full military support, including their readiness to accept British commanders for any joint expedition.[21]

They found that, at least so far as Eden and Chancellor of the Exchequer, Harold Macmillan, were concerned, they were preaching to the converted. The cabinet, having resolved 'in the last resort' to use military force over the canal, if necessary alone, delegated the day-to-day handling of the crisis to a specially constituted Egypt Committee, under Eden's chairmanship. At its first meeting the committee identified the overthrow of Nasser as the prime objective, to be followed by the international takeover of the management of the canal. Because this order of priorities had been laid down, albeit in the greatest secrecy, by politicians, the military planners, working in the cramped, depressing quarters of a wartime bunker several floors underground, replaced the initial concept of a landing at Port Said with a more ambitious plan to seize Alexandria and follow this up by an advance on Cairo, the heartland of Nasser's power. After all, Alexandria was a port of much greater capacity than Port Said and thus a rapid build-up could be achieved. The French planners joined the troglodytes after an embarrassing delay caused by British lack of confidence in French security, which was only completely overcome when Mollet agreed to the very stringent regulations that the British laid down.[22]

British ministers were shocked at discovering the level of unpreparedness of their own forces for swift response. The earliest that an invasion force could appear off Alexandria was six weeks. Those British leaders, including the Prime Minister, who were convinced from the start that force would be necessary were therefore faced with the challenge of first filling up the intervening time with political and diplomatic activity and then of showing ruthlessness in terminating such activity when D-Day approached. Somewhat similar demands would be made of another British Prime Minister in the case of the Falklands War and of the US president at the time of the Gulf War.

While the French leadership, having on this issue no fear of domestic public opinion, was anxious to parade the war preparations of the allies by an immediate and conspicuous move of a French unit to Malta or Cyprus and a visit to Paris by the British force commanders in full uniform,[23] Eden insisted on circumspection so long as the diplomatic phase continued. When the presence of General Stockwell, who was to be the allied land force commander, was absolutely required in Algiers, he was smuggled there in mufti and only allowed to change into uniform when he was inside the headquarters building. When the French arrived in some style to establish their *point d'appui* in Cyprus Eden blanched at the publicity surrounding the act and found himself being reprimanded by the United States for aggravating the tension.[24]

There were two aspects of the original *Musketeer* plans which gave the British trouble. For an opposed landing at Alexandria, followed by a march on Cairo and, presumably, a pitched battle with the Egyptian army if it would offer itself for annihilation, a major expedition would be needed, which in turn would require a long succession of trigger points that could scarcely pass in peacetime without public attention. But Eden wanted his public image to be that of a man who, while being firm, was sincerely backing the plans endorsed by 18 powers including the United States for a peaceful resolution of the future international management of the canal. John Foster Dulles had indeed been induced to propose the scheme himself though he knew his chief, President Eisenhower, had doubts as to its effectiveness[25] and, what was more important, was unprepared to use more than moral suasion towards carrying it out. Eden, anxious to have US support, unnerved the military by repeatedly postponing those components in the carefully interlocked plan that might be thought to jar with his peaceful intent. The service chiefs themselves began to feel that, with this kind of civilian direction, they should be working towards a different plan.[26]

The second worry arose from a degree of military caution that exasperated the Prime Minister, who considered the Egyptians 'yellow.'[27] He was disconcerted to learn from General Templer, chief of the Imperial General Staff, that, while there was sufficient logistical backing to get the British expeditionary force to Cairo, there would not be enough to go further if by then organized military resistance had not been brought to an end and the Egyptian government had not been overthrown. 'If these two results do not follow from the plan', said General Templer, 'it will be necessary to pause for approximately two months to enable the logistical build up to support a second phase.'[28] Eden commented that 'as so often happens in situations like the present, we were being unnecessarily gloomy'.[29]

At this stage Eden absolutely ruled out any Israeli participation. Shimon

Peres, director-general of the Israeli Defence Ministry, was told by his opposite number in Paris on 1 August that though Britain and France had decided on military action Israel should neither take part nor be told it was happening.[30] It was true that Harold Macmillan had favoured Israeli participation from the outset, if only, as he said, to 'make faces' at the Egyptians, thus drawing in more Egyptian troops across the canal into Sinai. But this view, though supported by the retired Winston Churchill, was comprehensively rejected.[31] As with Bush over the Gulf War, Eden took the position that it would be a major political error to confuse Britain's quarrel with Nasser with the Arab–Israeli question.

But in September Eden, worried about the steadiness of British opinion, told the marquess of Reading, who represented the Foreign Office in the House of Lords, to enlist the active support of British Jews behind the policy of taking a firm line with Nasser. The marquess consulted Baron Edmund de Rothschild, who replied, first, that there was no such thing as 'Jewish opinion', and, second, that if the Prime Minister really wanted Jewish support, he would do well to change British policy of not supplying arms to Israel and of not pressing Egypt for the opening of the Suez Canal to Israeli ships. Lord Salisbury, one of Eden's most influential ministers, commented, 'This, I am afraid, is rather in the nature of blackmail . . . My reaction is that we should be very chary of letting them feel that we need them too much.'[32]

By the middle of September the chiefs of staff were telling the Egypt Committee that *Musketeer* as it stood 'becomes less attractive with every day's postponement. Maximum further postponement is only eight days.' Furthermore, they – and primarily the First Sea Lord, Earl Mountbatten of Burma – were increasingly concerned that the plan 'must inevitably result in great destruction and loss of life in built up areas', especially as the capture of Alexandria was to involve preliminary naval bombardment. The alternative, which would not require starting off with a full-scale expeditionary force launched from Britain, called for an assault primarily from the air, beginning with the elimination of the Egyptian Air Force and then targeting oil storage tanks, refineries and pipelines, Cairo Radio, government buildings, military targets and key points of road and rail communications. Only when Egyptian morale had been broken would the landing of a smaller force by then already in the region be made at Port Said and other points on the canal. It would not be ordered until organized military resistance had ceased, and hopefully the Nasser government looked as if it was about to collapse.[33] To this end strong emphasis was put on the importance of psychological warfare, which was defined by Lenin as 'the corruption of the human mind, the dimming of the intellect and the disintegration of the moral and spiritual fibre of one nation by the influence of the will of another'.[34]

Eden, though less than charmed by this change of professional advice, was eventually brought round to it by the man whom he had appointed as allied commander-in-chief, General Sir Charles Keightley. Keightley had only taken over on 22 August and had never liked the *Musketeer* concept, which he had no part in shaping, and felt much happier with its successor, which was called *Musketeer Revise*, though according to Air Marshal Denis Barnett, who was to command the air operation, none of the task force commanders considered it militarily sound.[35] Everything was now dependent on the success of the air operation, which, joined to the psychological offensive, was to determine the other deadlines. For instance, D-Day, which under *Musketeer* was the time of landing on Egyptian soil, became under *Musketeer Revise* the moment for the opening of the air assault on Egypt. The subsequent date for landing ground troops (and hence also the dates for setting sail from Malta, Cyprus and Algeria) would only be decided later by the progress of the air campaign. It would probably not be sooner than 14 days after the first attack, unless Egyptian resistance disintegrated fast. If that happened, the troops in Malta would be too far away to act swiftly. Units could only be landed swiftly provided the sea was calm, because the island's unsuitable harbours made it necessary to ferry men, vehicles and stores to the troopships and stores ships by lighters.[36]

When Admiral Grantham, commander-in-chief, Mediterranean, asked Keightley what would happen if all the Egyptian tanks, guns and transport were hidden in towns and villages, he said they would go for them there and the civilian population would have to take it. 'This would form part of the breaking of the will to resist', he concluded. Grantham, reporting this to Mountbatten, added, 'I understood...that the Chiefs of Staff, or anyway you, do not consider that the *Musketeer* plan is to bomb civilians.'[37]

Air Chief Marshal, Sir Dermot Boyle, in turn, was worried that in practice Keightley's plan would run the danger of being an uneasy 'compromise between an all-out air plan and an assault landing leading to occupation [which] carries with it the danger of being neither the one nor the other'. He and his staff objected to bureaucratic suggestions that such targets as bridges, oil pipelines and storage tanks should be spared in order to make the subsequent task of British civil affairs administrators easier. 'An all-out air plan is certain to succeed if the air commander is given a political directive which allows him to carry it out logically and ruthlessly to the point where the Egyptians' will to resist is broken and they are prepared to negotiate with us.'[38]

On the other hand, Boyle went on, 'The great weakness of an all-out air plan, is that of Ministers losing their nerve under pressure of public opinion during the possibly protracted period whilst bombing [is] going on.' If this resulted in crippling restrictions being placed on the air commander's freedom of action, the air plan might well fail 'with disastrous consequences...for the place of the air in our future overall strategy'.[39] The outbreak of the Suez crisis had overtaken a major defence review which Eden was directing personally with a view to a drastic reduction to fit Britain's strained resources. The RAF was fearful that an air-driven campaign that went off at half cock would directly prejudice the future of the service. At the same time the First Sea Lord, Earl Mountbatten, who had political grounds for being opposed to a Suez campaign, was urging his colleagues to register their misgivings about the consequences in defence expenditure terms of the occupation of Egypt. After weeks of nagging he persuaded them to agree on a paper which foresaw that the intention to depose Nasser and maintain a 'co-operative government' in Cairo would require an indefinite commitment of three or four divisions to an occupation force.[40] As the British air chief in the Middle East put it to Boyle, 'Even with a puppet regime in Egypt favourable to us I believe we shall have to face a basically hostile and uncooperative population.'[41]

Misgivings about the impact of the operation on civilians were also expressed by at least one of those who were to be at its sharp end. Vice-Admiral, Manley Power, who was to command the expedition's aircraft carriers, wrote to his superior:

My aircraft are the only ones in the force capable pin-point bombing...However good their aiming is – and it *is* good – they cannot fail to have a good many outside the bull's eye with resulting civilian casualties. Our pilots are trained for war, not for indiscriminate killing...I do not consider it either right or fair that they should be used in a manner which can only earn the obloquy of our own people and of the whole world.[42]

It was, after all, only a decade since the Nuremberg trials, which had established the principle that war crimes were not to be excused by superior orders. No one was more conscious of this than Mountbatten, who, once the crisis was over, drew up two briefs as if he were the defendant in a war crimes trial, entitled respectively 'The First Sea Lord's Part in the Suez Canal Operation up to 7 September 1956' and 'Naval Responsibility for Inflicting Civilian Casualties', in which are listed the successive points at which his interventions had a life-saving or politically challenging thrust.[43] It was relevant to this that the government lawyers had held that seizure of the Canal Company did not give legal warrant to the use of force[44] and also that the decision had been made in Whitehall that there would be no declaration of war against Egypt.[45]

In Whitehall there were protracted wranglings over the wording of the political directive to be issued to the allied commander-in-chief. According to the logic of the revised (really, totally altered) plan, General Keightley wanted it understood that whatever time was needed should be allowed for air action to take full effect. (Boyle had rather unhelpfully suggested that this might take a month.) But the political pressures on the general were all the other way. Reflecting Eden's views, Sir Norman Brook, the cabinet secretary, told Keightley that it might be found essential to land on the canal when Nasser was still in power. In that case, once the canal had been secured, he would need 'to send a force to Cairo to overthrow his government and enable a successor regime to be established'. But this contingency was not provided for in the existing draft of the directive 'since the forces made available for the present plan would not be adequate for that purpose'.[46]

Eden had been forced to recognize that he would be unable to take a united cabinet or hope to take a united country into battle unless there had been a further provocation from Colonel Nasser. Public opinion, which had given an impression of near-unanimity in the immediate aftermath of nationalization, had perceptibly gone off the boil during subsequent weeks. A fresh Egyptian provocation was required to galvanize public enthusiasm for military action. But, contrary to the expectations of many, Nasser was clever enough to avoid opening himself to attack. The belief that Egyptian management of the canal would be either incompetent or maliciously partisan or both was not at all upheld. When the British and French canal pilots were withdrawn in the middle of September, nothing went wrong despite a British attempt to crowd ships at the entrance in order to overwhelm the inexperienced management.[47] At the same time on the diplomatic front Dulles and Eden were constantly circling each other, each seeking to be the manipulator. Dulles tried to entangle the British in long drawn-out negotiations until a military conclusion would appear unfeasible while Eden was hoping to utilize US suggestions as a means to manoeuvre the United States into a confrontation with Nasser. And all the time military deadlines were not being kept, British reservists were getting restless at seemingly purposeless military inactivity, the equipment, badly packed and often inappropriate (because of changes of plan) was mouldering on vessels that had been loaded hastily at the beginning of the crisis[48] and could not be unloaded because the dock labour now showed signs of being politically unreliable, and winter was approaching. The politicians had at last taken the Suez crisis to the United Nations. The military were insisting on switching to a winter plan which would have meant, should events come to a head, a slower response with diminished assets – 14 days between warning and air assault and another ten days before a landing.[49] Admiral Power ordered two of his three British aircraft carriers to Gibraltar for rest and maintenance.[50]

It was in these circumstances that Eden made the strategic decision to reverse his policy of not working with Israel though to do so at arm's length and in conditions of the utmost secrecy. The Israelis would have preferred not to go to war at this particular time. Though they thought a 'second round' with Egypt very likely, they did not consider the Suez Canal to be their issue and they had not had time to absorb fully the sudden flow of armaments they were now receiving secretly from France. But what Ben-Gurion considered to be of greatest importance was that Israel had for the first time acquired in France a Great Power ally. This relationship had begun before Suez at the Vermars intelligence conference on 23–24 June, which also launched a stream of arms secretly conveyed from France to Israel and the planning of joint covert actions.[51] Ben-Gurion's desire to prove that Israel was a reliable ally could see Israel drawn further into French plans against Nasser. At the St Germain conference of 30 September–1 October these possibilities were explored, with service collaboration still running ahead of French and Israeli political commitment.[52] Some news of these bilateral talks must have reached Eden for on 3 October he was heard for the first time by 'an absolutely trustworthy Minister'[53] to comment that 'the Jews had come up with an offer'. It is possible, though there is no positive evidence of it, that his mind was turning round this possible option during the next fortnight.

There had been and would continue to be on the British side speculation that Anglo-French action might supply a trigger for opportunistic Israeli intervention, but the reverse – that Israel should deliberately supply the trigger for Britain and France to intervene in the guise of impartial peacemakers – was new. When put to Eden on 14 October by French Deputy Chief of Staff General Maurice Challe, it seemed to him to offer a way out of his dilemmas. It might at the same time offer an escape from the very real danger of Britain getting involved in a war against Israel on account of the mounting scale of Israeli reprisal raids against Jordan. In the circumstances in which he was placed, Eden took the bait. From this point onwards only a few senior ministers, a handful of civil servants and the chiefs of staff fully knew what was afoot. Agreement in principle was reached between the British and French in Paris on 16 October in a conference without civil servants. On 18 October Bomber Command, which had just relaxed the readiness of its crews under the winter plan, ordered full deployment of its Canberras and Valiants in the Middle East.[54] On the same day Keightley put the winter plan in abeyance, thus reinstating *Musketeer Revise* though the effect of this was somewhat diminished when Admiral Grantham ruled three days later that the weather in the Mediterranean had broken, so that shipping could no longer be held in the exposed anchorages off Cyprus. That meant that except for paratroops all forces would have to come the long way from Malta.[55]

Israel was involved directly at the highest level in a secret conference at Sèvres on 22–24 October, where Ben-Gurion was present with General Dayan and Shimon Peres, and where Britain was represented on the opening day by the unenthusiastic foreign secretary Selwyn Lloyd. He had come to find out whether the putative Israeli offensive would be such as to impress the world that the Suez Canal and the ships on it were in imminent danger. While between the French and Israelis there was a genuine atmosphere of positive connivance, between the British and the Israelis there lay a heavy mutual suspicion. Lloyd's report back resulted in Eden telling the cabinet on 23 October that 'from secret conversations which had been held in Paris with representatives of the Israeli Government' he had concluded that the Israelis were not after all about to launch a full-scale attack.[56]

Eden told General Keightley, who had been recalled to London, that the 'hot' news had gone cold, not that it had not been true in the first place but that 'the people concerned' had had second thoughts and had cancelled this D-Day. Mountbatten grumbled about 'this fantastic degree of secrecy' which 'made us all, Charles [Keightley] and the three chiefs of staff look pretty silly'.[57] The chiefs were not even allowed to explain the rationale behind the rapid changes of orders to their vice-chiefs (though Mountbatten did to his) nor could Keightley enlighten his force commanders. Boyle suspended Bomber Command's deployment in Cyprus and Malta on 23 October and it did not resume until 26 October, so that it was only completed as late as the 30th.[58]

The atmosphere was changed thanks to the eager inventiveness of General Moshe Dayan who was willing to change his campaign plan to make it look more like a credible attack on the canal and to the active advocacy in London of French Foreign Minister Christian Pineau. These factors, together with Eden's readiness to be persuaded, enabled the Sèvres conference to end in agreement on 24 October. It committed Israel to a large-scale attack on the evening of 29 October 'with the aim of reaching the Canal Zone the following day'. Then would come the 'appeals' to Egypt and Israel to desist and to accept the temporary occupation of key positions on the canal by Anglo-French forces to guarantee free passage 'until a final settlement'. The ultimatum (effectively only to Egypt and concerning exclusively Egyptian territory) would be a 12–hour one and, if rejected, the Anglo-French forces would 'launch military operations against Egyptian forces in the early hours of the morning of 31 October'.[59]

As ultimatums go this was to be an unusually short one. That sent by Austria–Hungary to Serbia in 1914 was for 48 hours; and Air Chief Marshal Dickson recalled from his time on the North-West Frontier of India that at least 'you gave the tribesmen twenty-four hours to get their goats and women away before you bombed the mud huts'.[60] Rather naturally Ben-Gurion and Dayan, who had insisted on paring down the interval during which Israeli cities would be vulnerable to the high-performance planes of the Egyptian air force, expected that British and French bombs would drop on Egyptian air bases in the early hours of 31 October.

So determined was Eden that not only operational surprise should be achieved but that no one should ever be able to uncover evidence of British collusion in the Israeli attack that scarcely anyone was given advance warning of what was to take place. Almost the entire civil service, including all the ambassadors and all except half a dozen people in 10 Downing Street and the Foreign Office, was excluded. The Foreign Office communications network was not used; intelligence channels, presumably to a limited extent, took its place. A senior intelligence figure (Nicholas Elliot) was sent to Israel and his cables were withheld from even the holders of very sensitive posts.[61]

Some effort was made to overcome the operational handicaps of total secrecy. General Templer, chief of the Imperial General Staff, told the acting quartermaster-general to the forces: 'The PM has decided that the landing must take place as soon as possible but has said that no-one is yet to be told.'[62] By such indirect means units at Malta which were at seven days' notice for embarkation were told to be ready for it within three days. Fortunately, there was already a planned communications exercise called *Boathook*; there is an unsigned note headed 'Points for the Prime Minister' in the Air Ministry files dated 26 October (one of the very few traces of plans for the operation that have survived) which says, 'We will not make any overt moves that are not essential. We will use the signal exercise as a cover plan.'[63] 'Many officers and other ranks left the UK ostensibly to take part in [*Boathook*] and the social life attached thereto', said General Stockwell, 'only to find themselves in the real thing, slightly inadequately and inappropriately equipped.'[64]

When the operation was over exceptional steps were taken to try to ensure that any record that might point to previous knowledge of what was to come was made to disappear. Parts of the naval task force commander's report had to be held 'under lock and key' and destroyed 'by fire' and eventually another admiral was given the task of rewriting it.[65] Similarly one page of the air task force report had to be hastily withdrawn.

Meanwhile the new deadline of 29 October had leaked to the land

and naval force commanders by way of the French and they succeeded in some beefing up of the elements committed to *Boathook*. On Saturday 27 October Power's Carrier group left Malta; HMS *Tyne*, which was to be the command ship though she proved to be ill-suited for the purpose, being too crowded and with woefully inadequate communications, also sailed for Cyprus. The next morning a loading exercise at Malta was brought forward to take place immediately on a Sunday and it was to be 'as for war'. On the morning of 29 October HMS *Jamaica*, the sole cruiser in the Mediterranean Fleet, was sent by Mountbatten at top speed to Port Said, for reasons unexplained to her captain but in fact to be ready to receive Egypt's surrender if by chance the ultimatum was accepted. He was later told to arrive by the time 'the ultimatum' expired without being informed what the ultimatum was.[66] In an unfinished and unsigned note in the Admiralty files for use by Mountbatten in talks with the Prime Minister and his fellow-chiefs, which, though undated, was clearly written on the morning of 29 October, the ultimatum is openly discussed. The first sea lord was to suggest that, 'directly it is established [that] heavy fighting has broken out between Jews and Egyptians', the canal should be proclaimed a 'dangerous area' for British shipping. 'If this is issued about 24 hours before the expiry of our ultimatum there is a sporting chance [that] about half of our merchant ships [in transit] will get away (say 15 out of 30).'[67]

The Israeli parachute drop took place 35 miles from the Suez Canal at the time stipulated, 5 P.M. on 29 October. The ultimatums were delivered in London at 4.30 P.M. on 30 October for expiry at 4.30 A.M. (6.30 A.M. local time) on the 31st. Within hours they were denounced on the floor of the House of Commons by Hugh Gaitskell. After remarking that, 'I do not think anybody will accuse me of lack of sympathy with Israel', he said there was nothing in the United Nations Charter which justified a nation appointing itself as world policeman. The following day, he declared that the whole world looked on the present action as a transparent excuse to seize the canal. But, Gaitskell went on, there was an even worse story going round. 'It is the story that the whole business was a matter of collusion between the British and French Governments and the Government of Israel.'

A source for Gaitskell's 'story' is now known. William Yates, a maverick pro-Nasser Tory, was approached by a Lebanese businessman on the morning of 29 October, who alleged, on the strength of loose talk by a French senator in a Paris night-club, that 'Mr Ben-Gurion met Mr Guy Mollet and a representative of the British Government at a house near [the French air force base at] Villacoublay and they have worked out a plan for Israel to attack Egypt and then intervene themselves in the Suez Canal.' Yates failed to get his informant in to see Edward Heath, the Tory chief whip, but succeeded with Gaitskell. Doubting that he would be called to speak in the debate, he then tried a little clumsily to ventilate his key allegation as a point of order but was shouted down.[68]

Once Gaitskell had launched the idea of 'collusion' the epithet stuck, especially when the truth began to emerge bit by bit and was fully confirmed by Dayan and Pineau 20 years later. There has been much discussion since over what, given the acknowledged need for secret diplomacy, intelligence and the making of contingency plans, was accounted peculiarly objectionable about the proceedings at Sèvres. Probably the best answer was this by a retired diplomat: 'the intentional creation of a situation in which we would claim the right to intervene to stop what we had conspired to start'.[69]

The only tool to hand in the new emergency was *Musketeer Revise*, so that the concept of the impartial separation of belligerents following an Israeli attack had to be grafted at no notice onto an offensive project directed against Egypt. Last minute improvisations were attempted to adapt it to the new scenario. A senior RAF officer was sent out to the region with fresh instructions about targets. Most of those designed to paralyze the Egyptian civil economy were struck off. Even Cairo Radio, which to Keightley with his strong views on psychological warfare was an absolutely prime target, was not to be touched, though this proved to be due to a misunderstanding of where the transmitters and masts actually were. When it was clear that they were not, as thought in London, alongside the studios in a populated area, they were finally attacked but rather too late for genuine impact.

Since Eden felt unable to give his commanders a political briefing about Sèvres, the rationale of an initial attack at dawn when the ultimatum ran out in the early hours of 31 October did not appeal to them. True the chiefs of staff issued an order to Keightley two hours before the ultimatum that 'planning should be completed for day air attack' and another half an hour after its delivery: 'You should be prepared to commence daylight air attacks on bomber airfields starting as soon as possible after receipt of executive order.'[70] But the RAF had its own doctrine about how to deal with enemy air bases – first the runways should be cratered at nightfall and then ground attack aircraft should take out the trapped planes at or shortly before dawn. It did not feel happy at changing the sequence now. The air commanders were reinforced in this view by four interceptions of reconnaissance planes, one of them at 47,000 ft, which suggested that Egyptian radar control was working considerably better than had been expected. Keightley sought permission to stick to the standard drill and it was granted. The failure of the British and French to deliver what they felt had been promised them at Sèvres was a severe blow to those few Israelis who knew what to expect; it was all Dayan could do to avoid Ben-Gurion calling for the withdrawal of the troops that had constituted the 'threat' to the canal. It had, after all, been a big concession on his part to agree that Israel should risk bombing raids on her cities for the first 36 hours until Britain and France entered the war.

Even so when the first British and French bombs began to fall on military objectives around Cairo, Egyptian sources indicate that the Egyptian leadership was divided and for a while paralyzed.[71] If at that moment the British and French had been ready to land and take ruthless advantage of Nasser's evident disorientation their immediate purposes might well have been attained. But this would have required the convoys to be 'just over the horizon' and that would have betrayed the British and French collusion with Israel.

In Washington President Eisenhower and Secretary of State Dulles were disposed to believe a false agency report which reached them to the effect that this landing had in fact occurred.[72] While furious at Eden's failure to alert him in advance and at Eden's having chosen the last week before the US presidential election despite having been asked specifically to avoid anything happening until the election was over, Eisenhower at least expected a swift operation.[73] But of course the delay was the essence of the plan and was in fact several days less than the planners had had in mind. But then the plan, now hijacked for use in a completely different political context, had called for the ruthless smashing of key features of the Egyptian economy and iron nerve in resisting international pressures. Now the last-minute emphasis, in keeping with the picture of an impartial fire-fighter, was all on gentleness except for unambiguously military targets.

The British and French night bombing attacks, once they had begun on the evening of 31 October, although in fact very inaccurate, had demoralized the Egyptian air force to the extent that their high-performance planes had failed altogether to take to the skies. They provided instead sitting targets for the ground-attack planes which struck at 20 minutes before dawn on 1 November, doing great damage. But Keightley's worries about an air attack on his own forces were not over. On the uncompleted runways of Nicosia and Akrotiri in Cyprus, bombers and transport planes for paratroops were so packed wing-tip-to-wing-tip that they seemed wide open to attack from Syrian air bases only a few minutes' flight away. 'The essential point', the Air Ministry's chief planner had reminded Boyle in September, 'is that, once one attack (which might indeed be flown by "volunteer" pilots) has been mounted, the damage will have been done.'[74] This dread haunted Keightley before, during and after the operation.

His other great worry was that Israel's advance was so rapid that it could only be explained by the deliberate withdrawal of Egyptian troops from Sinai, thereby greatly increasing the likely strength of the defenders of Port Said. Consequently, Keightley's hope of an unopposed landing there was gone. Either he would now need to have a 'devastating bombardment' of Port Said to cover the assault or he should be allowed to land unopposed with Israeli permission in Haifa or Gaza. A third option was to revert to the old idea of taking a fortnight to bomb Egypt to the point of surrender before landing.[75] He absolutely rejected urgent pleas from the French to authorize the immediate landing of their paratroops who were champing with frustration on Cyprus.

The volume of world protest at British and French action continued to be turned up, all the more in that it was being orchestrated by the United States and that the Suez War coincided with the savage repression of the Hungarian rising against Soviet imperialism. The yearning, as the United States prepared to go to the polls on 6 November, was for the world scene to be transformed into a morality play in which communism, caught in the beam of a searchlight resting unblinkingly on what was occurring in Budapest, would be forever damned. Thanks to the Suez campaign the moral absolutes seemed confused.

US unfriendliness over the Suez operation was at its most concrete in the waters of the Eastern Mediterranean where the ships of the Sixth Fleet manoeuvred while the US population was evacuated slowly from Egypt, past Cairo West, an air base that had for that reason to be excluded at the last minute from the target list. The encounter at sea was ironic, since if they could have had their way the American naval chiefs would have strongly backed action in support of Britain and France. On 11 August US Chief of the Naval Staff Admiral Arleigh Burke had sent a signal to Mountbatten noting

> with interest and admiration the speed and efficiency with which the British Navy had been able to undertake and perform its many additional tasks... The present Suez situation demonstrates once again that when the chips are down it is the Navy who must first act.

Burke had been strong in support of a Joint Chiefs of Staff recommendation that Britain and France receive political, diplomatic, intelligence and logistical backing against Nasser. Eisenhower did not think this was right; instead Dulles asked Burke what he could do to hinder the Anglo-French operation. Admiral 'Cat' Brown of the Sixth Fleet was ordered to 'go to sea with bombs up, ready to fight anything'.[76]

They certainly succeeded in aggravating the task of the British admirals. 'Our combat air patrols were continually meeting one another', recalled Admiral Power.

> Since we were expecting attack by the Egyptian Air Force whose MiGs strongly resembled the US fighters, an international incident was an

ever present possibility. I felt it to be a distinct possibility that I might be presented with an ultimatum to cease attacking Egypt by the Sixth Fleet.[77]

On 2 November Power's superior Admiral Grantham replied to his complaints, 'It is clear that HMG are alarmed at the prospect of any untowards incident. Brown knows where you are operating. But he seems incapable of keeping his forces well clear of yours.'[78] The Admiralty signalled that, 'If an unidentified sub were sunk which turned out to be an American this would be a disaster of the first magnitude to our cause.'[79] US planes were liable to swoop quite low over British ships. Keightley later remarked that the action of the Sixth Fleet 'was a move which endangered the whole of our relations with [the United States]...this situation with the US must at all costs be prevented from arising again'.[80]

Before the landings at Port Said on 5–6 November, there were two key moments in the breaking of Eden's will to destroy Nasser and take over control of the canal. The first occurred as early as 1 November, when Eden was already shaken by the vehemence of US and world reaction and parliamentary rumblings at Westminster. The Suez group was not the only wing in the Conservative Party. The United Nations also had its loyal supporters. In 10 Downing Street Selwyn Lloyd had floated the idea that Eden should lessen the pressure on himself by showing himself to be willing to hand over the policing of the Suez Canal Zone to a UN peace force once this could be constituted. Lloyd left the meeting with Eden saying, 'The PM says that this is simply to throw our hand in. And wasn't it to keep the United Nations out that we have done this?'[81] Then he changed his mind, almost certainly having heard from R. A. Butler, Leader of the House of Commons. Eden put the suggestion into his speech on Labour's no confidence motion, and in next day's cabinet meeting Butler attributed the solidarity of the Conservative vote entirely to his having made it. The parliamentary position could only be maintained, he said, if it was exploited at once so that responsibility should be transferred to the UN 'as rapidly as possible'. At the same cabinet meeting, the first of two on 2 November, Selwyn Lloyd was showing signs of the strain the whole Foreign Office machinery was under. US feelings were of such an order that oil sanctions might be imposed, in which case 'we might be compelled to occupy Kuwait and Qatar'. Disastrous consequences threatened in Iraq: the friendly prime minister, General Nuri, would fall and the king himself might be overthrown.[82] (Both men were killed two years later.) The foreign secretary was clearly near the end of his tether.

The second defining moment was on 4 November, when the convoys had still not arrived, but Abba Eban, Israel's UN ambassador, had indicated around the previous midnight in New York that Israel would accept the UN General Assembly's call for an immediate cease-fire. This still seems in retrospect odd because the Israeli forces had not yet achieved the capture of what they had described as 'our Suez', namely Sharm al-Shaykh at the tip of the Sinai peninsula. But no doubt it says something about the weak liaison at that time between the Israeli Defence and Foreign Ministries and something too about the Israelis' confidence in their ability to improve their military position after the date of a cease-fire. In all respects other than this, the Israelis had completely attained their military objectives. They had never wanted to cross the canal and, though the speed of their success in Sinai was assisted by Nasser's order to withdraw behind the canal following the Anglo-French attack, they could still claim a great military victory. But the announcement had a devastating effect on the solidarity and resolution of the British cabinet. Because Egypt had already responded favourably to the cease-fire resolution, there now seemed to be no fire for a self-constituted 'fire brigade' to put out.

The cabinet now found itself divided. Thanks to an overnight visit to Cyprus by Brigadier Antony Head, the new minister of defence, and General Templer, Keightley had been persuaded that, so desperate were the political pressures, he must risk parachute landings on 5 November. The British paratroop commander seemed confident that he and his French colleague would be able to take Port Said between them and disarm the artillery pointing out to sea. This should enable an unopposed landing to take place next day. The cabinet debated whether to call off the whole programme. Lord Salisbury, one of Eden's senior ministers and hitherto a hawk, wanted to do so as the whole purpose was gone; so did two others. The second ranking minister, R. A. Butler either wanted to do that or wanted to defer the parachute landing until matters were clearer. (There is a conflict of testimony about this.) The latter course was favoured by another three. The remainder, a majority, still backed Eden who wanted to go ahead. When after a long and desultory discussion news came through that, thanks to urgent French pressure, the Israelis had changed their minds about the cease-fire, orders were given for the military action to go forward. But the fragility of the consensus behind the policy of using the Israeli attack as a cover for smashing Nasser had been exposed.

The paratroops established themselves on 5 November on the outskirts of Port Said but did not take the town, partly because the resistance was quite stiff but also because time was lost while the local Egyptian commander sought terms of surrender which he was eventually not allowed by Nasser to accept. The main convoy had actually arrived off

Port Said ahead of time on 5 November – the slowest ships in it, the tank landing craft, having made a speed of 8 knots when they were only supposed to be able to make 6½ – and the marines proposed going ashore immediately to back the paras up and take the town. But there does not seem to have been the sense of great urgency that the unfavourable political setting would have suggested. Drastic alterations to a carefully thought out plan were considered highly undesirable.[83]

On 6 November when the landing took place, General Keightley reported: '[The Egyptians] fought extremely stubbornly except under naval gunfire . . . Throughout the day they fought a battle in the town; and streets had to be cleared systematically. There is no doubt that both in fighting spirit and in equipment the Egyptian Army is very much improved.'[84] But the effort was in vain. Overnight the Soviet Union had sent threatening messages to Britain, France and Israel, pointing out suggestively its status as a nuclear power and also an audacious note to Eisenhower proposing that they undertake a joint intervention of the superpowers on behalf of the United Nations. Signed by Premier Bulganin but drafted by Khrushchev, these may not have had a decisive effect on the British but they certainly reinforced awareness of the basic strategic dependence of Britain on the United States. The last straw was the realization by Harold Macmillan, chancellor of the exchequer, who had stood by Eden in the cabinet debate of 4 November, that the sterling reserves were running out – not, it has been pointed out by a US scholar,[85] as fast as he made out, but running out nevertheless. He spent all night on the telephone to the United States which was then on the eve of election day. There was going to be no help from that quarter so long as Britain defied the United Nations.

Guy Mollet, the French prime minister was not effectively consulted about ordering a cease-fire. He was simply told by Eden on the phone on 6 November that he had already informed Eisenhower that there would be an immediate cease-fire.[86] This took place at 2 A.M. local time on 7 November, leaving the British and French in possession of Port Said, Port Fuad on the opposite bank of the canal and a short stretch of the canal itself.

Eden, suffering from the effects of a botched operation, was now obviously showing signs of sleeplessness and strain. His pronouncements seemed to lose all touch with reality. He spoke of the continued occupation of Port Said as if the holding of this 'gage' would enable him to make deals with the Egyptians, the Israelis and the United Nations, which, if the terms were right, would be encouraged first to reinforce and then take over from Britain and France. The UN should not leave until both the management of the canal and the Arab–Israeli dispute were settled.[87] The reality was that, first, the state of his health obliged him to withdraw for a rest to Jamaica; then his colleagues were faced with the bitter truth that nothing whatever would be discussed with them until they had given up the 'gage'.

So ended Britain's last serious effort to play the Great Power in the Middle East and its last effort to carry out on the ground a foreign policy in face of US dissent. The armed services felt that they had achieved what had been asked of them and been exposed to ridicule by indecisive political leadership. In his unpublished autobiography Admiral Sir Manley Power summed up the great anti-climax to the months of fevered preparation and the week of action in unforgiving bitterness about Eden, whose health had finally forced him from office in January 1957 and who later was created the Earl of Avon: 'Now after all the odium incurred and with complete success within our grasp we were stopped in a position of the greatest possible disadvantage. It was mad, bad and stupid – and to think that they subsequently made the villain of the piece an Earl!'[88]

NOTES

1. Avon Papers, University of Birmingham. AP20/34/40 Eden's Paper on Suez, January 1957. 'We should have had no help if Israel had attacked Jordan'.
2. *Foreign Relations of the United States (FRUS) 1955–1957*, Vol. XV, Doc. 54, 30 January 1956, pp. 101–7; Doc. 56, 31 January, pp. 109–11; Doc. 65, 1 February, pp. 125–6; Doc. 143, 1 March, pp. 263–5.
3. Cited by Motti Golani, *Israel in Search of a War: The Sinai Campaign, 1955–1956* (Brighton: Sussex Academic Press, 1998), p. 21.
4. *Documents Diplomatiques Français 1956*, Vol. III, Doc. 138, pp. 231–8. Procès-Verbal Mollet/Adenauer, 6 November 1956. On the day of the Anglo-French assault landing at Port Said, Adenauer repeatedly alleged to French Premier Mollet that Eisenhower, through back channels, was working in collusion with the Kremlin.
5. The arms were not very numerous and consisted largely of reconditioned tanks. The emotional force of the attack derived from the news in September 1955 of the huge Soviet upgrading of Egyptian armaments.
6. Public Record Office, Kew (PRO) FO, 371/119221, *Voice of the Arabs*, 1700 hrs GMT, 25 April 1956. Sadat, 'I accuse [the Labour MPs]...of receiving bribes through the Jewish Zionist companies...I accuse the leader of the British Labour Party of being a puppet and hireling of world Zionism. It is well known to all of us that he is married to an ardent Zionist Jewess...'
7. PRO FO, 371/118842/JE 1022/23, Halford (Tripoli) to Adam Watson (FO).
8. PRO [Kew] PREM, 11/859, 27 October, 1 November 1955.
9. Nigel Nicolson, 'Diary of a Suez Rebel', *The Sunday Telegraph*, 27 October 1996, p. 26.
10. PRO PREM, 11/1626, 'Visit of the Soviet Leaders to the UK, April 1956', pp. 13–14.
11. *FRUS XV*, doc. 143 pp. 263–5, Memo from Admiral Radford to J. F. Dulles.
12. PRO FO, 371/121761/VR 1076/64, ACM Dickson to Gen. Whiteley (Head of British Joint Services Mission, Washington), 15 March 1956.
13. PRO FO, 800/734 Top Secret PM/MS/56/57, Anthony Nutting (Minister of State, FO) to Eden, 14 March 1956.
14. PRO FO, 371/121761, Dickson to Whiteley, 16 March 1956. Makins to Eden, 18 March 1956. Dulles Oral History Project, Princeton; interview with Admiral Arleigh Burke.
15. PRO FO, 371/119069 JE1424/63, Makins to Selwyn Lloyd, 6 April 1956, Lloyd to Makins 6 April 1956.

16. PRO FO, 371/113681/JE 1194/369, Bell (British Agent, Kuwait) to FO, 6 November 1955. The ruler's excuses were that he relied on Egypt for much of Kuwait's educational service and that Egyptian pressure was very strong. He assured HMG of his loyalty.
17. Dulles Oral History Project, Princeton; interview with Admiral Arleigh Burke.
18. *FRUS XVI*, doc. 151 pp. 334–5 Memorandum of conversation between Eisenhower and Dulles, 30 August 1956.
19. PRO FO, 124244/V1072/21 Gladwyn Jebb (British ambassador, Paris) to FO, 20 January 1956. 'Too much importance ought not to be attached to *Le Monde*, which is almost incorrigible and incapable of finding any virtue in any British policy anywhere in the world.'
20. PRO FO, 800/734, 'Record of a Meeting Held at Chequers', Sunday, 11 March 1956, FO 371/124430/WF 1022/24 Eden to Jebb, 12 March 1956, Jebb to Eden, 19 March.
21. Mountbatten Papers, University of Southampton: 'The First Sea Lord's Part in the Suez Canal Crisis 1956'; Jean Chauvel, *Commentaire, Tome III De Berne A Paris* (Paris: Fayard, 1973), pp. 182–3.
22. PRO PREM, 11/1099, f. 133 'Minutes of a Staff Conference Held at Chequers, 11 August 1956'. Even after the French were admitted, for the first few days the British planners had to pretend to be going to Port Said whereas they were really going to Alexandria. This, said General Stockwell, the land force commander, was 'both distasteful and foreign to British principles'. General Sir Kenneth Darling, 'The Suez Crisis: the Problem of Intervention', Imperial War Museum; PRO WO, 288/77; Stockwell, 'Report on Operation *Musketeer*', p. 14; General André Beaufre, *The Suez Expedition* (London: Faber & Faber, 1969).
23. PRO DEFE, 13/47, ACM Sir William Dickson to Sir Walter Monckton (Minister of Defence).
24. John Foster Dulles Papers, Eisenhower Library, Abilene, Kansas. Box 82, US Ambassador Douglas Dillon to Dulles, 2 September 1956. FO, 800/740 f. 10, 'Conversation between secretary of state and Mr Barbour, the U.S. Chargé d'Affaires', 3 September.
25. *FRUS XVI*, Doc. 98, pp. 232–3 Eisenhower to Dulles, 19 August, 1956.
26. PRO WO, 288/77, Stockwell Report no. 13, pp. 17–18. ADM 116/6209 Vice-Admiral Richmond's Report no. 44 p. 30.
27. Mountbatten Papers. Earl Mountbatten of Burma, 'The First Sea Lord's Part in the Suez Canal Crisis up to 7 September 1956.' 'The PM was of the opinion that the Egyptians were yellow and would crumble [and that] our forces would be in Cairo within five days.'
28. PRO DEFE, 13/47, Templer, 'Limitations of Operation *Musketeer*', 10 August 1956.
29. PRO DEFE, 13/47, Note by Sir Walter Monckton (Minister of Defence).
30. Ben-Gurion Diary for 3 August 1956. S.I. Troen and M. Shemesh (eds), *The Suez–Sinai Crisis 1956: Retrospective and Reappraisal* (London: Frank Cass, 1990) p. 292.
31. PRO PREM, 11/1099, ff. 270–2. 'Record of a Meeting in 11, Downing Street', 3 August 1956. PREM, 11/1098, ff. pp. 278–9 EC (56) 8 'Action Against Egypt. Note by the Chancellor of the Exchequer', 7 August 1956. Sir Martin Gilbert, '*Never Despair': Winston S Churchill 1945–1965* (London: Heinemann, 1988), pp. 1203–4.
32. PRO PREM, 11/1115, Rothschild to Reading, 11 September 1956; comment by Eden, 16 September, PM's Personal Minute M198/56; Salisbury to Eden, 16 September.
33. PRO CAB, 134/1217 Terrapin EC (56) 47, 10 September 1956. FO 371/118997 JE11924/76 and /76 'C', Draft Note by Egypt (Official) Committee.
34. PRO ADM, 205/154, Psychological Warfare PSW (56) 4 (Final) 17, August 1956.
35. PRO AIR, 20/10746, Air Marshal Barnett, 'Summary of Operations during Operation *Musketeer*', 19 February 1957.
36. PRO WO, 288/77, Stockwell Report, pp. 24–30: 'Joint Task Force Commanders' Appreciation of the *Musketeer Revise* Concept.'
37. PRO ADM, 205/133, Admiral Sir Guy Grantham to Mountbatten, 24 September 1956. Signal 241634Z.
38. PRO AIR, 8/2081, Brief for Sir Dermot Boyle at Chiefs of Staff Committee, 25

September 1956; ADM, 205/132; Captain Duncan Lewin (Director of Plans, Admiralty) to Mountbatten. 'Major bridges, etc. which would be expensive to replace after hostilities would be left intact.'

39. PRO AIR, 8/2081, Brief for Sir Dermot Boyle at Chiefs of Staff Committee, 25 September 1956.
40. PRO ADM, 205/132, Mountbatten (whose nickname was Dickie) to Air Chief Marshal Dickson (Dickie to Dickie), 27 September 1956. DEFE, 4/91 COS (56) 97th Meeting, 9 October 1956, item 6; PREM, 11/1100, ff. 21–7; Memorandum of the Chiefs of Staff, 'Military Implications of Mounting Operation *Musketeer*', 25 October 1956.
41. PRO AIR, 20/9968, 'Suez Records'. CINC to Boyle 24 August 1956, Signal 240835Z.
42. Mountbatten Papers. Admiral Power to Admiral Grantham, 16 September 1956.
43. Mountbatten Papers, N.106. On 1 September the First Sea Lord consulted the Minister of Defence and the First Lord of the Admiralty (Lord Cilcennin) about whether he should resign. 'I drew their attention to the fact that the British had been instrumental in laying down at the Nuremberg war criminal trials that a senior officer could not escape the guilt of ordering the shooting down of women and children merely because his Government had told him to do so. If I failed to resign I would therefore be held responsible under this ruling for the deaths that were caused.'
44. PRO FO, 800/747, for correspondence of government lawyers; FO, 800/748, 'We are on an extremely bad wicket legally as regards using force in connection with the Suez Canal. Whatever illegalities the Egyptians may have committed…these do not in any way…justify forcible action on our part.' G. G. Fitzmaurice, Legal Adviser to the Foreign Office. CAB, 134/1225, ff. 15–16 EOC (56) 3rd Meeting, 30 August 1956. Annex: 'Nature of Hostilities Contemplated in Egypt'.
45. PRO FO, 371/118838/JE 1018/1.
46. PRO FO, 371/118997 JE11924/76, 24 September 1956. CAB 134/1217 EC(56)53, 25 September.
47. PRO CAB, 128/30 Pt.2 JE 14211/1784, Memorandum on Operation *Pile-up* by Harold Watkinson, Minister of Transport, 10 September 1956.
48. PRO WO, 288/77, Stockwell Report p. 24. 'The considered War Office opinion was that unless vehicles and certain other equipment were unloaded by 1 November 1956 or shortly after for servicing they would not be battle-worthy.'
49. PRO WO, 288/77, Stockwell Report.
50. Admiral Sir Manley Power, unpublished memoirs, Churchill College, Cambridge.
51. Mordechai Bar-On, *The Gates of Gaza* (New York, NY: St Martin's Press, 1994) pp. 169–71. Golani, *Israel in Search of a War*, pp. 26–36.
52. Golani, *Israel in Search of a War*, pp. 76–88.
53. Hugh Thomas, *The Suez Affair* (London: Weidenfeld & Nicolson, 1966), p. 96.
54. PRO AIR, 9967, HQ Bomber Command, 'Report on Operation *Musketeer*'.
55. PRO ADM, 116/6106, Richmond Report: The Winter Plan no. 49–50, p. 32.
56. PRO CAB, 128/30 ff, 610–1; CM (56) 72, Confidential Annex. Only one of the copies of this annex contains the sentence quoted.
57. Mountbatten Papers N.106. Mountbatten to Grantham, 23 October 1956.
58. PRO AIR, 9967, Bomber Command Report, 9967 HQ Bomber Command, 'Report on Operation *Musketeer*'.
59. Keith Kyle, *Suez* (London: Weidenfeld & Nicolson, 1991) Appendix 'A' 'The Protocol of Sèvres, 24 October 1956', pp. 565–7; Avi Shlaim, 'The Protocol of Sèvres: Anatomy of a War Plot', in this volume.
60. Interview with Marshal of the RAF Sir William Dickson, 1986.
61. Information from Nigel Clive, formerly of the Foreign Office.
62. General Sir John Cowley, unpublished memoir, Churchill College, Cambridge.
63. PRO AIR, 8/2081, 'Suez Canal Crisis: Planning for Military Operations. Points for PM', 26 October 1956.
64. PRO WO, 288/77, Stockwell Report.
65. PRO ADM, 205/161, Mountbatten to Admiral Durnford-Slater, 7 and 8 January 1957.
66. Eden was informed of this, according to Mountbatten's 'Speaking Notes' for 29 October. Captain A.D. Lenox-Conyngham, DFC, RN (commander of *Jamaica*) to

Commander (ret.) Conrad Rawnsley, 13 November 1986.

67. PRO ADM, 205/139, 'Top Secret Guard', n.d. but clearly 29 October, 1956.
68. William Yates, 'Forty Years After the Amesa Conference', address to seminar at Deakin University, Australia, 22 September 1996.
69. Sir Brian Barder, 'Letter to the Editor', *The Times*, 1 August 1996.
70. PRO AIR, 8/1940, C[hiefs]O[f]S[taff-]KE[ightle]Y 2, Signal 301440Z (i.e. 30 October 2.40 P.M., Z=Zulu=GMT); COSKEY 4, Signal 301700Z.
71. Troen and Shemesh, *The Suez–Sinai Crisis 1956*, Ch. 22, 'Abd al-Latif al-Bughdadi's Memoirs'.
72. Dulles Papers, Eisenhower Library, Abilene, General Telephone Conversations, 10 P.M., 29 October l956; President's telephone calls, 8.40 A.M., 30 October.
73. PRO PREM, 11/1102, ff. 302–4 Macmillan, 'Note of a Private Talk with Mr Dulles, 25 September 1956'; *FRUS XVI*, Doc. 265, 25 September, pp. 580–1.
74. PRO AIR, 20/9965, 'Operation *Musketeer*'. Assistant Chief of Air Staff (Plans) to Boyle, 10 September 1956.
75. PRO AIR, 1940 KEYCOS 17, Signal O22135Z.
76. Dulles Oral History Project, Princeton. Interview with Admiral Arleigh Burke.
77. Manley Power, unpublished memoirs, pp. 101–2.
78. PRO ADM, 116/6117, 'Admiralty Signals, *Musketeer*', Grantham to Power, 2 November 1956. 021702Z.
79. PRO ADM, 116/6136, Admiralty to Task Force, 1 November 1956.
80. PRO AIR, 8/1940, Keightley, 'The Lessons of Suez.'
81. William Clark papers, Bodleian Library, Oxford. Clark was Eden's press secretary. Keith Kyle, 'Suez and the Waldegrave Initiative', in *Contemporary Record*, 9, 1 (Summer 1995), pp. 384–5.
82. PRO CM, (56) 77, Cabinet Minutes, 2 November 1956.
83. PRO ADM, 116,6209, Richmond Report, no. 227, p. 64.
84. PRO DEFE, 11/111, 'Strategic Policy Middle East'. Keightley to Chiefs of Staff, KEYCOS 54, 7 November 1956.
85. Diane B. Kunz, *The Economic Diplomacy of the Suez Crisis* (Chapel Hill, NC: University of North Carolina Press, 1991), pp. 131–3.
86. Kyle, *Suez*, p. 467.
87. Parliamentary Debates (Hansard) House of Commons, Vol. 560, 6 November l956, cols 75–81. Kyle, *Suez*, pp. 472–3.
88. Admiral Sir Manley Power, unpublished memoirs.

6

The Protocol of Sèvres, 1956:
Anatomy of a War Plot

AVI SHLAIM

The tripartite aggression against Egypt in 1956 involved an extraordinary reversal of Britain's position in the Middle East. The French were the matchmakers in bringing Britain and Israel into a military pact whose principal aim was the overthrow of Gamal 'Abd al-Nasser. The war plot against Egypt was hatched towards the end of October 1956 in a secret meeting at Sèvres, near Paris. The discussions lasted three days and culminated in the signing of the Protocol of Sèvres. British, French and Israeli sources are used here to reconstruct the sequence of events that produced the most famous war plot in modern history.

SECRECY AND THE SOURCES ON SÈVRES

On 24 October 1956, in a private villa in Sèvres on the outskirts of Paris, representatives of the British, French and Israeli governments, at the end of a three-day meeting which was concealed behind a thick veil of secrecy, signed a most curious document which later came to be known as the Protocol of Sèvres. The document set out in precise detail the plan of the three governments to attack Egypt. The plan, in a nutshell, was that Israel would attack the Egyptian army near the Suez Canal, and that this attack would serve as the pretext for an Anglo-French military intervention. Written in French and typed in triplicate, this protocol was signed by Patrick Dean, an assistant under-secretary at the Foreign Office for Britain, by Foreign Minister Christian Pineau for France, and by Prime Minister David Ben-Gurion for Israel. To the end of his days Sir Anthony Eden, the driving force on the British side on the road to war, denied that there had been any collusion with Israel or even foreknowledge that Israel would attack Egypt. The Protocol of Sèvres tells a different story. The British copy was in fact destroyed on Eden's orders, the French copy was lost and the Israeli copy was kept under lock and key in the Ben-Gurion Archives in Sde Boker. In 1996 permission was given to photocopy the protocol for a BBC documentary shown on the fortieth anniversary of the Suez war.[1] With the release of the protocol, the tripartite meeting at Sèvres became not only the most famous but also the best-documented war plot in modern history.

Rumours and accusations of collusion started flying around as soon as the Suez war broke out but no hard evidence was produced at the time, and certainly no smoking gun. Over the years, however, a great deal of information has come to light about the meeting at Sèvres at which the war plot was hatched. A number of participants have written about the meeting in their memoirs. Sir Anthony Nutting was not a participant at this particular meeting, but he was the first insider to publish the story of the collusion.[2] Christian Pineau spilled the beans on the twentieth anniversary of Suez, and even gave an annotated version of the Protocol of Sèvres.[3] Moshe Dayan gave a much more accurate and more detailed account of this meeting in his autobiography.[4] Selwyn Lloyd wrote a whole book on Suez which includes a vivid description of his embarrassment at the encounter with the Israelis at Sèvres.[5] Abel Thomas wrote an account which is not always accurate on the details and wholly unconvincing in its central claim that France got involved in the Suez affair out of concern for the security of Israel.[6] Shimon Peres was the principal source for a book on Suez published in Hebrew in 1965.[7] More recently, Peres shed interesting new light in his memoirs on the background of the conference of Sèvres, and particularly on his own private discussions with the French.[8] Ben-Gurion's diary is governed by Israel's 30-year rule and the main entries on Suez have been translated and published in English.[9]

But the principal, most prolific and most reliable chronicler of the proceedings of the Sèvres conference is Colonel Mordechai Bar-On, chief of bureau of the Israel Defence Forces (IDF) Chief of Staff, who served as the secretary of the Israeli delegation and took copious notes throughout. In 1957, at Dayan's request, Bar-On, who had a degree in history, wrote a detailed account of the events that led to the Suez war with access to all the official documents, and in 1991 this study was published as a book.[10] Bar-On also published another book, which started life as a doctoral thesis, as well as numerous articles on various aspects of Suez.[11] Sir Donald Logan, who attended the Sèvres conference as Lloyd's private secretary, was allowed to see a copy of the Protocol of Sèvres in the Israeli Embassy in London before its release and he in turn guided Keith Kyle in publishing an English translation of the protocol as an appendix to his book on Suez.[12] Logan also wrote a personal account of the meetings at Sèvres.[13] With the benefit of all these first-hand sources, it is now possible to reconstruct the discussions and decisions that immediately preceded the tripartite attack on Egypt in late October 1956.

INVITATION TO A CONSPIRACY

The French were the matchmakers in the Anglo-French–Israeli military pact whose undeclared aim was the overthrow of Egyptian President Gamal 'Abd al-Nasser. Ever since his nationalization of the Suez Canal Company on 26 July 1956, the French and the British had been making plans for military action against Egypt if negotiations failed to achieve their aims. By early October it looked as if these plans might have to be abandoned because no suitable excuse could be found to justify the attack. The French, whose relations with the Israeli defence establishment were increasingly intimate, came up with the idea of using an attack by Israel as a pretext for Anglo-French intervention. On 14 October, General Maurice Challe, the deputy chief of staff of the French armed forces, accompanied by Albert Gazier, the acting foreign minister, visited the British prime minister in his country house at Chequers. At this meeting the French general presented a plan of action which quickly became known as 'the Challe scenario': Israel would be invited to attack the Egyptian army in Sinai and pose a threat to the Suez Canal and this would provide Britain and France with the pretext to activate their military plans and occupy the Suez Canal Zone, ostensibly in order to separate the combatants and protect the canal.

Eden liked the idea. According to Anthony Nutting, the Minister of State for Foreign Affairs who was present at the meeting, 'he could scarcely contain his glee'. The question of whether Israeli aggression might not require Britain and France to come to Egypt's aid under the terms of the Tripartite Declaration of May 1950 was disposed of when Gazier reminded Eden that the Egyptians themselves had recently said that this declaration did not apply to Egypt. Nutting records Eden as saying excitedly: 'So that lets us off the hook. We have no obligation, it seems, to stop the Israelis attacking the Egyptians.'[14] The only aspect of the Challe scenario that Eden did not like was the idea of Britain inviting Israel to move against Egypt. He preferred Israel to move of its own accord; he did not want Britain to be implicated in anything that might be construed as collusion in an alliance with Israel against an Arab country. In short, he hoped for divine intervention.

For Eden the Chequers meeting was the turning point. The 'Suez Group' within the Conservative party had been intensifying the pressure on him to get tough with Nasser. Selwyn Lloyd, the Foreign Secretary, was at the United Nations in New York, working towards a peaceful settlement of the dispute with Mahmud Fawzi, his Egyptian opposite number. Up to this point, Eden had been thrashing around. He did not think that the United Nations could produce a solution and he was not enamoured with Lloyd's diplomatic efforts but no alternative policy was available. Now the Frenchmen landed at Chequers like two angels from heaven and offered an alternative. Eden seized this alternative with great alacrity and made a sudden jump from the diplomatic track to the military track. He telephoned Lloyd in New York and ordered him to drop everything and return home immediately.[15]

Lloyd arrived on 16 October in the middle of a meeting to which Eden had invited several ministers to discuss the French proposal. The meeting was held in the cabinet room at 10 Downing Street and Anthony Nutting was also there. Nutting took Lloyd to an ante-chamber and gave him a very brief report on the Chequers meeting. Lloyd did not like the French proposal. He said to Nutting: 'You were quite right to reject it. We must have nothing to do with the French plan.' After the meeting a tug-of-war developed between the two Anthonys, with the hapless foreign secretary in the middle. Eden won. He took Lloyd to lunch and convinced him to go along with the French plan. Originally, Eden had told Challe and Gazier that he would send Nutting to Paris with a reply to their proposal. But given Nutting's strong opposition to this proposal, Eden decided to keep the matter in his own hands and more or less ordered Lloyd to accompany him to a meeting in Paris that very day. Lloyd was very reluctant to embark on this venture but he felt that he had no real choice.[16]

On the evening of 16 October, Eden and Lloyd had the follow-up to the Chequers meeting at the Palais Matignon, the official residence of the French Prime Minister, with Guy Mollet and his Foreign Minister, Christian Pineau. No officials were present at this meeting. The first matters to be discussed were the recent efforts to settle the canal dispute by negotiation. Attention then turned to the possibility that Israel would launch an attack against Egypt. Pineau enquired about the British reaction to such an attack. Eden replied that if Israel attacked Jordan, they were bound to go to Jordan's help but if Israel attacked Egypt, they would not regard themselves as bound to intervene under the Tripartite Declaration. Mollet then asked whether the United Kingdom would intervene in the event of hostilities in the vicinity of the canal and Eden said that he thought the answer to that question would be 'yes'. On the following day, 17 October, Eden confirmed in writing to Mollet the answers he had given to the two questions at the meeting, again making a distinction between an Israeli attack on Jordan and an attack on Egypt.[17] The French wasted no time in conveying to the Israelis these indirect assurances and in encouraging them to launch an independent attack near the canal in accordance with the Challe scenario.[18]

Ben-Gurion was greatly excited by the prospect of a military partnership with the Great Powers against Egypt but extremely suspicious of the British in general and of Sir Anthony Eden in particular. Only a week earlier, following an IDF attack on the police station in Kalkilya, across the border in Jordan, the British had reminded the Israelis of their obligation to come to Jordan's aid under the terms of the Anglo-Jordanian Treaty of 1946. A private source warned Ben-Gurion that the British were preparing to take military action against Israel.[19] Although he knew that the plan to attack Egypt originated with General Challe, he repeatedly referred to it as 'the English plan.' He had no faith in vague and indirect British assurances and he feared that Britain might turn its back on Israel or even turn against it. Moreover, he greatly resented the suggestion that Israel should be used merely to provide services for the Great Powers. What he deeply longed for was a partnership between equals and an explicit coordination of military plans, preferably at a face-to-face meeting with Eden.[20] When news reached Ben-Gurion of the planned Anglo-French summit meeting, he urgently cabled the Israeli defence ministry's representative in Paris:

In connection with the arrival of the British representatives in Paris, you should contact the French immediately and ask them whether the meeting can be made tripartite. The Israeli representatives are ready to come immediately, in utmost secrecy. Their rank will equal the ranks of the British and French representatives.[21]

The French understood that only a face-to-face meeting might allay Ben-Gurion's suspicions. The following day Guy Mollet cabled Ben-Gurion to suggest that he should come to Paris and, if the need arose, a member of the British government could also be invited. Ben-Gurion replied that the British proposal was out of the question but that he was still willing to come if Mollet considered that his visit would serve a useful purpose in spite of the disqualification of the British idea. In his diary Ben-Gurion recorded: 'It seems to me that the English plot is to embroil us with Nasser, and in the meantime bring about the conquest of Jordan by Iraq.'[22] Whether the British would be represented at the talks in Paris would not become clear until after Ben-Gurion's arrival.

BEN-GURION'S GRAND DESIGN

The senior members of the Israeli delegation to the talks in Paris were David Ben-Gurion, who was defence minister as well as prime minister,

Moshe Dayan, the IDF chief of staff, and Shimon Peres, the director-general of the Ministry of Defence. France was represented by Guy Mollet, Christian Pineau and Maurice Bourgès-Maunoury, the Minister of Defence. Also present were General Challe, Louis Mangin, Bourgès-Maunoury's friend and adviser, and Abel Thomas, the director-general of the Ministry of Defence. Although it was essentially a political meeting, with the politicians bearing the ultimate responsibility for decisions, it was the military men who had pressed for the meeting and who provided most of the ideas that were finally agreed upon.[23]

Most of the French delegation had been active in the Resistance against Nazi Germany during the Second World War. All of them saw Nasser as a dangerous new dictator, not least because of his support for the Algerian rebels, and all of them were united by the conviction that military action was urgently required in order to seize the canal and knock Nasser off his perch. The French military had three priorities at that time: Algeria, Algeria and Algeria. And they proceeded on the assumption, for which there was no solid basis, that if only Nasser could be toppled, the Algerian rebellion would collapse. The French politicians were haunted by the spectre of another Munich. The spacious villa, in rue Emanuel Girot in the leafy suburb of Sèvres, belonged to a family that had supported General de Gaulle against the Vichy regime. It had been used by Bourgès-Maunoury as a Resistance base during the war. The collective determination of the French that this time there must be no appeasement was conveyed by Abel Thomas to the Israeli leader soon after his arrival at the villa. 'One day the Sèvres conference will no doubt be publicized', said Thomas. 'It therefore depends on us whether it is remembered as the Yalta conference or as the Munich conference of the Middle East.'[24]

The first session started at 4 P.M. on Monday, 22 October, in the conservatory of the villa and it was intended to enable the leaders of the two countries to get to know each other and to have a preliminary discussion. Ben-Gurion opened the discussion by listing his military, political and moral considerations against 'the English plan.' His main objection was that Israel would be branded as the aggressor while Britain and France would pose as peacemakers but he was also exceedingly apprehensive about exposing Israeli cities to attack by the Egyptian air force. Instead, he presented a comprehensive plan, which he himself called 'fantastic', for the reorganization of the Middle East. Jordan, he observed, was not viable as an independent state and should therefore be divided. Iraq would get the East Bank in return for a promise to settle the Palestinian refugees there and to make peace with Israel while the West Bank would be attached to Israel as a semi-autonomous region. Lebanon suffered from having a large Muslim population which was concentrated in the south. The problem could be solved by Israel's expansion up to the Litani River, thereby helping to turn Lebanon into a more compact Christian state. The Suez Canal area should be given an international status while the Straits of Tiran in the Gulf of Aqaba should come under Israeli control to ensure freedom of navigation. A prior condition for realizing this plan was the elimination of Nasser and the replacement of his regime with a pro-Western government which would also be prepared to make peace with Israel.

Ben-Gurion argued that his plan would serve the interests of all the Western powers as well as those of Israel by destroying Nasser and the forces of Arab nationalism that he had unleashed. The Suez Canal would revert to being an international waterway. Britain would restore its hegemony in Iraq and Jordan and secure its access to the oil of the Middle East. France would consolidate its influence in the Middle East through Lebanon and Israel while its problems in Algeria would come to an end with the fall of Nasser. Even the United States might be persuaded to support the plan for it would promote stable, pro-Western regimes and help to check Soviet advances in the Middle East. Before rushing into a military campaign against Egypt, Ben-Gurion urged that they take time to consider the wider political possibilities. His plan might appear fantastic at first sight, he remarked, but it was not beyond the realm of possibility given time, British goodwill and good faith.

The French leaders listened patiently to Ben-Gurion's presentation but they showed no disposition to be diverted from the immediate task of launching a military campaign against Egypt with British involvement. They told Ben-Gurion politely that his plan was not fantastic, but added that they had a unique opportunity to strike at their common enemy and that any delay might be fatal. They also considered that while Eden himself was determined to fight, he faced growing opposition in the country and the cabinet, with Selwyn Lloyd showing a preference for a diplomatic solution. The United States usually trailed behind events, as its record in the two world wars had shown, and it was therefore unlikely to support military action to get rid of Nasser. Technical considerations, such as the onset of winter, were also cited by the French in support of immediate action. In the end Ben-Gurion was persuaded that priority had to be given to the campaign against Egypt but he continued to insist on full coordination of their military plans with those of Britain.

THE RELUCTANT CONSPIRATOR

Ben-Gurion hoped to meet Eden but the British prime minister did not want to be seen to be allied to him in any way. The French had in fact suggested to Eden that he should come to the meeting but Eden decided to send Selwyn Lloyd instead, travelling incognito. Selwyn Lloyd, accompanied by his private secretary, Donald Logan, arrived at the villa and, after being briefed by the French, joined in the discussions. As the French had feared, their allies did not take to one another. Moshe Dayan gives a vivid description of the encounter in his memoirs: 'Britain's foreign minister may well have been a friendly man, pleasant, charming, amiable. If so, he showed near-genius in concealing these virtues. His manner could not have been more antagonistic. His whole demeanour expressed distaste – for the place, the company and the topic.'[25] To Selwyn Lloyd, however, 'Ben-Gurion himself seemed to be in a rather aggressive mood, indicating or implying that the Israelis had no reason to believe in anything that a British minister might say.'[26]

It was immediately apparent that Selwyn Lloyd was still hoping for success in the negotiations and that he was reluctant to get involved in any collusion with the Israelis. It was not difficult to guess that he was only attending the meeting on his master's orders. Whereas the purpose of the meeting was to discuss military action, Lloyd began by saying that, on the basis of his recent discussions with Egyptian Foreign Minister, Mahmud Fawzi, he estimated that a diplomatic solution to the dispute over the canal could be reached within a week.[27] On the possibility of tripartite military action, Lloyd explained that his government could not go beyond the statement which Eden had made in the Palais Matignon on 16 October and subsequently confirmed in writing. In practical terms this meant that Israel would have to initiate a full-scale war and remain alone in the war for about 72 hours, while Britain and France issued an ultimatum to Israel which implied that Israel was the aggressor. It was, of course, precisely the role of aggressor that Ben-Gurion did not want to play. He bristled with hostility at the very idea of Israel incurring all the opprobrium for the attack on the common enemy while Britain posed as the peacemaker and basked in self-righteousness. The only encouraging element in what Lloyd had to say was the admission that his government wanted to destroy Nasser's regime. The one important drawback of a compromise with Egypt, he remarked, was that Nasser would remain in power. Lloyd defined the aim of any allied military operations as 'the conquest of the Canal Zone and the destruction of Nasser'.

When they got down to brass tacks, Ben-Gurion demanded an agreement between Britain, France and Israel that all three should attack Egypt. He also wanted an undertaking that the Royal Air Force would eliminate the Egyptian air force before Israeli ground troops moved forward because otherwise Israeli cities such as Tel Aviv could be wiped out. Lloyd understood Ben-Gurion's anxiety but declined to have any direct cooperation with Israel. In his memoirs he claimed that throughout the meeting he tried to make it clear that an Israeli–French–British agreement to attack Egypt was impossible. All he agreed to was the French proposal that if Israel attacked Egypt, Britain and

France would intervene to protect the canal.[28] As Ben-Gurion categorically rejected this proposal, the discussion came to a dead end.

At this juncture Ben-Gurion presented a new proposal which lowered the price demanded by Israel for providing the pretext for allied intervention. The proposal came from General Dayan who had been pressing very persistently for a 'preventive war' against Egypt ever since the Czech arms deal was announced by Nasser in September 1955. The proposal envisaged an Israeli retaliatory raid near the canal, an Anglo-French ultimatum to Egypt to evacuate its military forces from the Canal Zone, an appeal to Israel not to approach the canal, and aerial bombardment of Egypt's airfields following the expected rejection of the ultimatum. Lloyd responded by pointing out that only a real act of war on Israel's part would justify Britain's intervention in the dispute. On re-examining the timetable, however, Lloyd concluded that the gap between the Israeli attack and the allied intervention might be reduced to 36 or 24 hours but he emphasized that he only had authority to conduct negotiations based on allied intervention two days after D-Day. To bridge the remaining gap, Bourgès-Maunoury offered to use the French air force from bases in Israel and Cyprus to protect Israeli cities in the first two days of fighting. Lloyd hastily ruled out the use of Cyprus because it would have provided proof of collusion, but he was less categorical in rejecting the idea of stationing French aircraft in Israel as a defensive precaution.

At no point did the French and the Israelis threaten to go it alone. They knew that only the RAF had the heavy bombers, the Canberras, near enough to the theatre of operations and they needed the RAF to launch an attack on Egypt's airfields from its bases in Cyprus. The main question at issue therefore was the time at which the RAF would intervene by an attack on the Egyptian air force. The meeting concluded, as far as Lloyd was concerned, with an undertaking from Lloyd to go back to London and to ask the cabinet whether RAF intervention could be advanced and to return with the answer the following day.[29]

Fearing that Lloyd would present the Israeli conditions in a manner calculated to bring about their rejection, Pineau decided to go to London the following evening to speak to Eden directly. Ever the pessimist, Ben-Gurion feared that Pineau's trip would be in vain because Lloyd would secure a decision which would go against the wishes of the French and Israeli delegations.[30]

THE SECOND DAY AT SÈVRES

On the second day of the conference, Tuesday 23 October, in the absence of the British, the atmosphere was markedly more relaxed and friendly and there was more time for informal discussions. The French continued to search for the magic formula that would satisfy all the parties concerned. In the late morning there was a meeting of the military men in the house of Louis Mangin. General Challe suggested that Israel might simulate an 'Egyptian' air raid on Beersheba and that this would serve as the trigger for Franco-British intervention. Although Dayan saw no merit in this proposal, Challe decided to present it to Ben-Gurion in the afternoon at the meeting with French ministers. When he heard this proposal, Ben-Gurion looked grim and said sternly that the one thing he could not do was to lie to the world. The atmosphere in the room became very tense and the French general mumbled an apology. To defuse the tension, Pineau revealed that, after consultations with the President of the Republic, René Coty, it was decided to offer Israel a formal guarantee to carry out whatever was finally agreed between the three countries. Bourgès-Maunoury followed up with the offer of a military guarantee in the form of air squadrons to be stationed in Israeli bases and naval forces to protect Israel's coast. France, he said, would continue to do its best for Israel whatever happened but there would never be a better opportunity for joint action. Under the impression of this dramatic statement, the two delegations adjourned for private consultations.

Ben-Gurion was inclined to show flexibility. One of his motives in coming to Paris was to consolidate the alliance with France. Dayan now came up with a revised proposal: an IDF paratroop drop on the strategic Mitla Pass, deep in Sinai and about 30 miles from the Suez Canal, and the westward thrust of a mechanized brigade which together would constitute 'a real act of war' and thus provide the pretext for intervention by Britain and France 36 hours later. Ben-Gurion instructed Dayan to present this scheme as an informal idea that Pineau could take with him to London.

To underline the informal nature of the proposal, Ben-Gurion left it to Dayan and Peres to meet alone with Pineau. But this was simply a tactical ploy. Ben-Gurion was only too well aware that if Pineau were to go to London empty-handed, the whole conference would end in failure. Pineau, who by now knew how the Israeli delegation worked, was delighted to learn of the unofficial shift in Israel's position and he took down in writing a series of eight points made by Dayan which constituted Israel's minimum conditions. Particularly noteworthy is the last point for it was included at Ben-Gurion's specific request and it defined Israel's territorial aims which were only tenuously related to the Suez Canal crisis:

> Israel declares its intention to keep her forces for the purpose of permanent annexation of the entire area east of the El Arish–Abu

Ageila, Nakhl–Sharm al-Shaykh, in order to maintain for the long term the freedom of navigation in the Straits of Eilat and in order to free herself from the scourge of the infiltrators and from the danger posed by the Egyptian army bases in Sinai. Britain and France are required to support or at least to commit themselves not to show opposition to these plans. This is what Israel demands as her share in the fruits of victory.

After Pineau's departure, many of the other members of the French and Israeli delegations gathered in the large sitting-room and chatted about various subjects in a relaxed and convivial atmosphere. Guy Mollet talked about France's difficulties in North Africa. Ben-Gurion gave a lecture on the history of the Sinai peninsula, on the oil deposits that had been discovered there, and on the problems of atomic energy.

Pineau arrived in London in the evening and went to dinner with Selwyn Lloyd after which they were joined by Eden for discussions that lasted a couple of hours. Once again no officials were present and there is no official record of the meeting.[31] Nutting relates that, from talking to Lloyd the following day, he had the impression that Eden's enthusiasm for the French plan waxed stronger than ever and that he assured Pineau that Israel need have no fear of being left in the lurch and, if it led the way with an attack in Sinai, Britain would lend its fullest support.[32] Lloyd, on the other hand, gives no details of the meeting but merely states that it was decided that it was worthwhile having another meeting at Sèvres and since he could not go, it was agreed to send Patrick Dean, an assistant under-secretary at the Foreign Office, and that Donald Logan should go with him. Lloyd feared that Pineau might make more of their talk than was warranted so he wrote him a letter that evening for his officials to deliver by hand. In the letter he said that he wished to make it clear that they had not asked Israel to take any action. They had merely stated what would be the British reaction if certain things happened.[33]

THE THIRD DAY AT SEVRÈS

Very early next morning, 24 October, Dean was summoned to 10 Downing Street and given a fifteen-minute briefing by the Prime Minister before breakfast. Eden impressed on Dean his anxiety that Nasser intended to inflict great damage on British interests in the Middle East. Eden also told Dean, without going into detail, that the French and the Israelis shared his opinion and that it might be necessary for the three countries to take action if the canal itself was threatened as a result of hostilities between Israel and Egypt. Dean's brief was to make it absolutely clear to the other parties that there would be no British military action unless the Israelis had advanced beyond their frontiers and a threat to the canal had definitely emerged. If the other parties did not accept this position, Britain would not participate in any military contingency plan. Eden stressed that it was very important to keep the visit secret because it involved possible military operations and he told Dean that a private military aeroplane would take him to Paris and fly him back to report the same evening.[34]

October 24 was the third and last day of the conference. Ben-Gurion finally made up his mind to commit the IDF to the battle. In his diary he summarized the main considerations that led to this fateful decision. He thought that the operation had to be undertaken if Israel's skies could be effectively defended in the day or two that would elapse until the French and the British started bombing Egypt's airfields. The aim of destroying Nasser had pervaded the entire conference and it was uppermost in Ben-Gurion's mind. 'This is a unique opportunity', he wrote, 'that two not so small powers will try to topple Nasser, and we shall not stand alone against him while he becomes stronger and conquers all the Arab countries...and *maybe* the whole situation in the Middle East will change according to my plan.'[35]

In the late morning Ben-Gurion summoned his young lieutenants to the villa in Sèvres where he had been staying. They found him in the garden, enjoying the sunshine and the autumn colours on the trees. He did not announce his decision but from the expression on his face they could tell, to their great relief and satisfaction, that 'the old man' had made up his mind. He began by asking Dayan to go over the main moves in the operational plan he had proposed. This was best done with the help of a map but as they had no paper, Peres tore open a packet of cigarettes and Dayan drew the outline of the Sinai peninsula on it, showing in bold arrows the proposed lines of advance. Dayan was rather glad that he did not have a proper map at the time because on the smooth cigarette packet, with no signs of mountains, sand dunes, or wadis, the plan looked deceptively easy to carry out. Ben-Gurion then pulled out a sheet of paper on which he had jotted down a long list of questions, some of them military, some political and some simply unanswerable. All the questions, however, were of the 'how', 'what' and 'when' variety and this confirmed the impression that a positive decision on joining the campaign had already been reached.[36]

At 3 P.M. Pineau returned from London and they were immediately called to the conference room. Pineau reported that he had found Eden's approach much warmer than Lloyd's and that once he had conveyed Israel's agreement to a timetable that met Britain's needs, Eden was inclined to accept most of Israel's remaining conditions. Pineau claimed that Eden had agreed to a six-point plan which was based on Dayan's latest proposal. The first point of the plan was that Israel would decide how precisely to initiate hostilities in Sinai but the governments of France and Britain recommended action connected with the Suez Canal. Second, Israel had to carry out an operation that would look like a real act of war so that the French and British governments could argue that the canal was in danger. Third, the air forces of France and Britain would go into action not more than 36 hours after Israel launched its attack. Fourth, on the day after D-Day, the French and British governments would send two somewhat differently worded messages, to be called an appeal rather than an ultimatum in order to preserve Israel's good name. Fifth, to reinforce the air defence of Israeli cities in the period between the opening of hostilities and the allied intervention, France undertook to station fighter bombers in Israel but these planes were to be given Israeli air force markings to conceal their true identity. Finally, D-Day was to be Monday, 29 October 1956, at 19.00 hrs Israeli local time.

This six-point plan represented a rough draft of the final agreement. The Israelis were satisfied with Pineau's achievements. At 4.30 P.M. the British representatives, Patrick Dean and Donald Logan, arrived. The bilateral talks became trilateral and they assumed a more official air. The French and the Israelis spoke from Pineau's six points of which Dean and Logan were ignorant. Ben-Gurion, however, raised two new points. First, he demanded that, in return for an Israeli pledge not to attack Jordan, the agreement should explicitly commit Britain to refrain from activating the Anglo-Jordanian Treaty if either Jordan or Iraq attacked Israel. Second, he wanted the British and French governments to note Israel's territorial demands, even if they could not officially support them. 'France and Britain have a vital interest in the Suez Canal', he said forcefully. 'The Straits of Tiran are the State of Israel's Suez Canal...We intend to capture the Straits of Tiran and we intend to stay there and thus ensure freedom of navigation to Eilat.'[37]

Dean confined himself to the narrow brief Eden had given him: make plain to the Israelis and the French that British forces would not move unless the Israelis had advanced beyond their frontiers against Egypt and presented a clear threat to the canal. The British officials then asked a number of questions about Israel's operational plans, evidently inspired by the fear that the Israeli operation would not amount to a real act of war and that, consequently, Britain would not have a credible *casus belli* for military intervention. Would Israel issue a formal declaration of war? Ben-Gurion replied that Egypt's repeated violations of the armistice agreement made a declaration of war superfluous. Dayan retorted more bluntly: 'We will not declare – we will simply strike!' He declined to give any details about their operational plans beyond demonstrating on the same cigarette packet that there would be significant military activity at the Mitla Pass. Being a wise man, he did not give away military secrets easily but he did assure the British representatives that Israel would stand by its commitments on time, place and size of forces, and provide an adequate pretext.

Ben-Gurion took the initiative in suggesting to the French that a protocol be drawn up to summarize the decisions that had been reached and that this document should be signed by the three parties and be binding on them.[38] The fact that the idea for drawing up a formal document came from Ben-Gurion is worth underlining because it is glossed over in the first-hand Israeli accounts of the meeting, presumably with the intention of minimizing his part in the collusion. A drafting committee, consisting of French and Israeli officials, was set to work in the neighbouring kitchen. It was heavy going and an attempt to compose a preamble had to be abandoned. The protocol was drafted in French, the language of the hosts and the language of international diplomacy. As soon as they had finished, a secretary was rushed into the kitchen and she typed the draft in a great hurry on a portable typewriter, in three copies. By 7 P.M. the document was ready.

The British representatives were taken aback when they were presented with a copy of the protocol and asked to sign it. The protocol simply summarized the actions and reactions of the three states as they had been discussed during the week. But this was the first indication they had had that anybody intended to make a record of the conversation. When confronted with the text, Dean and Logan had a word together because there had been no earlier mention of committing anything to paper. Logan said that the document seemed accurate and that it might be useful to take it back to the prime minister to show that they had achieved an Israeli agreement to a significant military move against the canal. As a good civil servant, he believed that there was some merit in having an agreed record of what was a rather elaborate scenario. To refuse to sign a summary to which they could take no exception would only have increased suspicion of their intentions in an exploit to which the prime minister was wedded. Dean agreed. He initialled each page and signed the document at the end. He made it clear that he was signing ad referendum, subject to the approval of his government.[39] Pineau signed the document for France and Ben-Gurion signed it for Israel. Although the document had to be ratified by all three governments, Ben-Gurion made no effort to conceal his excitement. He studied his copy of the document, folded it carefully and thrust it deep into the pocket of his waistcoat.

While the drafting was in progress, two other private conversations took place in another part of the villa. Ben-Gurion had a conversation with his French opposite number at which no one else was present. In his diary Ben-Gurion recorded the next day:

I told him about the discovery of oil in southern and western Sinai, and that it would be good to tear this peninsula from Egypt because it did not belong to her; rather it was the English who stole it from the Turks when they believed that Egypt was in their pocket. I suggested laying down a pipeline from Sinai to Haifa to refine the oil and Mollet showed interest in this suggestion.[40]

In the absence of any other record of this conversation, one is left with the impression that the French Prime Minister played the part of the polite host to the very end even when his Israeli guest was making cynical plans to share the territorial spoils of war.

An even more intriguing conversation took place at the end of this one. It concerned French assistance to Israel in developing nuclear technology. Details of this second conversation emerged only in 1995 when Shimon Peres published his memoirs. The relevant passage reads as follows:

Before the final signing, I asked Ben-Gurion for a brief adjournment, during which I met Mollet and Bourgès-Maunoury alone. It was here that I finalized with these two leaders an agreement for the building of a nuclear reactor at Dimona, in southern Israel... and the supply of natural uranium to fuel it. I put forward a series of detailed proposals and, after discussion, they accepted them.[41]

The development of nuclear power was a subject dear to Ben-Gurion's heart. He saw in it a technological challenge which would help to transform Israel into an advanced industrial state. The negotiations with the French were about a small nuclear reactor for civilian purposes. Nothing was said at this stage about possible military applications of this nuclear technology. But that was Ben-Gurion's ultimate aim: to produce nuclear weapons. He believed that nuclear weapons would strengthen Israel immeasurably, secure its survival and eliminate any danger of another holocaust.

Shimon Peres was the moving force behind the Israeli attempt to get French help in building a nuclear reactor. Pineau opposed this request, Bourgès-Maunoury strongly supported it, and Mollet was undecided. On 21 September 1956, a month before Sèvres, Peres reached an agreement with the French on the supply of a small nuclear reactor. He used the occasion of Sèvres to try to commit France at the political level. Against this background, the broaching of the nuclear issue by Peres at Sèvres could not have come as a complete surprise. A year later, in September 1957, when Bourgès-Maunoury was Prime Minister, France delivered to Israel a nuclear reactor which had twice the capacity previously promised.[42]

Israel did not join in the Franco-British war plot in order to get a French nuclear reactor. The sensitive question of nuclear power was raised only towards the end of the conference and after the basic decision to go to war had been taken. Nevertheless, the nuclear deal concluded at the private meeting at Sèvres is interesting for at least three reasons. In the first place, it shows that the French were determined to go to war at almost any price and for their own reasons, not, as Abel Thomas later claimed, in order to save Israel. Second, it reveals the full extent of the incentives that the French were prepared to give Israel in order to induce it to play the part assigned to it in the war plot against Egypt. Third, it confirms the impression that Israel did not face any serious threat of Egyptian attack at that time but colluded with the European powers to attack Egypt for other reasons. Taken together, the two private conversations at Sèvres thus drive a coach and horses through the official version which says that Israel went to war only because it faced an imminent danger of attack from Egypt.

For Ben-Gurion the high-level French political commitment to assist Israel in the nuclear field was one of the greatest achievements of the gathering at Sèvres. It would be wrong to suggest that participation in the war against Egypt was the price he paid for this assistance because by this stage he had decided to go to war for his own reasons. The reactor was an added bonus. His overall aim at this time was to consolidate the alliance with France. He already had an intimate political partnership with France, French military hardware, and French air cover in the coming war. The nuclear reactor reinforced the value of the alliance with France in his eyes.[43]

THE PROTOCOL OF SÈVRES

An English translation of the Protocol of Sèvres is reproduced in the Appendix.[44] The original protocol shows some signs of having been prepared in a hurry: there are some minor typing errors and the layout is erratic. There is no preamble as in most international treaties because there was no time to compose one. Instead of a preamble, the first line simply says: 'The results of the conversations which took place at Sèvres from 22 to 24 October 1956 between the representatives of the governments of the United Kingdom, the State of Israel and France are the following.' There are seven articles.

In substance the protocol corresponds closely to the draft used by

Pineau for his discussion with Eden on the previous day, with one amendment and two additions. The amendment concerns the 'appeals' to the Egyptian and Israeli governments (Article 2); the additions concern Israel's territorial aims (Article 4) and Jordan (Article 5). The first Article states simply that Israel will launch a large-scale attack on the evening of 29 October with the aim of reaching the Canal Zone the following day. This wording was designed to underline, as Selwyn Lloyd had insisted in his letter of 23 October to Pineau, that the British and French governments had not invited or incited the Israeli government to attack Egypt but only intimated what their reaction would be to such an attack.

Article 2 describes the Anglo-French appeals to the belligerents to stop fighting and to withdraw their forces to a distance of ten miles from the canal. Egypt alone is asked to accept the temporary occupation of key positions on the canal by the Anglo-French forces. This demand was inserted in order to ensure that Egypt could not possibly accept the appeal. The last 'temporary occupation' of Egypt by Britain had lasted 74 years, from 1882 until June 1956. If the appeals were not accepted within 12 hours, Anglo-French forces would intervene to enforce compliance but Israel would not be required to comply in the event of an Egyptian refusal. This article reflects a compromise between the British desire to maintain an appearance of even-handedness towards Egypt and Israel, and Israel's refusal to be placed on exactly the same footing as Egypt.

Article 3 says that if Egypt failed to comply, the Anglo-French attack on the Egyptian forces would be launched in the early hours of the morning of 31 October. This article differs from the previous one in that no military actions against Israel are envisaged. As signatory to the agreement, Israel could not agree to be subject to its sanctions. Article 4 notes the intention of the Israeli government to occupy the western shore of the Gulf of Aqaba and the islands of Tiran and Sanafir in order to ensure freedom of navigation. The British and French governments did not undertake to support this plan but neither did they express any opposition to it.

In Article 5 Israel promises not to attack Jordan during the period of hostilities against Egypt, and Britain promises not to help Jordan if it attacks Israel. The purpose of this provision was to minimize the risk of a military clash between Israel and Britain on the Jordanian front. It did not directly concern France, except as a signatory to the Tripartite Declaration, but it underlined the complexity of Britain's relationships in the Middle East. For both Britain and Israel Jordan was a rather sensitive issue and a major source of mutual distrust. Article 5 embodied Britain's agreement to Israel's request that in the event of a Jordanian attack on Israel, the Anglo-Jordanian Treaty would not come into force. In effect, it meant that Britain and Israel were guilty of collusion against Jordan as well as against Egypt.

Article 6 requires all three governments to keep the provisions of the accord strictly secret. Finally, Article 7 says that the provisions of the protocol will enter into force as soon as they have been confirmed by the three governments.

Once the protocol had been signed, champagne was produced but there was little sparkle in the atmosphere and no comradely backslapping. The first to leave the rue Emanuel Girot were the British. They left, writes Dayan, 'mumbling as they went words of politeness tinged with humor and not quite comprehensible'.[45] After the departure of the British, another bottle of champagne was produced and drunk *en famille*, with much sparkle in the atmosphere. Peres whispered something in Ben-Gurion's ear and the latter nodded in approval. Peres then asked Mollet loudly whether they could also celebrate the nuclear deal and Mollet said 'yes'. So they all drank a toast to the nuclear reactor about which some of the more junior members of the two delegations heard for the first time.[46]

The secret meeting at Sèvres had a farcical sequel. Dean reported to Eden at 10 Downing Street late on Wednesday night. When Eden learnt that the war plot had been recorded in a formal document, he was clearly surprised and very put out. He made it clear to Dean that he had not expected anything would be written down, but he did not suggest that Dean and Logan ought to have known that this was his intention. At no time did Eden say or imply that Dean and Logan had acted improperly or exceeded their authority but he was seriously worried about the possible consequences.[47]

So worried was Eden, that he ordered Dean and Logan to return to Paris the next day to persuade the other parties to destroy the protocol. Pineau was not sympathetic but said he would consult his colleagues, adding that Ben-Gurion was already airborne with his copy. The British pair were shown into one of the grand reception rooms in the Quai d'Orsay. At lunchtime they tried to get out but the door was locked. Since the entire Quai d'Orsay had been kept in the dark about the meeting at Sèvres, their presence there would have been acutely embarrassing if discovered. The unfortunate envoys were kept under lock and key until 4 P.M. when Pineau returned to inform them that Ben-Gurion would not accede to their request, nor would the French government. Dean and Logan returned to 10 Downing Street to report the failure of their mission. Eden then ordered all the copies of the protocol and the English translation made in the Foreign Office to be rounded up and delivered to Number 10 for destruction. He knew, however, that two smoking guns remained.[48] In the event neither gun was discovered until much later. But within days, rumours of the meeting at Sèvres were circulating in Paris. The discipline of the Resistance had not held.

Eden's reluctance to leave additional traces of the collusion accounts for the peculiar manner in which he ratified the Protocol of Sèvres. Ben-Gurion was under the impression that each government would send two letters, one to each partner, ratifying the protocol. But he was far from confident that a British letter would arrive. Ben-Gurion's suspicion was justified: he received no letter from Eden. Eden only wrote to Mollet to ratify the agreement reached at the tripartite meeting. The most charitable explanation of Eden's behaviour is that he followed the usual diplomatic practice of addressing ratification to the depository power, in this case France. On 25 October Ben-Gurion received a batch of letters from Paris. The first letter confirmed the pledge of an air umbrella and a naval belt. The pledge came in the form of an 'Annex to the Protocol of Sèvres' and it was signed by Maurice Bourgès-Maunoury. An English translation would read:

> The French government undertakes to station on the territory of Israel to ensure the air defence of Israeli territory during the period from 29 to 31 October a reinforced squadron of Mystères IV A, and a squadron of fighter bombers. In addition two ships of the Marine Nationale will during the same period put into Israeli ports.[49]

This document discharged France's promise of a guarantee of military support to Israel during the war against Egypt. Pineau observed in his memoirs that this annex, unlike the protocol, at least had the merits of honesty and clarity.[50]

The second letter was from Guy Mollet, confirming the agreement of the French government to 'the results of the conversations of Sèvres and the terms of the final protocol to which they gave rise.'[51] Mollet also enclosed, for Ben-Gurion's personal information, a copy of a letter he had just received from the British Prime Minister. The letter said that 'Her Majesty's Government have been informed of the course of the conversations held at Sèvres on October 23–24 and confirm that in the situation there envisaged they will take the action described.'[52] Ben-Gurion noticed immediately that the letter did not refer specifically to the protocol. In his diary he wrote: 'This letter is typical of the British Foreign Office for it can be interpreted in various ways, while the French state clearly to what they have committed themselves, as was discussed with them, without adding or subtracting.'[53] The Foreign Office had not even seen the letter which was written at Number 10, signed by Eden, and probably drafted by him. In any case, Ben-Gurion wrote to Mollet on 26 October to thank him for the two letters and to confirm the agreement of the government of Israel to the results of the conversations held at Sèvres and to the terms of the protocol.[54]

CONCLUSION

The documentary evidence does not leave any room for doubt that at Sèvres, during those three days in late October 1956, an elaborate war plot was hatched against Egypt by the representatives of France, Britain and Israel. The Protocol of Sèvres is the most conclusive piece of evidence for it lays out in precise detail, and with a precise timetable, how the joint war against Egypt was intended to proceed and shows foreknowledge of each other's intentions. The central aim of the plot was the overthrow of Gamal 'Abd al-Nasser. This aim is not explicitly stated in the protocol but it emerges clearly and unambiguously from all the records of the discussions surrounding it. Yet each of the three partners had a very different perspective on this war plot, and it was not at all clear how even the agreed aim was to be achieved.

The French were the most straightforward, unwavering and unabashed advocates of military force. As far as they were concerned, Colonel Nasser supported the Algerian rebels and that, along with his nationalization of the Suez Canal Company, was enough to justify a war to overthrow him. For their part, the French did not need any further pretext for taking military action. It was the British, unwilling to incur Arab hostility by appearing as an ally of Israel, who needed a pretext and Israel was able and willing to provide it but only at a price. Israel also required the elimination of Nasser's air force, for which task Britain alone had the heavy bomber bases sufficiently near at hand. Thus, willy-nilly, the French became the matchmakers between the stand-offish British and the suspicious Israelis. It was the French who issued the invitation to the conspiracy and it was they who wooed, cajoled and applied subtle pressure on their partners to participate in what was bound to be a risky joint venture. And it was only the French who could have brought about this improbable *ménage à trois*.

On the British side, Anthony Eden bore the ultimate responsibility and received most of the opprobrium for the collusion with France and Israel. Eden was desperate for a pretext to go to war in order to get rid of Nasser, and the alliance with Israel was the price he reluctantly paid to procure such a pretext. The elaborate plot embodied in the protocol was so transparent that it is still difficult to understand how Eden could have believed that it would not be seen as such. What is clear is that having got embroiled in the war plot, Eden became desperate to hide the traces. His attempt to round up and destroy all the copies of the Protocol of Sèvres has to be seen in this light. He wanted to expunge the war plot, in which Britain had been a reluctant but a full and formal participant, from the historical record. What he embarked on was a massive attempt to deceive. This attempt ended in miserable failure, like all the expedients that Eden resorted to in his vendetta against the Egyptian leader whom he perceived, for no good reason, as another Hitler.

On the Israeli side the most senior figure was David Ben-Gurion and all the important decisions connected with the war plot were made by him. The idea of a secret, high-level tripartite meeting came from him. The Suez Canal was not his prime concern and ideally he would not have wished the attack to take place then, or there, or in that way. He badly wanted to join the Great Powers club and he found that subscribing to the Suez campaign at the end of October was the only way of doing it. Although he was pompous and prolix about the moral issues involved, his abrupt change of position regarding Israel's participation in the campaign against Nasser was dictated exclusively by practical considerations. Initially, he opposed the Challe scenario because it did not treat Israel as an equal member of the club, but he ended up by joining the club essentially on the basis of this scenario. Three days of bargaining at Sèvres improved the conditions offered to Israel but its role in enacting the Challe scenario remained fundamentally unchanged.

Having settled for this inglorious role, Ben-Gurion took the lead in proposing that a record of the decisions be drawn up and signed by the representatives of the three countries concerned. The Protocol of Sèvres was the result. For him the protocol was not something to be ashamed of but a major achievement. It represented a military pact with two Great Powers against a common enemy, albeit a secret and awkward pact. Britain's persistent cold-shouldering of Israel was disappointing and disconcerting. But Ben-Gurion felt that the protocol at least gave him a guarantee against betrayal by perfidious Albion.

The three partners in the war plot against Nasser thus differed markedly in their attitude to the Protocol of Sèvres. The French were largely indifferent to the protocol but they agreed to it in order to get Israel on board in their bid to topple Nasser. Eden was shocked and dismayed when he discovered that the war plot had been committed to paper but, hard as he tried, he could not destroy the incriminating evidence. Ben-Gurion was the only leader who was proud of the protocol which was really his brain-child. His mistrust of Britain verged on paranoia and he saw the protocol as a means of keeping Britain to the decisions that had been reached at Sèvres. In the final analysis, the Protocol of Sèvres was thus a monument to French opportunism, Eden's duplicity and Ben-Gurion's paranoia.

APPENDIX

Protocol

The results of the conversations which took place at Sèvres from 22 to 24 October 1956 between the representatives of the Governments of the United Kingdom, the State of Israel and of France are the following:

1. The Israeli forces launch in the evening of 29 October 1956 a large scale attack on the Egyptian forces with the aim of reaching the Canal Zone the following day.

2. On being apprised of these events, the British and French Governments during the day of 30 October 1956 respectively and simultaneously make two appeals to the Egyptian Government and the Israeli Government on the following lines:

A. To the Egyptian government
   a) halt all acts of war.
   b) withdraw all its troops ten miles from the Canal.
   c) accept temporary occupation of key positions on the Canal by the Anglo-French forces to guarantee freedom of passage through the Canal by vessels of all nations until a final settlement.
B. To the Israeli government
   a) halt all acts of war.
   b) withdraw all its troops ten miles to the east of the Canal.

In addition, the Israeli Government will be notified that the French and British Governments have demanded of the Egyptian Government to accept temporary occupation of key positions along the Canal by Anglo-French forces.

It is agreed that if one of the Governments refused, or did not give its consent, within twelve hours the Anglo-French forces would intervene with the means necessary to ensure that their demands are accepted.

C. The representatives of the three Governments agree that the Israeli Government will not be required to meet the conditions in the appeal addressed to it, in the event that the Egyptian Government does not accept those in the appeal addressed to it for their part.

3. In the event that the Egyptian Government should fail to agree within the stipulated time to the conditions of the appeal addressed to it, the Anglo-French forces will launch military operations against the Egyptian forces in the early hours of the morning of 31 October.

4. The Israeli Government will send forces to occupy the western shore of the Gulf of Aqaba and the group of islands Tiran and Sanafir to

ensure freedom of navigation in the Gulf of Aqaba.

5. Israel undertakes not to attack Jordan during the period of operations against Egypt. But in the event that during the same period Jordan should attack Israel, the British Government undertakes not to come to the aid of Jordan.

6. The arrangements of the present protocol must remain strictly secret.

7. They will enter into force after the agreement of the three Governments.

(signed)

DAVID BEN-GURION PATRICK DEAN CHRISTIAN PINEAU

NOTES

This chapter was previously published under the same title in *International Affairs*, 3 (1997).

1. 'The Suez Crisis – BBC Version' was shown on BBC 1 on 22 October 1996. Jeremy Bennett was the producer, Keith Kyle and I were the historical consultants. Shimon Peres, who was Israel's Foreign Minister at the time, gave us permission to photocopy the Protocol of Sèvres after protracted negotiations and only after we produced letters from the British and French governments saying that they had no objection to our request. The protocol is now available at the Ben-Gurion Archives in Sde Boker and in the Israel State Archives in Jerusalem. Selwyn Ilan Troen, 'The Protocol of Sèvres: British/French/Israeli collusion against Egypt, 1956', *Israel Studies* 1, 2, (1996), pp. 122–39, reproduced the original French text of the protocol, a translation into English, the annex to the protocol, and the letters of ratification.
2. Anthony Nutting, *No End of a Lesson: The Story of Suez* (London: Constable, 1967).
3. Christian Pineau, *Suez 1956* (Paris: Robert Laffont, 1976).
4. Moshe Dayan, *Story of My Life* (London: Weidenfeld & Nicolson, 1976).
5. Selwyn Lloyd, *Suez 1956: A Personal Account* (London: Jonathan Cape, 1978).
6. Abel Thomas, *Comment Israël fut sauvé: les secrets de l'expédition de Suez* (Paris: Albin Michel, 1978).
7. Yosef Evron, *Beyom sagrir: Su'etz me'aborei bakla'im* [In stormy days: Suez behind the scenes] (Tel Aviv: Ot Paz, 1965).
8. Shimon Peres, *Battling for Peace: Memoirs* (London: Weidenfeld & Nicolson, 1995).
9. 'Ben-Gurion's Diary – the Suez–Sinai Campaign', edited and introduced by Selwyn Ilan Troen in Selwyn Ilan Troen and Moshe Shemesh, eds, *The Suez–Sinai Campaign: Retrospective and Reappraisal* (London: Frank Cass, 1990), pp. 289–332.
10. Mordechai Bar-On, *Etgar ve-tigra* [Challenge and quarrel] (Sde Boker: The Ben-Gurion Research Center, 1991).
11. Mordechai Bar-On, *The Gates of Gaza: Israel's Road to Suez and Back, 1955–1957* (New York: St Martin's Press, 1994).
12. Keith Kyle, *Suez* (London: Weidenfeld & Nicolson, 1991), Appendix A, pp. 565–7.
13. Donald Logan, 'Suez: meetings at Sèvres, 22–25 October 1956'. I am grateful to Sir Donald Logan for giving me a copy. An edited version of this account was published as 'Collusion at Suez', *Financial Times*, 2 Jan. 1986.
14. Nutting, *No End of a Lesson*, pp. 90–95. General Challe's account of the Chequers meeting to the French Chief of Staff is reported in Paul Ély, *Mémoires* (Paris: Plon, 1969), pp. 136–40.
15. Interview with Sir Anthony Nutting, London, 12 March 1997.
16. Ibid.

17. Selwyn Lloyd wrote a six-page top secret minute of this meeting for his personal file. Minute by Selwyn Lloyd, 18 Oct. 1956, FO 800/725, Public Record Office (PRO), London.
18. Ben-Gurion's diary, 17 and 18 Oct. 1956, the Ben-Gurion Archives, Sde Boker; and Mordechai Bar-On, 'In the web of lies: Anthony Eden and the collusion with France and Israel in the autumn of 1956' (in Hebrew), *Iyunim Bitkumat Israel*, vol. 2, (1992), pp. 169–96.
19. Interview with Shimon Peres, Tel Aviv, 20 Aug. 1982.
20. Interview with Colonel Mordechai Bar-On, Ditchley Park, 8 Dec. 1996.
21. Quoted in Mordechai Bar-On, 'David Ben-Gurion and the Sèvres Collusion', in Wm. Roger Louis and Roger Owen, eds, *Suez 1956: The Crisis and its Consequences* (Oxford: Clarendon Press, 1989), pp. 149–51.
22. Ben-Gurion's diary, 17 Oct. 1956.
23. Motti Golani, 'The Sinai Campaign, 1956: Military and Political Aspects' (in Hebrew) (unpublished PhD thesis, University of Haifa, 1992), p. 235. This thesis gives the most comprehensive account available of the military aspect of the talks at Sèvres, based on exhaustive research in the IDF Archive. Also, see Golani's chapter in this volume.
24. Bar-On, *Etgar ve-tigra*, p. 251. In the following account of the discussions at Sèvres, I have drawn very heavily and with gratitude on Bar-On's account in pp. 250–79 of his book. All the quotations are from this source unless otherwise stated.
25. Dayan, *Story of My Life*, p. 180.
26. Lloyd, *Suez 1956*, p. 183.
27. On the talks between Selwyn Lloyd and Mahmud Fawzi in New York see Lloyd, *Suez 1956*, pp. 153–63; and Mahmoud Fawzi, *Suez 1956: An Egyptian Perspective* (London: Shorouk International, n.d.), ch. 5.
28. Lloyd, *Suez 1956*, pp. 181–5.
29. Interview with Sir Donald Logan, Suez Oral History Project, Liddell Hart Centre for Military Archives, King's College London.
30. Ben-Gurion's diary, 22 Oct. 1956.
31. Selwyn Lloyd did write a minute of this meeting and asked his private secretary to put it with his other top secret minutes. But the minute deals only with the talks at the United Nations on the canal dispute; it does not make even an oblique reference to the talks at Sèvres. Minute by Selwyn Lloyd, 24 Oct. 1956, FO 800/725, PRO.
32. Nutting, *No End of a Lesson*, p. 104.
33. Lloyd, *Suez 1956*, p. 186.
34. Memorandum by Sir Patrick Dean, 1986. I am grateful to Sir Donald Logan for giving me a copy of this memorandum.
35. Ben-Gurion's diary, 24 Oct. 1956. Emphasis in original.
36. Dayan, *Story of my Life*, pp. 189–91.
37. Bar-on, *Etgar ve-Tigra*, p. 276.
38. Ben-Gurion's diary, 25 Oct. 1956.
39. Lloyd, *Suez 1956*, p. 188; Logan, 'Meetings at Sèvres' and Dean, 'Memorandum.'
40. Ben-Gurion's diary, 25 Oct. 1956.
41. Peres, *Battling for Peace*, p. 130.
42. Yossi Melman, 'A Royal Present', *Ha'aretz*, 11 Oct. 1992.
43. Interview with Colonel Mordechai Bar-On.
44. The English translation appears in Kyle, Suez, pp. 565–7. I am grateful to Keith Kyle for giving me permission to reproduce this translation.
45. Dayan, *Story of My Life*, p. 193.
46. Interview with Colonel Mordechai Bar-On.
47. Interview with Sir Donald Logan, Ditchley Park, 8 Dec. 1996; and comments by Donald Logan on Richard Lamb, *The Failure of the Eden Government*, box 30, the Selwyn Lloyd Papers, Churchill College, Cambridge.
48. Kyle, *Suez*, p. 331; Robert Rhodes James, *Anthony Eden* (London: Weidenfeld & Nicolson, 1986), pp. 530–2; interview with Donald Logan, Suez Oral History Project, Liddell Hart Centre for Military Archives, King's College, London and Sir Donald Logan, 'Collusion at Suez', *Financial Times*, 8 Jan. 1986.

49. 'Annexe au Protocole de Sèvres', 24 Oct. 1956, the Ben-Gurion Archives. The French text is also given in Pineau, *Suez 1956*, pp. 153–4. Ben-Gurion writes that in addition to the two squadrons of Mystères, the French promised 'volunteers' to fly some of Israel's Mystères. Ben-Gurion's diary, 25 Oct. 1956.
50. Pineau, *Suez 1956*, p. 153.
51. Mollet to Ben-Gurion, 25 Oct. 1956, the Ben-Gurion Archives.
52. Eden to Mollet, 25 Oct. 1956, the Ben-Gurion Archives.
53. Ben-Gurion's diary, 26 Oct. 1956.
54. Ben-Gurion to Mollet, 26 Oct. 1956, the Ben-Gurion Archives.

7

Origins of the Czech–Egyptian Arms Deal: A Reappraisal

RAMI GINAT

With the conclusion of the Second World War the world witnessed the rise of two superpowers: the Soviet Union, the leader of the emergent Eastern bloc, and the United States, the new leader of the Western bloc. This historical development was concurrent with the evolution of a new international conflict – the Cold War between the two blocs. Both superpowers vied for influence and domination in areas which were not fully identified with either of the two camps. One of these areas was the Middle East. One of Stalin's main foreign policy goals in the war's immediate aftermath, in the Middle East in particular, was to end British and French hegemony in various colonies, and to fill the vacuum as soon as conditions would allow. This policy was translated into action at the United Nations when the Soviet Union supported the demands of Lebanon and Syria in 1946 and Egypt in 1947 for a complete and speedy evacuation of foreign troops from their countries. The Soviets were also actively involved in terminating the British Mandate in Palestine and were one of Israel's major supporters in its struggle for independence in 1947–48. Soviet post-war policy contradicts the traditional concept that their interests and political activity in the Middle East during the Stalinist period were marginal. It also negates, as will be seen, the belief held by contemporary scholars that arms supplies from the Soviet bloc began reaching Arab countries in 1955; in fact, such supplies reached Egypt and other Arab countries as early as 1948.[1] Furthermore, Soviet–Egyptian commercial relations increased steadily from 1948 until 1955.[2] These pre-1955 agreements, thus far neglected in the professional literature, were of crucial importance in the establishment of Soviet hegemony over Egypt and other Arab countries.

The growth of Soviet influence and its improved position in Egypt in the second half of 1955 was the result of a gradual process of political and ideological development in Egypt, beginning in the late 1940s and early 1950s. The process was coupled with a concrete change in Soviet Middle Eastern policy in the late 1940s. Indeed, the dynamics of Soviet penetration of the region can be better understood by tracing the roots and motives of Soviet foreign policy after the Second World War.

The Czech–Egyptian arms deal, announced officially in September 1955, has been the subject of many studies. Most of them suggest that the deal was concluded as a result of the following events: the formation of the Baghdad Pact in February 1955 (a defence pact between Iran, Turkey, Pakistan and Iraq), the Israeli attack on Gaza on 28 February 1955; the Bandung Conference in April 1955 (of Asian and African peoples); and the Western refusal to supply Egypt with arms. These studies also claim that the first discussions on this subject between Egypt and the Soviet Union were initiated by the former at the Bandung Conference when Nasser first met Chinese Premier Zhou Enlai and examined with him the possibility of obtaining Soviet arms. The next contact is said have taken place in May, when Nasser met with Soviet Ambassador Daniil Solod in Cairo. These studies base their accounts on what are considered to be Egyptian primary sources. However, the versions given by these sources do not conform to the facts.[3]

A few studies have rejected the conventional account and argued, correctly, that Nasser later used the developments in the Middle East as a pretext to justify his application to the Soviet bloc for arms. Thus, Uri Ra'anan in his book *The USSR Arms the Third World*, says that the arms deal was concluded in mid-February, i.e. two weeks before the Israeli attack on Gaza, and that the first contacts between Egypt and the Soviet Union took place at the very beginning of 1955. Ra'anan maintains that by 12 January 1955, when the Turkish–Iraqi military pact became known publicly, the interests and policies of Egypt and the Soviet Union temporarily converged, though they were not identical. The *rapprochement* between the two countries was a result of this development in the Middle East, and coincided with domestic political changes in the Soviet leadership which led to the conclusion of the arms deal in mid-February.[4] P. J. Vatikiotis takes a similar view in his book, *Nasser and his Generation*.[5]

In his work *The Soviet Union and the Middle East*, Walter Laqueur argues that anyone seeking the motives behind the arms deal and the dramatic change in Egyptian policy towards the Great Powers must go back some years at least, perhaps even several decades. He focuses on two points: the evolution of anti-Western feeling and the growing radicalization of the Arab intelligentsia from the late 1930s. Laqueur's conclusion that the idea of an Egyptian alliance and even an arms deal with the Soviet Union was far from new, is indeed quite correct.

However, this theme is only sketched; moreover, regarding the genesis of the arms deal, Laqueur bases his arguments on the same disputable Egyptian sources.[6]

An exceptional – and partly acceptable – approach is presented by Mohrez Mahmoud El-Hussini. In his book, *Soviet–Egyptian Relations, 1945–85*, he says it is not clear whether the Soviets or the Egyptians were the first to initiate the arms dialogue. He notes, however, that 'from circumstantial evidence it seems plausible that the USSR, motivated by certain ideological and strategic requirements, made the first move'. In this view, the Soviet offer of arms to Egypt was part of a long-term Soviet plan to acquire naval and air facilities in Egypt.[7] The strategic arguments adduced by Hussini make sense. However, it would be a mistake to disregard the political and economic considerations which were the motivating force behind the arms deal and formed the corner-stone in the Soviet–Egyptian *rapprochement*.

I would like to suggest that the so-called Czech–Egyptian arms deal, announced officially in September 1955, was in fact a combination of two separate deals. The first, smaller one was concluded in the first quarter of 1955 between Egypt and Czechoslovakia; and the second, the larger and more famous, was concluded towards the end of July with the Soviet Union, and signed in September 1955 with Czechoslovakia. In fact, the second deal was a direct continuation of the first. Both deals were the result of several stages of negotiations, which started at the end of 1953, gathered momentum at the end of 1954 and reached their conclusion in 1955. These contacts were conducted at official and unofficial levels and were motivated and affected by the political and economic climate which prevailed between the two countries. Both deals were actually concluded by the Soviets, and Czechoslovakia was given the green light to go ahead with sales.[8]

This chapter focuses on the first period of negotiations, which I consider to be the formative stage which culminated in the deals of 1955. The process of *rapprochement* between Egypt and the Soviet Union had begun long before the signing of the Baghdad Pact. Soviet interest in the area had been increasing steadily since the second half of the 1940s. Towards the end of Stalin's period in power, the Soviets made many attempts to improve relations with Arab governments which conducted anti-Western or neutralist policies. This was the case with Egypt's Wafdist government (1950–52). Salah al-Din, the Wafdist foreign minister, shaped and implemented Egypt's new policy of neutralism. He resolutely rejected Western proposals to establish a Middle East Command, and he was the driving force behind his government's decision to abrogate the treaty of 1936 with Britain. The possibility of an arms deal with the Soviet Union was discussed seriously in Cairo. As a result of this policy, relations between

Egypt and the Soviet Union improved significantly; several commercial agreements were concluded, and greater understanding and cooperation was furthered at the UN. During the second half of 1951, the idea of concluding a non-aggression pact between the two countries was seriously considered. In fact, the roots of the later Soviet–Egyptian 'honeymoon' can be traced to this period.[9]

The downfall of the Wafd government in January 1952 generated a period of mutual suspicion and distrust in Soviet–Egyptian relations. In his last months, however, Stalin moderated his negative attitude towards the Free Officers' regime in Egypt. The Soviets now adopted a wait-and-see tactic. Eventually, the Free Officers' position *vis-à-vis* the Western powers did, to some extent, satisfy Soviet policy-makers. They believed that Western failure in the region would serve Soviet interests. In the meantime, the Soviet media supported Egypt and the Arabs in their 'just struggle' and their 'right' to full independence. At the 19th Congress of the Communist Party of the Soviet Union (CPSU), held in Moscow in October 1952, Soviet officials called for the full liberation of the colonial and dependent countries. In practice, the Soviet Union stepped up its efforts to encourage disorder and to stir up revolts against the West in the Arab world. The Wafd period in power had taught the Soviets how to exploit the substantial opportunities created by differences between Egypt and the Western powers, in order to promote their interests. They realized that Egypt could defect from the West to the East without being brought under direct communist control. To enhance its position in the Arab world and to demonstrate good will towards the Arabs, the Soviets attacked Israel and Zionism. Two significant events took place on the international scene during the first quarter of 1953: first, the end of Truman's presidency and the accession of President Eisenhower in January 1953; second, the beginning of a new era in the Soviet Union after the death of Stalin in March 1953. In the long term, these changes were to have great importance for the policy of both superpowers towards Egypt and the Middle East.

In their first year in power, Stalin's successors acted to turn the Middle Eastern clock back to the days of cooperation and cordial relations with neutralist Arab governments. In the latter part of 1953, many within Egyptian political circles urged the adoption of a policy of neutralism and the nurturing of good relations with the Soviet Union. Anti-Western feelings increased steadily because of Britain's refusal to evacuate its troops from Egypt. The inability of the military regime to implement the main clause of Nasser's political programme – the liberation of Egypt – caused the political atmosphere in the country to revert to what it had been during the Wafdist government. As far as the Anglo-Egyptian dispute was concerned, Nasser and his colleagues could not ask for less than Salah al-Din, the last Wafdist Foreign Minister, and his dominant but extreme group within Nahhas Pasha's government. This was what apparently induced Nasser to adopt Salah al-Din's policy of neutralism. He pursued that policy in order to manipulate both Western and Soviet interests, which he then intended to utilize to his own advantage – to further Egypt's foreign policy.[10] Perceiving that Egypt's new rulers had embarked on the road of neutralism, the new Soviet leadership decided to take a more variegated approach towards the Free Officers' regime – based on 'accommodationism' and pragmatism – thus bringing to an end the short 'wait-and-see' period.

Stalin's successors put considerable emphasis on presenting the Soviet Union as a friend of the Arabs. They attempted to persuade the Arabs that they had no reason to consider the Soviet Union a potential enemy, or to fear Soviet imperialist intentions. On the contrary, they cited Egypt's failure to reach an acceptable solution to its extended dispute with Britain as proof that Britain and not the Soviet Union was Egypt's real enemy. In its attempts to acquire goodwill in the Near East, the Soviet government invited non-communist guests from that region to visit the Soviet Union as guests of the state, and plied them with messages extolling the economic progress and peaceful intentions of the Soviet Union.

The Soviet media attacked all Western proposals for settling the Anglo-Egyptian dispute. US efforts to find a solution throughout 1953, by eliciting substantial British concessions when necessary, led the Soviets to conclude that this policy was intended to pave the way for Egypt to accept the Four-Power proposal of 13 October 1951 to establish a Middle East Command (MEC). Soviet propaganda organs constantly emphasized the 'contradictions' between the United States and its allies, mainly Britain – playing it both ways. When the United States showed sympathy towards British policy in a certain country, the Soviet press played up the incident as an example of the Anglo-American efforts to continue the oppression of colonial peoples. On the other hand, if the two allies disagreed on some issue, the Soviets commented that the United States was not sympathetic towards the nationalist aspirations of the Middle Eastern peoples but wanted only to weaken Britain's influence and replace it as the dominant power in the country concerned. This Soviet tactic was intended to drive a wedge between the two Western powers. The Soviet government also showed acute sensitivity towards any approaches to its frontiers as well as a desire to have friendly states on its borders. As this was a basic feature of Soviet policy towards the Near East, the Soviet Union made its opposition to any Western defence plans in this region very clear. The Soviets cautioned Middle Eastern governments against joining defence organizations, and warned Western powers to stop pressuring these governments to enter such military pacts.[11] In a speech before the Supreme Soviet on 8 August 1953, Prime Minister Georgii Malenkov reaffirmed that the new Soviet government wished to win international support and to spoil Western defensive plans wherever and whenever it could. To refute Western contentions of Soviet expansionism, he stressed that the Soviet Union had no territorial claims against any state and that this included every neighbouring state. The principle of Soviet foreign policy was to respect the national freedom and sovereignty of every country, large and small. The differences between the social and economic systems of the Soviet Union and some neighbouring states was not an obstacle to maintaining and strengthening friendly relations with them. The Soviet government, he said, had taken steps to reinforce 'good-neighbour relations' with such states, and now it was up to the governments to show their readiness to take an active part, 'not in words but in ideas, in bringing about this friendship, which presupposes mutual concern for strengthening peace and the security of our countries'.[12]

A turning point in Soviet–Egyptian relations occurred in the second half of 1953. Soviet political activity in the Middle East was gathering momentum – the Middle Eastern pot, as it were, was moved from the back of the Soviet stove to the front. One of the most important moves made by the Soviet government was the appointment of Daniil Solod on 11 October 1953, as Soviet minister to Egypt. Solod, who had served as the Soviet minister to Syria from 1946 to 1950, was considered one of his country's ranking Middle East experts. He had played a leading role in the process of *rapprochement* between the Soviet Union and Syria and Egypt in 1950. Solod's first mission in the Arab world had been in 1943, when he was appointed a counsellor at the Soviet legation in Cairo following the establishment of diplomatic relations between the Soviet Union and Egypt.[13] Towards the end of 1953, the international situation created a basis for greater understanding and cooperation between the Soviet Union and Egypt. A pro-Arab stand was taken by the Soviets in UN debates dealing with the Arab–Israeli conflict, and Soviet delegates at the UN also frequently attacked the Western powers for exerting pressure on Egypt and other Arab countries to join a military pact with them. During the last quarter of 1953 and the first quarter of 1954, Soviet vetoes caused Israel to lose its cases in the Security Council. By this time, the new Soviet leadership's decision to join the UN programme of granting technical assistance to underdeveloped countries, and particularly Malenkov's call to tighten cooperation with the Arab states, had fallen on attentive Egyptian ears. Western restrictions on supplying arms to Egypt, and Britain's refusal to evacuate its troops or to buy Egyptian cotton, had led Egypt's rulers to seek other sources of supply and export outlets. An official survey of Egypt's trade prospects, prepared by the country's Foreign Ministry, assessed that 'great gaps can be filled in Egypt's needs for arms, coal and heavy industry' by trading with the Eastern bloc. The report stressed that a Soviet–Egyptian trade agreement providing for the exchange of Egyptian cotton in return for Soviet wheat, coal and industrial equipment had already been initialled by representatives of both sides.[14] After lengthy secret negotiations, this agreement was signed on 18 August 1953. An Egyptian Foreign Ministry official said that in the course of the talks, the Soviet Union had agreed to furnish Egypt with military equipment if requested to do so, and that Egypt had already begun negotiations to purchase arms from the Škoda Works in Czechoslovakia.[15]

The zenith of this process of *rapprochement* occurred in December 1953, when an Egyptian trade mission headed by Hasan Rajab, deputy war minister went on a three-month visit to Eastern Europe, including nearly two months in the Soviet Union.[16] Although the declared purpose of the tour was to extend economic and industrial cooperation with the Eastern bloc, Rajab emphasized that the visit was also proof that Egypt's new regime 'wished to work with all peoples for the insurance of peace.'[17] The delegation was welcomed warmly by East European governments and its protracted visit was a turning point in political and economic relations between Egypt and the Soviet bloc. The timing was right, as both the Soviet Union and Egypt were reviewing economic policy with the aim of conducting trade with as many countries as possible. The new economic programme of Stalin's successors in their first year in power called for slightly increased imports of consumer goods and for a considerable increase in capital goods imports, largely though not exclusively, intended for the industries producing consumer goods and foodstuffs.[18] The Egyptian market could offer the Soviets two important items, cotton and rice, which, to a degree, were in line with the Soviet goal. For Egypt, sending experts in various fields to the Soviet bloc was intended to explore and discuss the various possibilities of increasing trade and barter. It should be pointed out that this visit was one of a series to many different countries for the same purpose.

Although not made explicit, Egypt's decision to send Brigadier Hasan Rajab, 'undersecretary for War Factory Affairs at the Ministry of War', as the head of an economic delegation was twofold. First, as officially stated, it was to widen economic relations with the Eastern bloc by sending a senior official. But second, as part of Egypt's endeavour to find alternative sources of arms, it was necessary to send a high-ranking military official who specialized in armaments. Indeed, reports from Prague confirmed that during its five-day visit there the delegation visited several munitions factories and the firm that manufactured the

MIG fighter-plane. In fact, no sooner had the delegation left Egypt, than the Israeli embassy in Prague reported that Egypt had ordered MiGs from Czechoslovakia.[19]

The Israeli newspaper *Yediot aharonot* reported on 19 January 1954 that a first shipment of Czech and Polish arms, which had been purchased by the Egyptian commercial delegation, had arrived in Egypt and was to undergo a routine inspection. The shipment contained rifles and machine-guns. The paper referred to 'political circles' in the Middle East who conjectured that the purchase was intended to put pressure on the United States and Britain to supply arms to Egypt.[20] On 14 February 1954, *al-Misri* quoted a statement made by Salah Salim (a prominent figure in the Revolutionary Command Council, or RCC) that Egypt had already submitted requests for arms to various countries, including the Soviet Union. Salim revealed that there was a possibility that the Soviets would agree to supply some of the requests.[21] Whether the sources quoted above are reliable or not, the question of purchasing arms from Soviet bloc countries had definitely come up during the three-month visit, as may be gleaned from a variety of archival and non-archival sources.[22]

Ahmad Hamrush, a former member of the Egyptian communist organization DMNL (Democratic Movement for National Liberation) who maintained close contacts with the Free Officers, adds an important dimension to the story. In his book *Qissat Thaurat 23 Yuliyo* (The Story of the 23 July Revolution), he claims that one of the main reasons for dispatching the commercial delegation was to put pressure on the Western powers to change their attitude towards Egypt. He says that attempts to purchase arms from the Soviet bloc were made by both Hasan Rajab in Prague and Muhammad Nagib in Cairo. According to Hamrush, in December 1953 Nagib held talks with Soviet Ambassador Daniil Solod, in which he explored the possibility of purchasing arms from the Soviet Union. Several weeks later, in January 1954, Solod replied positively, expressing Soviet readiness to begin supplying the Egyptian army with weaponry. Nagib told Solod that he would ask 'Abd al-Hakim 'Amer, the commander-in-chief of the Egyptian armed forces, to supply him with a list of required equipment. However, according to Hamrush, this dialogue was not crowned with success because of Nasser's objections.[23] Nasser's attitude stemmed from a series of internal and external political considerations.

When the existence of a power struggle between Nagib and Nasser became known, the Soviets, understandably, overestimated Nagib's power, as he was the key figure in the contacts with them. Towards the end of 1953 and at the very beginning of 1954, Nagib was still considered the strongest figure in Egypt. In fact, he was supported by most of the country's political circles, including radical groups, the Muslim Brotherhood and the communists. Furthermore, when the power struggle gathered momentum during February and March 1954, it appeared from the outside that Nagib had the advantage, owing to the massive demonstrations of support in his favour. Yet, inside the RCC, effectively the ruling body, Nagib found himself isolated. The RCC was fully controlled by Nasser, and of all its members, Khalid Muhyi al-Din, the well-known pro-communist, was Nagib's only supporter. The Soviet decision to reply positively to Nagib's request for arms derived, *inter alia*, from the wish to strengthen his position *vis-à-vis* Nasser, who was known for his anti-Soviet approach.[24] The Soviets and the Egyptian communists, who believed that Nagib would win the day, assumed that their firm support for him would advance their interests in the long term. At the beginning of 1954, the Soviets consistently expressed their satisfaction with Egyptian foreign policy.

However, Nagib's inability to persuade the RCC to welcome the Soviet approval to furnish Egypt with arms, reflected his weakness. The Soviets learned the lesson and henceforth insisted that every official negotiation with Egypt was to be 'subject to Colonel 'Abd al-Nasser's personal approval'.[25] The Soviets also avoided giving public support to either Nagib or Nasser when the power struggle reached its climax. News reports in the Soviet Union on the February–March events and on Nagib's ouster in November, were objective and balanced.[26] Nasser responded negatively to the Soviet agreement to supply arms because he did not want to provoke the Western powers on the eve of talks on British evacuation. His decision to abort the Nagib–Solod dialogue was also a tactical move intended to promote his personal ambitions; it was not due to his anti-Soviet policy, since only two months earlier he had supported the decision to dispatch the Rajab mission to Eastern Europe to seek arms. In fact, Nasser maintained contacts with the Soviets at both diplomatic and clandestine levels throughout 1954.[27]

From the economic aspect, Rajab's visit was a great success. On 11 February, an Egyptian official, described as reliable, told an officer at the US embassy that Kabanov, the Soviet minister of trade, had made an attractive offer to the Rajab delegation in Moscow. The Soviet Union, he said, would assist Egypt in building the High Dam at Aswan. The official added that two members of the Egyptian mission had returned to Cairo to transmit the Soviet proposals to Nasser. The latter then ordered the mission to bring back the fullest information on the Soviet offers, stressing that they would receive 'careful consideration'.[28]

Soon after the delegation returned to Cairo, in March 1954, Rajab said that the visit to the Soviet Union had shown that the possibilities of economic cooperation were unlimited.[29] Indeed, during March 1954, several agreements with the Soviet Union and its satellites were signed. For instance, on 27 March 1954 a barter agreement for the exchange of Soviet industrial equipment, petroleum and other products in return for cotton and other Egyptian products was signed between Egypt and the Soviet Union.[30] At the signing ceremony, held at the Egyptian Ministry of Foreign Affairs, V.D. Alekseenko, commercial counsellor of the Soviet embassy and the Soviet signatory, expressed willingness to extend commercial relations with Egypt, as the agreement would open an advantageous field for economic cooperation. Kamil 'Abd al-Nabi, director of the Economic Department in the Egyptian Ministry of Foreign Affairs and the Egyptian signatory, replied that the agreement would help to establish economic cooperation and would launch a new era in relations between the two countries.[31]

There is no doubt that the three-month visit did in fact open a new era in relations between Egypt and the Soviet bloc. It contributed to the renewal of the cordial understanding which had been interrupted with the downfall of the Wafd government in January 1952. The visit came at the right time for both Egypt and the Soviet Union. No doubt, Soviet willingness to supply Egypt with arms unconditionally reinforced Nasser's rejection of any military alliance with the West. Nasser realized that the Soviet option might be useful for two purposes. First, it could be a bargaining card to strengthen Egypt's position in the upcoming talks with Britain. In the meantime, it would lessen US pressure on Egypt to join a military pact. Second, in case of a deterioration in relations with the West, and the latter's refusal to support Egypt financially and militarily, Egypt could turn to the Soviet alternative. The visit revealed possibilities latent in purchasing arms from the Soviet bloc. Egypt had no longer to surrender to Western pressure to join a military alliance in order to acquire arms. Weapons could thus be obtained unconditionally while Egypt could maintain its neutral policy without committing to a particular bloc. There is no clear evidence to establish that the arms deal was concluded during the three-month visit of the Rajab mission. However, a basic inspection of the Eastern bloc's armaments industry and of the possibilities of adjusting it to the requirements of the Egyptian army, was certainly carried out. Hasan Rajab who specialized in military–industrial projects was not chosen to head the mission by accident. His visits to military factories and his hosts' requests to exchange Egyptian cotton in return for arms, laid the basis for the arms deals of 1955.

Hamrush tells us that Nasser continued his contacts with the Eastern bloc to purchase arms on the diplomatic and clandestine levels throughout 1954. According to him, 'Aziz 'Ali al-Misri, Egypt's ambassador in Moscow held talks with the Soviets on this subject throughout 1954. He revealed that these contacts gathered momentum towards the end of the year as a result of other political events in the Middle East. In October, after the conclusion of the Anglo-Egyptian agreement, Ahmad Lutfi Wakd, Nasser's office director, approached the Soviet embassy in Cairo to discuss Nasser's plan to be presented at the Bandung Conference. During his talks, the question of Soviet arms sales came up. This dialogue, noted Hamrush, remained at a low level and was intended more to learn about the Soviet attitude towards this issue than to formalize the framework of future negotiations. Another attempt was made towards the end of 1954, when Nasser asked Husayn 'Arafa, a member of the Egyptian Military Police, to check the possibility of purchasing arms from the Soviet Union. The results of 'Arafa's inspection, said Hamrush, remain unknown.[32]

The ascendancy of Khrushchev during January–February 1955 after a continuous power struggle with Malenkov, the then Prime Minister,[33] contributed significantly to the acceleration of the clandestine Soviet–Egyptian dialogue. As far as foreign policy was concerned, Khrushchev maintained that the attitude towards neutral countries had to be revised, 'rapprochement with their nationalist (though bourgeois) governments was imperative if the course pursued by these governments was to be directed against the West; abundant economic help, in addition to political rapprochement, must lead to the emergence of a firm coalition of Communist-controlled nations with the "neutrals"'.[34]

In fact, from the end of 1954, Khrushchev had ultimate control over clandestine operations. He dominated the CPSU's Central Committee apparatus, controlled the KGB, and maintained a close alliance with leading Red Army cadres, a matter which paved the way for a direct channel of communication with Soviet military intelligence.[35] By that time, undercover activities and contacts had already been taking place between Egyptian and Soviet intelligence. Soviet activity was handled by Soviet military intelligence, the *Glavnoe razvedyvatel'noe upravlenie* (GRU), which was attached directly to the General Staff. The GRU collected and evaluated military field intelligence and extensive foreign espionage. It was also in charge of Soviet military shipments to other countries. At that time, the organization was interested in using Egypt 'as an anti-capitalist military power in the Near East'.[36] Clandestine Egyptian activities were directed by 'Ali Sabri, Director of Egyptian Air Force Intelligence, who, according to some reports, negotiated Egypt's military requirements with a Soviet military representative, probably a member of the GRU, at the Soviet embassy in Cairo.[37] Secret contacts between diplomatic representatives of the two countries in Turkey also took place continuously in Ankara from the very beginning of 1955. Despite the Egyptian embassy's denial, US and British reports from Ankara, based on reliable sources, stated that such contacts were taking place. According to these reports, one of these meetings took place on 6 February: two diplomatic cars met at the Cubuk water reservoir, eight miles outside Ankara. The Egyptian ambassador emerged from the one car, and five officers from the Soviet embassy, headed by the chargé d'affaires, from the other. All met, walked together for some time in the adjoining park, then parted.[38] This information was also confirmed by Menderes, the Turkish Prime Minister, on 8 February, during his conversation with Sir James Bowker, the British ambassador to Turkey. Adnan Menderes blamed the Egyptian government for conducting a continuous violent campaign against Iraq and Turkey. Egypt, he said, aimed to isolate the Arab states from any defence association with the West. He believed that several moves made recently by the Egyptian government clearly indicated that Egyptian policy had basically taken a pro-Soviet orientation which could affect the security of the Canal Zone; he therefore called for the closest observation. According to him, this oscillation in Egypt's policy found its expression in:

• statements by Egyptian political leaders that 'Egypt should furnish the Arab states with all the arms they required';
• Egyptian criticism of Iraq for breaking off diplomatic relations with the Soviet Union;
• the recent clandestine contacts between Egypt and the Soviet Union.[39]

Despite Menderes' evaluation which was based on solid grounds, the British ambassadors in both Cairo and Ankara ruled out the possibility that Egypt's moves indicated a pro-Soviet reorientation. The two believed that Egypt would remain on the side of the West and that its present anti-Western policy derived from fears that Iraq was going to become the main ally of the West and would therefore replace Egypt as leader of the Arabs.[40] It is quite possible that Egyptian statements on furnishing the Arab states with arms came after they had received Soviet assurances that they would supply the arms. By that time, the interests of both the Soviet Union and Egypt were to prevent other Arab states from joining the Turkish-Iraqi pact. As Iraq received new modern weapons from the Western powers in return for siding with them, the Soviets realized that this state of affairs required them to take countermeasures in order to back the Arab states opposed to this. It is therefore reasonable to argue that the Soviets stood behind these statements and encouraged the Egyptian government to continue in the same direction.

On 28 January 1955, in a message to US diplomatic missions, Dulles informed them that: 'In recent months there have been several reports of Soviet bloc offers to provide technical assistance and equipment to non-communist countries, particularly to less developed countries.'[41] Intelligence reports which were being received as early as March 1955 indicated that the Soviets had been in direct contact with the Arabs, and was offering them economic and military aid.[42] But although US and British policy-makers were informed that relations between Egypt and the Soviet Union were converging and tightening, they did not pay the necessary attention to this development.

As argued earlier, in 1955 Egypt concluded two separate deals with the Eastern bloc. Both deals were actually concluded by the Soviets while Czechoslovakia was given the green light to go ahead with sales.[43] The first arms deal between Egypt and the Soviet bloc was concluded in Cairo in February 1955. This information was first officially revealed by the Soviets a decade later, when the Communist Party organ *International Affairs* confirmed that 'Nasser's government concluded in February 1955 a commercial agreement with Czechoslovakia for the delivery of arms.'[44] Indeed, on 10 February a Czech trade delegation arrived in Cairo for the reported purpose of general trade discussions and negotiation of the trade and payments agreement. The Czech delegation left Cairo towards the end of February without any official announcement regarding the results of its visit. Soon after its departure, on 24 March 1955, a Czech trade exhibition was opened in Cairo.[45] This move was presumably intended to demonstrate that relations between the two countries were based mainly on commercial interests. Such an industrial exhibition could be used as a cover for clandestine negotiation for arms, and to refute some Western reports which claimed that the purpose of the recent dialogue was to negotiate a barter agreement to exchange Egyptian cotton for Czech arms. For instance, a correspondent of Agence France Presse, reported on 14 February 1955:[46]

It has been learned from a well-informed source that Czechoslovakia is ready to exchange heavy arms for Egyptian cotton. A Czech mission headed by Dr. Otakar Teufer, director general of the Prague Foreign Trade Department arrived in Cairo and had its first conference on February 14 at the Foreign Ministry with Egyptian Under Secretary for Foreign Affairs Sami Abu al-Futuh and General Hassan Rajab, under secretary of the War Ministry.

The *New York Herald Tribune* reported that talks on this subject were going on between the two countries when the Czech government opened the industrial exhibition in Cairo in March.[47] In a report which evaluated Egyptian–Soviet bloc relations, Henry Byroade, the US ambassador in Cairo, stressed that in the spring of 1955, following the

Gaza incident of 28 February, Hasan Ibrahim, the Egyptian minister of production, and Hasan Mar'i, ex-minister of commerce, visited Eastern Europe in search of arms. According to him, they were apparently successful in obtaining tanks and possibly jet planes in Czechoslovakia. Later on, he said, in May 1955, Daniil Solod, the Soviet ambassador in Cairo, in response to Nasser's request, offered to furnish 'heavy artillery' to Egypt. In both cases, the arms were to be exchanged for Egyptian cotton 'without strings' as to their potential use. Byroade said that Solod's offer was not immediately accepted by Nasser since 'he would prefer for political and other reasons to obtain arms in the West if possible.' Byroade concluded incorrectly that, 'it is apparent that Nasser would be most reluctant to accept the [Soviet] offer since it would, of course, involve Egypt even more deeply with the Soviet bloc than is now the case as a result of the current exchanges of cotton for petroleum and industrial goods'.[48]

From Byroade's report and from other intelligence and non-intelligence reports and information, it can be established that an arms deal between Czechoslovakia and Egypt was indeed concluded in February 1955. Under this agreement Egypt was to exchange cotton for military equipment. It can also be established that soon afterwards, the Soviets offered Egypt military equipment which could not be supplied by the Czechs. This specific Soviet offer was made only in May 1955. This conclusion however requires elucidation. A close examination of Egypt's dialogue with Czechoslovakia and the Soviet Union after February 1955 will simplify this complex issue.

The mission of Hasan Mar'i and Hasan Ibrahim mission to Eastern Europe was not in order to obtain arms because of the Gaza incident. Two simple reasons indicate the opposite. First, the arms deal had already been concluded a few weeks before the Gaza incident; the visit was therefore undoubtedly made in order to discuss and complete technical details arising from the need to implement the already concluded deal. The decision to send ex-minister Hasan Mar'i was probably due to his previous experience and familiarity with the subject. As the former minister of commerce, he had conducted the talks with the Czech delegation in February.[49] Second, during Rajab's mission to Prague in 1954, he visited several arms factories including the firm which manufactured the MiG aircraft. This means that during his talks with the Czech delegation in February 1955 he already knew what the Czech armaments industry could supply. There was therefore no need to dispatch another Egyptian delegation to the Eastern bloc countries in order to get more information about their armaments industries. With his previous experience, Rajab could undoubtedly conclude such a deal. The fact that his dialogue with the Soviets was crowned with success and first led to a small arms deal with the Eastern bloc, was also noted by Khrushchev in his memoirs. In the chapter dealing with the Soviets relations with Nasser's Egypt he recalls:

> Soon after the coup, when the Egyptians decided to try to oust the English, Nasser's representatives came to us with a request for military aid. They said they needed to have their own army in order to put pressure on the English. We agreed. We gave them weapons ranging from rifles to regular artillery, but as I recall, we didn't give them any planes at first. We did, however, give them tanks and naval equipment. Nasser said he particularly needed torpedo boats. I think we gave them military aid on a commercial basis, but at a reduced price.[50]

By the time that talks with the Soviets for modern arms had been concluded at the end of July, Egyptian technicians had already flown to Prague to check the first consignment of MiG 15 aircraft.[51] On 19 July, a week before the technicians' departure, it was officially announced that Egypt and Czechoslovakia had concluded a trade and payments agreement.

In fact, they signed two separate agreements on the same date. The first agreement was for one year and provided for the exchange of Egyptian cotton, rice and other products for Czech machinery and equipment, chemicals, rubber products, glass, timber and sugar. The Egyptian government also agreed on the dispatch to Egypt of Czech technical advisers. A three-year agreement was the second to be signed. It applied 'only to government purchases', with a total exchange value of US$7 million. The agreements were concluded after a six-week visit by a Czech trade mission, headed by Kohout, vice-minister for foreign trade, who in March 1955 had handled the Czech industrial exhibition in Cairo. As officially announced by Richard Dvorak, Czech minister of foreign trade, the arms deal was a part of the trade accord.[52] Thus, it follows that the second agreement which related to 'government purchases' was probably a cover for arms purchases. From a close examination of similar barter deals between Egypt and other Eastern bloc countries in the 1950s, it follows that the conclusion of such deals did not require such a long period of negotiation. It is therefore certain that during the six-week visit, technical and financial details arising from the conclusion of the arms deal of February, were discussed and concluded before the departure of Egyptian technicians to Prague.

The Egyptian government's consent in the first agreement to facilitate the work of Czech technicians was in contrast to its policy of not allowing foreign advisers into the country. Its decision to allow many of the Czech technicians who entered Egypt in March 1955 (in connection with the industrial exhibition) to stay in Egypt (despite the end of the exhibition), and its consent to the arrival of some more, was intended to prepare the ground for the acceptance of the new military equipment, some of which had already arrived in Egypt. The Soviets were certainly involved, both directly and indirectly, in the Czech–Egyptian clandestine negotiations which led to the agreement. Their complete control of their allies' legations in Cairo, was well described by Zakariya Muhyi al-Din, Egypt's interior minister. According to him, 'more and more persons of Russian nationality are handling Soviet bloc affairs in Egypt', whereas in the past, he emphasized, the Soviets had left the handling of Middle East affairs to the 'satellite representatives'.[53] It can also be deduced that the Soviets were fully aware of Egypt's military needs from the fact that on 23 May, during a meeting between Solod and Nasser, on the latter's initiative, Solod provided a list of available military equipment and terms of purchase. They undoubtedly played a crucial role in the first half of 1955 in bringing the arms deal between Egypt and Czechoslovakia to a conclusion. Solod's offer was made after the conclusion of this deal and included a list of military equipment some of which was similar and in addition to the Czech equipment, and some, like submarines, heavy tanks and jet bombers, which could not be supplied by Czechoslovakia.[54]

Soon after the Nasser–Solod meeting, clandestine negotiations between Egypt and the Soviet Union took place in Cairo. 'Ali Sabri again represented the Egyptian government and his Soviet counterpart was Colonel Nimoshenka, military attaché at the Soviet embassy in Cairo. These negotiations were kept secret and only a few officials from both sides knew about them.[55] A US intelligence report indicated on 5 June that Nasser had designated Hasan Rajab to head a mission to the Soviet Union 'to negotiate the purchase of artillery items offered for barter against cotton'.[56] This deal was concluded at the end of July 1955 during a visit by D.T. Shepilov, editor of *Pravda*, secretary of the CPSU's Central Committee, a specialist in foreign affairs, and a favourite of Khrushchev. The decision to send Shepilov and not a representative of the Foreign Ministry to handle the final stage of the deal, was well-calculated by Khrushchev. Shepilov arrived in Cairo on 21 July, while talks on relaxing international tensions were going on in Geneva between the leaders of the East and West. Shepilov was in fact one of the key figures in shaping Soviet foreign policy, and was Khrushchev's choice. Officially, he was invited by the Egyptian government as the editor of *Pravda*, to attend Egypt's Liberation Day celebrations, on 23 July. The argument put forth by David Dallin in his book *Soviet Foreign Policy after Stalin*,[57] that 'with Shepilov rather than a representative of the Foreign Ministry conducting the negotiations, the proceedings would appear less official in case the issue should come up at Geneva', is fully acceptable. During his visit, all the details of the arms deal were decided upon, although the deal itself was not yet signed. Shepilov brought a message from Khrushchev that the Soviet Union was prepared to assist Egypt in every field. In his talks with Nasser, Shepilov made it clear that his government was willing to increase its latest offers substantially, and would provide Egypt with MiG aircraft and with the latest weapons. He promised quick delivery and consented to a barter with Egyptian cotton. The Soviets agreed to sell to Egypt among others, 100 MiGs, 200 tanks and jet bombers. The military shipments would begin to arrive within 30 days. The Soviet Union was also willing to finance the building of the High Dam in Aswan, and Egypt could repay in cotton over a period of up to 30 years and in terms suitable to Egypt. In addition, Shepilov also promised that the Soviet Union would also be of great assistance to Egypt in economic development and technical assistance.[58]

By the end of August the Egyptian government had decided to sign an agreement with the Soviet Union. The deal was signed on 20 September 1955 in Warsaw,[59] officially, with the Czech government, deputed by the Soviet government for this purpose. In fact, three communist countries were involved: the Soviet Union, Czechoslovakia and Poland.[60] Under this deal Egypt was to receive from the Soviets and the Czechs the following military equipment: between 120 and 200 MiG 15 fighters; between 30 and 60 IL 28 bombers; small numbers of training aircraft; small numbers of transport aircraft; 200 medium and heavy tanks, and light and heavy artillery and ammunition. Under this deal, Poland and the Soviet Union were to supply naval equipment. This included two Skory-class destroyers, two T-43 minesweepers, 12 MTBs-P6 and three submarines, two W-class and one Malutka-class. The total arms purchased was estimated at US$140 million.[61] On 27 September 1955, the day of Nasser's announcement of the conclusion of the arms deal with Czechoslovakia, a shipment of small arms, including machine guns, reportedly arrived in Egypt. According to this source, another shipment, including 60 heavy tanks, was to arrive within the week.[62] The arrival of these shipments, only a few days after the signing of the main deal, could be a result of two things. First, since the report concerned shipments of small arms, and according to the September deal Egypt was to receive heavy equipment, it is reasonable to assume that these shipments were part of the military equipment supplied by the Czechs under the agreement of February 1955. Second, the Soviets could make available for delivery, without special preparations, surplus stocks of military equipment, including tanks and planes, owing to their recent armed forces' re-equipment programme. As a result of the new programme, the Soviets could offer Egypt huge quantities of surplus arms with quick delivery.[63] Nevertheless, it is pointless to try to establish which shipment came from which country. One thing is certain, the decision to dispatch arms shipments from Soviet bloc countries to Egypt was definitely made by the Soviet leaders.

NOTES

1. This chapter is based on my book *The Soviet Union and Egypt, 1945–55* (London: Frank Cass, 1993), and includes some additions to the original. See also, Rami Ginat, 'Soviet Policy towards the Arab World, 1945-48', *Middle Eastern Studies*, 32, 4 (1996), pp. 321–35. The information and interpretations are based primarily on US, British and Israeli archival material. Many of the documents are classified as intelligence reports which generally derive their analyses from well-informed Egyptian, Soviet and other sources. I have made every effort to cross-reference these reports with other sources whenever possible. The chapter also relies on the Soviet and Arabic press, memoirs of Arab and Soviet leaders, official statements and publications and interviews with incumbent and former leaders. At the time when most of this research was first completed (early 1991), Soviet archives were not accessible. Since then I have managed to obtain direct and indirect access to some of these archives, but I have found nothing thus far which substantially alters the assessments and conclusions presented here. It would seem that the key to understanding the consolidation of the Soviet–Egyptian arms deals lies somewhere deep in the basements of the archives of Soviet military intelligence (GRU) and the KGB. Unfortunately, these archives, as well as Egyptian state archives, remain closed.
2. On commercial relations between the two countries see Ginat, *The Soviet Union and Egypt*, pp. 103–7, 134–43, 229–38.
3. A logical and acceptable criticism of these sources was made by Uri Ra'anan. He proved indisputably that the two main Egyptian sources, Muhammad H. Haykal and Salah Salim, were not primary sources containing full and precise information. Nor did their versions of the genesis of the arms deal correspond with the facts. See Uri Ra'anan, *The USSR Arms the Third World* (Cambridge, MA: MIT Press, 1969), pp. 62–8.
4. Ra'anan, *The USSR Arms the Third World*, Part I.
5. P. J. Vatikiotis, *Nasser and his Generation* (London: Croom Helm, 1978), p. 232.
6. Walter Laqueur, *The Soviet Union and the Middle East* (London: Routledge & Kegan Paul, 1959), pp. 213–17.
7. Mohrez Mahmoud El-Hussini, *Soviet–Egyptian Relations, 1945–85* (Basingstoke: Macmillan, 1987), pp. 55–64.
8. On the conclusions of the two deals, see Ginat, *The Soviet Union and Egypt*, pp. 209–19.
9. For details on this subject see Ginat, *The Soviet Union and Egypt*, pp. 107–43.
10. Muhammad Salah al-Din, former Wafdist foreign minister, was one of the only pre-coup politicians not to be hurt by the Revolutionary Command Council in its first years in power. See Jean Lacouture, *Nasser* (in Hebrew) (Tel Aviv: Am Oved, 1972), p. 85. See also Jean and Simonne Lacouture, *Egypt in Transition* (London: Methuen, 1958), p. 242; and Joel Gordon, *Nasser's Blessed Movement* (New York, NY and Oxford: Oxford University Press, 1992), pp. 85–6.
11. See a memorandum by J. Jefferson Jones, first secretary at the US embassy, Moscow, entitled 'Soviet Attitudes towards the Near Eastern Area', in despatch 20 from American Embassy, Moscow, 17 July 1953, General Records of the Department of State, Record Group (RG) 59, 661.80/7-1753, National Archives, Washington DC (hereafter cited as RG 59 with appropriate filing reference). The Soviet press attacked the Anglo-Egyptian agreement on the Sudan signed on 12 February 1953. The agreement was described by *Izvestiia* as a victory for US diplomacy which urged Egypt and Britain to reach an agreement. See for instace, I. Potekhin, 'K itogam Anglo-Egipetskikh peregovorov o Sudane', *Izvestiia*, 19 February 1953. See also Radio Moscow in Arabic, *SWB* (Summary of World Broadcasts) 24 February 1953, USSR, pp. 27–8.

12. See Papers of Harry N. Howard, File Subject: Middle East Chronological File, 1953, Box 14, Truman Library. The full text of his speech was published by Radio Moscow, 8 August 1953, *SWB*, USSR, pp. 1–21.
13. Ginat, *The Soviet Union and Egypt*, pp. 13, 69–70, 109, 170–2. Solod spoke Arabic as well as Balkan languages. Before he began his diplomatic career he was professor of Semitic languages in Leningrad. During his early years as a diplomat he was entirely concerned with Balkan affairs, mainly Yugoslavia. During his first mission in Cairo in 1943, he had displayed interest in the question of the Arab Union. On the diplomatic members of the Soviet Mission to Cairo in 1943, see despatch 502 from British Embassy, Cairo, 26 April 1944, FO371/41358, Public Record Office, London (hereafter cited as FO371 with appropriate filing reference). See also, Yaacov Ro'i, *Soviet Decision-Making in Practice* (New Brunswick, NJ: Transaction Books, 1980), p. 34.
14. *New York Times*, 10 August 1953. The agreement was signed between Egypt and the Soviet Union on 18 August 1953. On the agreement, see despatch 287 from US Embassy, Cairo, 31 July 1953, RG 59, 461.7431/7-3153; and despatch 398 from US Embassy, Cairo, 12 August 1953, RG 59, 461.7431/8-1253. Despatch 444 from US Embassy, 18 August 1953, RG 59, 461.7431/8-1853.
15. *New York Times*, 18 August 1953.
16. On the commercial aspect of the visit see Ginat, *The Soviet Union and Egypt*, pp. 229–38.
17. See Radio Cairo, *SWB*, 20 December 1953, *SWB*, Egypt, p. 35. Prior to this visit, an Egyptian military mission in August 1953 had already visited military factories and installations as well as units of the Yugoslav army. The mission was headed by Admiral Sulaiman 'Izzat, the Chief of Naval Staff, and comprised ten officers. Yugoslav officials confirmed it but stressed that no orders were placed by the Egyptians. On this visit, see FO371/102829, JE/1193/102, 102(A), 102(B). See also Radio Cairo, *SWB*, 18 August 1953, *SWB*, Egypt, p. 26.
18. See a review of developments in the Soviet Union since Stalin's death, in despatch 22 from British Embassy, Moscow, 5 March 1954, FO371/111671, NS1015/18A. See also David Dallin, *Soviet Foreign Policy after Stalin* (Philadelphia, PA: Lippincott, 1961), pp. 187–8.
19. The first report on the Egyptian government's decision to send a military delegation to the Soviet Union was broadcast by Radio Cairo on 21 May 1953, almost six months before the actual visit. On the MiG order, see letter 3896/PR from Israel Legation, Prague, 8 December 1953, Records of Israel Foreign Ministry (FM)2506/5/A, Israeli State Archives, Jerusalem (hereafter cited as ISA, FM, with appropriate filing reference), and letter 421/408D from the Eastern European Department, Israel FO, to Israel Legation, Prague, 27 December 1953, ISA, FM2506/5/A. On the Egyptian Legation's visit to arms factories, see letter 601/PR, from Israel Legation, Prague, 29 December 1953, ISA, FM2506/5/A.
20. See letter 412/408/Z from Eastern European Department, Israel FO, to Israel Legation, Prague, 26 January 1954, ISA, FM2506/5.
21. Ahmad Hamrush, *Qissat Thaurat 23 Yuliyo*, Vol. 2 (Cairo: Maktabat Madbuli, 1983), p. 65.
22. Several months later, the Israeli embassy in Moscow reported that the Egyptian request for arms had been rejected by the Soviet Union. No reasons or explanations were given. See, letter 3/1702/SM from the Israeli Embassy, Moscow, 3 August 1954, ISA, FM2506/4. On the dialogue with the Czechoslovak government see Hamrush, *Qissat Thaurat*, Vol. 2, p. 64. Hamrush claimed that after considering the Egyptian request for arms, the Czechoslovak government replied negatively, stating: 'We are a peace loving state and will not supply arms to others.' Khalid Muhyi al-Din, at the time a member of the RCC, confirmed that Rajab's delegation visited the Soviet Union and negotiated purchasing arms from the Soviet Union. See his version of the story in a collection of interviews and dialogues by Muhammad 'Awda, Filib Jallab and Sa'd Kamil in: *Qissat al-Sufyat ma'a Misr* (Jerusalem: Manshurat Salah al-Din, 1977), pp. 52–4. See also Intelligence Report No. 7292: 'The Evolution of Egyptian Neutralism', 9 July 1956, R & A Reports, NA, Washington. In his book *Soviet Foreign Policy after Stalin*, p. 389, David

Dallin says that the purpose of the visit was to submit and discuss various Egyptian industrial projects; under the heading of 'agricultural machines' the Egyptians included arms. The Egyptian proposals, Dallin claims, were coolly received by the Soviets.
23. Hamrush, *Qissat Thaurat*, pp. 64–6. Several years later, Nasser confirmed that Egypt's decision to break up the Western monopoly of arms supplies to the Middle East had first been made in 1954. In his speech in Alexandria, on 26 July 1962, he said *inter alia*: 'In 1954 and 1955...we did not hesitate to break up the arms monopoly.' Quoted in Ra'anan, *The USSR Arms the Third World*, p. 42.
24. On the power struggle between Nagib and Nasser during the first quarter of 1954, see Vatikiotis, *Nasser and his Generation* pp. 138–49; Lacouture, *Nasser*, pp. 86–92 and Mohammed Neguib, *Egypt's Destiny* (London: Gollancz, 1955), pp. 213–36. See also, US Department of State, *Foreign Relations of the United States, 1952–1954*, Vol. IX (Washington, DC: Government Printing Office, 1986) pp. 2222–9, 2242–5. Despatch 1022 from Caffery, Cairo, 3 March 1954, RG 59, 774.00/3-254; despatch 161 from Caffery, Cairo, 28 July 1954, RG 59, 774.00/7-2854.
25. This information was given to a US Embassy Officer 'in strictest confidence' by a 'reliable Egyptian source'. See despatch 902 from Caffery, Cairo, 12 February 1954, RG 59, 661.74/2-1254.
26. Most of the Soviet reports on the events were based on Egyptian and Western accounts. See for instance, Tass, 25 and 27 February 1954, *SWB*, USSR; and Tass, 9 March 1954. See also reports on the RCC's announcement of Nagib's removal, in Radio Moscow, *SWB*, 14 and 15 November 1954, *SWB*, USSR, p. 30.
27. This continuous dialogue will be discussed below.
28. Despatch 902 from Caffery, Cairo, 12 February 1954, RG 59, 661.74/2-1254.
29. See despatch 2362 from American Embassy, Cairo, 2 April 1954, RG 59, 661.74/4-254.
30. On the agreement see, FO371/108403, JE11338/1-3; Despatch 1169 from US Embassy, Moscow, 30 March 1954, RG 59, 461.7431/3-3054; Despatch 2232, US Embassy, Moscow, 20 March 1954, RG 59, 461.7431/3-2054; Despatch 2157, US Embassy, Moscow, RG 59, 461.7431/3-1254.
31. Alekseenko was quoted in *al-Ahram*, 28 March 1954, in despatch 2362 from US Embassy, Cairo, RG 59, 661.74/4-254.
32. Hamrush, *Qissat Thaurat*, p. 65.
33. On 8 February 1955, Malenkov announced his resignation. A new government was formed, headed by Bulganin. However, the regime was dominated by Khrushchev who continued to hold the post of first secretary of the CPSU. On his ascendancy and on the internal power struggle and their influences on Soviet foreign policy, see Ra'anan, *The USSR Arms the Third World*, pp. 86–130. Ra'anan claims that a power struggle between Khrushchev and Molotov continued after Malenkov's downfall. According to him, Soviet foreign policy was in fact conducted by Khrushchev, while Molotov remained passive. The question of selling arms to Egypt was one of the bones of contention between the two. Molotov was sceptical as to Nasser's intentions and feared that dangerous results might arise from such a move. However, as the highest Soviet authority, Khrushchev made the decision to sell arms to Egypt. See also, Dallin, *Soviet Foreign Policy after Stalin*, pp. 218–23; Isaac Deutscher, *Russia, China, and the West 1953–1956* (Harmondsworth: Penguin Books, 1970), pp. 28–38.
34. Dallin, *Soviet Foreign Policy after Stalin*, p. 222.
35. Ra'anan, *The USSR Arms the Third World*, p. 72.
36. See, Ra'anan, *The USSR Arms the Third World*, pp. 70–2 and Oleg Penkovsky, *The Penkovsky Papers* (London: Collins, 1965), p. 61. On the GRU, see Barton Whaley, *Soviet Clandestine Communication Nets* (Cambridge, MA: MIT, Center for International Studies, 1969), pp. 84–108. US intelligence reports confirmed that details of the nature and extent of Moscow offers were obtained through intelligence channels. See Report on the Near East by the director at the White House to a bi-partisan congressional group, 9 November 1956, White House, Office of the Staff Secretary Records, 1952–1961, in US Declassified Documents Reference System, US, 1978, 18A.
37. Ra'anan, *The USSR Arms the Third World*, pp. 70–2.
38. See despatches 894 and 903 from American Embassy, Ankara, 9 and 10 February 1955,

RG 59, 661.82/2-955 and 661.82/2-1055; Telegram 93 from Bowker, Ankara, 9 February 1955, FO371/115489, V1073/193; Letter 1073/289/55 from Bowker, Ankara, 14 February 1955, FO371/115493, V1073/311; Telegram 9, from Bowker, Ankara, 18 February 1955, V1073/318. See also Ra'anan, *The USSR Arms the Third World*, pp. 72–3.

39. See telegram 93, from Bowker, Ankara, 9 Feb. 1995 FO 371/115489.

40. See telegram 220 from Stevenson, Cairo, 10 February 1955, FO371/115489, V1073/212, and also V1073/220.

41. See message CA-4913 from Dulles to all American Missions, 28 January 1955, Foreign Office Posts of the Department of State, Record Group (RG) 84, Cairo Embassy–General Records, 1955, File Subject: Soviet Bloc Trade, 511.12, Washington National Records Center, Suitland, Maryland (hereafter cited as RG 84 with appropriate filing reference).

42. See report on the Near East given by the Director of the White House, 9 November 1955, RG 84, Cairo Embassy–General Records, 1955, File Subject: Soviet Bloc Trade, 511.12. The Egyptian War Minister and Commander-in-Chief, Major General 'Abd al-Hakim 'Amer, confirmed on 27 June, during a conversation with the British oriental counsellor that a Soviet offer of arms had already been made in March 1955. See despatch 161 from Sir Humphrey Trevelyan, British Ambassador to Cairo, 24 October 1955, FO371/113680, JE1194/368. See also telegram 812 from British Embassy, Cairo, 28 June 1955, FO371/113672, JE1194/107. Sir Humphrey Trevelyan also claimed that the Soviets had offered Nasser arms in the spring after the conclusion of the Baghdad Pact. See telegram 1325 from Trevelyan, Cairo, 26 September 1955, FO371/113674, JE1194/161.

43. British and US reports from Cairo claimed that the negotiations were with the Soviet government. Some of these reports suggested that there were two separate contracts, one with Czechoslovakia and one with the Soviet Union. Referring to this information, Trevelyan said: 'This is quite possible, but I have no confirmation of this.' See letter 1191/123/55 from Trevelyan, Cairo, 29 September 1955, FO371/113675, JE1194/241. The French military attaché in Cairo confirmed that there were two separate deals; one with Czechoslovakia and one with the Soviet Union. See telegram 1455 from US embassy, Paris, 29 September 1955, RG 59, 774.56/9-2955. The US Embassy in Prague thought that it was quite possible that the question of selling Czech arms to Egypt, or other Arab states, was under study in Prague from the end of 1954, or the beginning of 1955. The embassy suggested that owing to the need of the Czech industry for markets outside Eastern Europe and China, in order to expand its exports, the Middle East was in fact a good choice for the Czechs. Indeed in the second half of 1954, Syria purchased 44 German Mark IV tanks from Czechoslovakia at extremely favourable prices. Towards the end of 1955, it was reported by the US embassy in Prague, that 50 tanks of the same type but with modifications had already been delivered to Egypt. See telegram 128 from American Embassy, Prague, 5 October 1955, RG 59, 774.56/10-555. 'USA Objectives and Policies with respect to the NE', 2 November 1955, White House, Office of the Special Assistant for National Security Affairs, Records 1951–61, File Subject: NSC 5428, Near East (Deterrence of Arab–Israeli War) (2), Box 12, Eisenhower Library; Patrick Seale, *The Struggle For Syria* (London: Oxford University Press, 1965), p. 233; Telegram C-121 from American Embassy, Prague, 6 December 1955, RG 59, 774.551/12-655. On the extent of trade relations between Czechoslovakia and Egypt, see Ginat, *The Soviet Union and Egypt*, pp. 103–7, 134–43, 229–38.

44. K. Ivanov, 'National Liberation Movements and the Non-Capitalist Path of Development', *International Affairs*, 5 (1965), p. 61; quotation taken from Ra'anan, *The USSR Arms the Third World*, p. 76.

45. See report on Egypt's economy for the first quarter of 1955, in despatch 1937 from American Embassy, Cairo, 11 April 1955, RG 59, 874.00/4-1155.

46. Quoted in Ra'anan, *The USSR Arms the Third World*, p. 79.

47. Ansel E. Talbert, 'Nasser's Effort to Lessen Mid-East Tension Seen', *New York Herald Tribune*, 7 April 1955. On 19 July 1955, after the six-week visit to Egypt of a Czech trade mission, it was announced officially in Cairo, that a new trade and payments agreement between the two countries had been concluded. The fact that the arms deal

was concluded before its official announcement was first revealed by a senior Czech official on 28 November 1955. In a press conference in Cairo, Richard Dvorak, Czechoslovak Minister of Foreign Trade, who headed a Czech trade delegation that visited Egypt in November 1955, said that the agreement to supply arms to Egypt was a part of the trade accord between the two countries. Officially, the talks on a trade agreement had begun in February 1955. On the July agreement, see report on Egypt's economy for the third quarter of 1955, despatch 448 from American Embassy, Cairo, 22 October 1955, RG 59, 874.00/10-2255. despatches 125 and 126 from George C. Moore, second secretary at American Embassy, Cairo, 28 July 1955, RG 84, Cairo Embassy–General Records, 1953-1955, File Subject: 510.1, Trade Agreement, Box 4, and File Subject: 510.1 Trade Agreements & Missions, Box 266. ISA, FM2506/5/B, 421/408/Z. On Dvorak's statement see, despatch 598 from James N. Cortada, second secretary at American Embassy, Cairo, 29 November 1955, RG 84, Cairo Embassy–General Records, 1953–1955, File Subject: 510.1 Trade Agreements, Box 4.

48. Dispatch 95 from Byroade, Cairo, 20 July 1955, RG 59, 661.74/7–2055. The Office of Intelligence Research (OIR) of the Department of State, confirmed that soon after the Gaza incident, Egyptian officials purchased some arms from Czechoslovakia. The Czechs, it also said, 'have recently also offered military planes in exchange for cotton.' See, United States Government, Office Memorandum by Philip H. Trezise (OIR), 'Soviet Arms Offer to Egypt', 6 September 1955, in US Declassified Documents Reference System, US, 1976, 182 E. According to the British Embassy in Cairo, the Soviet ambassador in Cairo had already offered arms to Egypt in March 1955, shortly after the Gaza incident. See despatch 56(10321/50/56) from British Embassy, Cairo, 19 April 1956, FO371/118846, JE1024/1. On the commercial agreement for the exchange of Egyptian cotton for Soviet petroleum and industrial goods, see Ginat, *The Soviet Union and Egypt*, pp. 229–38.
49. Radio Cairo, *SWB*, 13 February 1955, in Ra'anan, *The USSR Arms the Third World*, p. 78, n. 23.
50. Nikita Khrushchev, *Khrushchev Remembers* (with an introduction commentary and notes by Edward Crankshaw) (London: Book Club Associates, 1971), p. 433.
51. This information was given by Salah Salim. See his statement in Seale, *The Struggle for Syria*, pp. 234–6.
52. On the agreement and Dvorak's statement, see n. 47. See also, 'Soviet Bloc Economic Activities in the Near East and Asia as of November 25, 1955', Report, Office of Research, Statistics, and Reports, Clarence Francis Papers, Eisenhower Library.
53. See a report made by an anonymous US officer on his conversation with Zakariya Muhyi al-Din, which took place on 19 June 1955, in despatch 2298 from American Embassy, Cairo, RG 59, 674.00/6-2155.
54. According to the British assistant military attaché in Prague, the Czechs did not themselves produce very heavy tanks (T-34), though they did assemble them. However, they produced lighter tanks of their own design, 75 mm. self-propelled guns, other armour and artillery as well as MiG 15 aircraft. See letter 1192/2/55 from British Embassy, Prague, 28 September 1955, FO371/116193, NC1192/1.
55. From a conversation between Nasser and Byroade which took place at Nasser's home on 16 June 1955, it appears that even Mahmud Fawzi, minister of foreign affairs, knew nothing about the negotiation. A memorandum of the conversation is attached to despatch 2311 from Byroade, Cairo, 23 June 1955, RG 59, 674.00/6-2355. See also Hamrush, p. 69; and M. H. Heikal, *Nasser: The Cairo Documents* (London: New English Library, 1972), p. 55.
56. See, Trezise, 'Soviet Arms Offer to Egypt'.
57. Dallin, *Soviet Foreign Policy after Stalin*, p. 394. The Geneva Summit Conference opened on 18 July. The Soviet Union was represented by Nikita Khrushchev, CPSU first secretary and Nikolai Bulganin, Soviet prime minister.
58. On the visit and its results see, Trezise, 'Soviet Arms to Egypt'. See also Dallin's interviews with high-ranking employees (Gilin, Chase, Johnston and Dick Mitchell) of the External Research Division of the State Department, Washington DC, 15 December 1958, in David J. Dallin Papers, File E, MSS. & Archives Section, New York Public

Library. See also a record of conversation between Byroade and Ahmad Husain, Egyptian ambassador to US, in Cairo, on 14 August 1955, in despatch 234 from Byroade, Cairo, RG 59, 774.56/8-1555. Hamrush, p. 70. In a press statement before his departure on 29 July 1955, Shepilov expressed his satisfaction about the visit and thanked the Egyptian government for its hospitality. He said, *inter alia*: 'They [the Egyptians] have demonstrated their great energy in the struggle against the imperialist oppressors. They have shown their implacable resolve to defend their national rights, their freedom...The sentiments of the Soviet people are wholly on the side of the Egyptian people's aspirations.' Tass announcement, 29 July 1955, *SWB*, USSR, p. 36. See also *Daily Telegraph*, 5 November 1955, in: FO371/113680, JE1194/368(A).

59. This information is taken from the Egyptian Naval Archives, 'A Collection of Special Reports and Messages on Armaments', 5 November 1955, in M. N. El-Hussini, *Soviet–Egyptian Relations, 1945–85*, pp. 57, 235–6. Byroade reported on 21 September: 'last night we were told by highly reliable source that Egypt's arms deal with Russia was now definitely decided'. See telegram 518 from Byroade, Cairo, 21 September 1955, RG 59, 774.56/9–2155. A week later Byroade pointed out that the actual agreement was with Czechoslovakia. However, he emphasized, the Soviet Union was behind the agreement. According to him, Daniil Solod had told Nasser that the deal could be arranged through 'a satellite country if this is better from Nasser's point of view'. See telegram 600 from Byroade, Cairo, 29 September 1955, RG 59, 774.56/9-2955.

60. CIA, 'The Communist Economic Campaign in the Near East and South Asia', 30 November 1955, in: US Declassified Documents Reference System, US, 1986, 002516; El-Hussini, *Soviet–Egyptian Relations, 1945–85*, p. 57.

61. Intelligence Report No. 7117, 'The New Soviet Approach to Syria: Diplomacy rather than Ideology', 15 December 1955, Office of Intelligence Research, Department of State in memorandum to the Secretary of State, 21 December 1955, RG 59, 661.83/12-2155. 'Soviet Bloc Economic Activities in the Near East and Asia', op. cit. note 52. See also Annual report (No. 6) on the Egyptian Air Force during the year 1955, prepared by Air Commodore C.M. Heard, former air attaché at the British Embassy in Cairo, in: despatch 111(1221/8/56G) from British Embassy, Cairo, 19 July 1956, FO371/119009, JE1224/4. Egypt: Annual report for 1955, in: despatch 13(10113/1/56), from British Embassy, Cairo, 31 January 1956, FO371/118830, JE1011/1. The data on the naval equipment were taken from El-Hussini, *Soviet–Egyptian Relations*. The first submarine for Egypt was on its way from Poland when Israel launched its attack in Sinai. See, 'Report on the Near East given by the Director at the White House to a bi-partisan Congressional group', 9 November 1956.

62. 'Soviet Bloc Economic Activities in the Near East and Asia', op. cit. note 52.

63. See despatch 56(10321/50/56), FO371/118846, JE1024/1. United States Government, Office Memorandum, 'Soviet Intentions Regarding Egypt', from William A. Crawford, Eastern European Department, to Wilkins, Near Eastern Department, 17 August 1955, RG 59, 774.56/8-1755. In addition to the re-equipment programme, Crawford said, that the Soviets were apparently engaged in reducing the size of their ground forces, as indicated by their announcement of a cut of 640,000 men in the Soviet armed forces. This move, he stressed, would undoubtedly free considerable amounts of military equipment for use elsewhere. He concluded that the initial stocks of weapons and equipment to Egypt were probably available. Both Britain and the US suggested that this equipment might not be of the very latest models, yet, could be serviceable and not entirely obsolete.

8

The Sinai War, 1956:
Three Partners, Three Wars

MOTTI GOLANI

The most recent historical research on the Sinai War provides telling descriptions of the war as a coalition endeavour involving Britain, France and Israel. This basic fact was denied for years by the three governments. There appears to be little to add to the historiographic discussion on the partnership as such.[1] However, the question of the character borne by the partnership has yet to be fully addressed. Various studies have described and analysed the vicissitudes of the political–diplomatic process that preceded the final decision to go to war. Similarly, the different motives of each of the three partners has been dealt with. In this chapter I will argue that the application of the Sèvres agreement during the war (29 October–6 November 1956) demonstrated clearly, not to say flagrantly in some cases, the differences of motivation, the divergent interests and the separate goals of each of the three nations that sent their armed forces into war. From many points of view the military collaboration was a moment of truth, when it was no longer possible to conceal the fact that each of the three ostensible partners had compartmentalized the other two and that the communications between the three nations that were supposedly fighting shoulder-to-shoulder against Nasser's Egypt were, at best, fraught with misunderstandings and half-truths. What follows will highlight the disparities between the three partners; the focus will be on Israel's perception of the military collaboration, though similar problems can also be identified with regard to both Britain and France.

RETROSPECTIVE UNEASE

In the war's aftermath some in Israel sought to downplay the French (not to say the British) assistance that Israel had received. Summing up the war some 12 months or so later, the commander of the Israel Air Force (IAF), Major-General Dan Tolkovsky, wrote:

Although air activity by the enemy was brought to an 'artificial' end by Anglo-French intervention...it will be untrue to say that the IDF's [Israel Defence Forces] success was possible because of the active participation of foreign forces in the Suez/Sinai campaigns. There is no doubt, however, that this participation allowed the Air Force to achieve what it did with minimal losses. And this was the real military achievement of these forces.[2]

Many years after the war Major-General Meir Amit, then the IDF's chief of operations wrote

collaboration with the French and the British was damaging to the IDF, operationally speaking. The IDF was placed under severe constraints: It was ordered not to cross a line 10 kilometres [actually 10 miles] from the Suez Canal, nor to use its air force and armoured forces prior to a specified date. These restrictions tied its hands in a very significant way...I would have thanked God if those restraints had not been put on us. Without them, we would have achieved much better results.[3]

When the war began, on 29 October, Israel's military collaboration with France, and through the French with Britain, already bore a blatant operational character. Concretely, the cooperation was effected in part in Israel through French air squadrons stationed there and by liaison officers (for land and sea forces), and in part through the joint Anglo-French HQ in Cyprus. The French military mission, led by Colonel Jean Simon, was based at the Supreme Command Post (SCP) in Ramla. From time to time General André Martin, the personal representative of the French Chief of Staff Paul Ely and of Admiral Pierre Barjot, the senior French officer attached to Operation *Musketeer* (the code-name of the Anglo-French invasion of Egypt), flew into Israel from Cyprus.

On the Israeli side the brunt of the liaison work was assigned to Lieutenant-Colonel Shlomo Gazit, formerly the chief of staff's bureau chief, and in Cyprus, to the Deputy Director of Military Intelligence Colonel Yuval Ne'eman (and afterwards to Lieutenant-Colonel Yosef (Paul) Kedar from the air force). For all practical purposes, the director-general of the Defence Ministry, Shimon Peres was also involved in the liaison activity, as he was responsible for procuring arms supplies (a task that continued during the war), and had excellent ties with the French. Also taking part in the contacts was Colonel Nehemia Argov, Ben-Gurion's personal representative. In Paris, Yosef Nahmias, together with Asher Ben-Nathan, his designated successor as head of the Defence Ministry mission in the French capital and Colonel Emanuel Nishri, the military attaché, stayed in touch with Major-General Maurice Challe, the French deputy chief of staff for air force affairs, who engineered the triple conspiracy, and with Colonel Louis Mangin, adviser to the French defence minister. These personal relations played an important role in ensuring that wartime collaboration – which was manifested more in coordination and aid than in actual joint operations – ran smoothly.[4]

KEEP A LOW PROFILE WITH THE FRENCH, DISAPPEAR FROM BRITISH VIEW

At the beginning of the war the IDF sent two officers to Cyprus: Yuval Ne'eman representing the General Staff and Yosef Kedar as the representative of the air force. Ne'eman arrived in Israel from France on 29 October, the day the war broke out. Before proceeding to Cyprus he met with the French and British military attachés in Israel with the aim of expediting the announcement of the Anglo-French ultimatum to Egypt, which Israel was anxiously awaiting. The attachés, who had been victims of the deception campaign conducted by their Israeli hosts and their own governments, now received for the first time, a few hours after hostilities had already begun, an explanation of what was afoot in Sinai.[5]

On 30 October Israeli Chief of Staff Lieutenant-General Moshe Dayan ordered Yuval Ne'eman to Cyprus, as a liaison to Anglo-French HQ. Dayan told Ne'eman that he should keep in mind that the IDF's goal was to conquer all of the the Sinai Peninsula, apart from the Canal Zone, and to try to induce the allies to internationalize the waterway and not to interfere with Israeli operations. 'It is important for us that the French [rather than the British] control the east bank of the canal', Dayan said. He also authorized Ne'eman to promise the French all the assistance the IDF could render them east of the canal: 'We shall put at their disposal more bases, hospitals, convalescence facilities.' Dayan issued no instructions to Ne'eman about working with the British as it was clear that contacts with them would be effected by the French throughout the war. There was no direct connection between the IDF and the British army. Ne'eman's mission was more to observe developments in Cyprus and less to liase with the allies. Actual coordination was handled by Dayan in Israel, via the French mission in the country.[6]

Ne'eman sent his first report from Cyprus on the afternoon of 31 October. No one had expected him, and 'in general they are not fighting yet' – whereas for Israel the war had been on for 48 hours already. Ne'eman eventually tracked down Martin and Barjot in the joint Supreme HQ near Episkopi. Barjot, Ne'eman reported, was 'scared stiff of the British – what will he do if they don't want [Israel] in'. The French convinced Ne'eman that he should go into hiding at their Akrotiri base until they could secure British approval for his presence on the island. The base's location, far from the joint HQ, kept Ne'eman from maintaining regular communications with the French who obviously found it more convenient to hide their close ties with Israel even if this hindered the joint prosecution of the war.

Finally the French persuaded General Sir Charles Keightley, the commander of Operation *Musketeer*, that operational and technical coordination with Israel was essential. It was agreed that the British 'knew nothing' about the presence of an Israeli mission in Cyprus. Evidently nonplussed by the situation, Ne'eman reported, 'All sorts of Englishmen told me (privately): "It never crossed my mind that we would be allies, but I must say I'm delighted." As for myself, I was less than delighted about their dubious fair play.'[7]

On 2 November, Ne'eman turned over responsibility for liaison in Cyprus to Yosef Kedar, who was his junior in rank and less informed than Ne'eman about the details of the conspiracy. But, in any event, neither the British nor the French apprised the Israeli liaison officer of their moves. As for the French, they were happy to keep knowledge of their direct military operations against Egypt that were launched from Israeli soil from their own personnel, and certainly from the British.

The Israeli liaison mission in Cyprus functioned until the end of the war. It was through the Cyprus station that Operation *Tushiya* (resourcefulness) was mounted, in which 65 Egyptian Jews were smuggled out of Port Sa'id without British knowledge and with minimal cooperation from French intelligence.[8]

COOPERATION IN THE AIR – 'THOSE BASTARDS, NOT EVEN AN APOLOGY'

Israel had pinned high hopes on the allies' intervention in the war, and the greater the expectation, the more intense the disappointment when it was delayed. On the night of 30 October, as reports – however unreliable – were received that the Egyptians were going to launch a concentrated bombing attack on Israeli cities the following morning, anxiety reached new heights. Still, no one bothered to examine whether the rumours of an attack had any foundation, and Dayan consoled himself with the hope that the Anglo-French bombing campaign, which according to the Sèvres plan was supposed to begin on the morning of 31 October, would prevent an Egyptian attack.

Then came the postponement, and Israel reacted with outrage – and fear. As Dayan summed it up: 'Those bastards. They make a political agreement in which one of the main clauses, one we insisted on, was an air strike on

Wednesday morning, and here they casually postpone the operation by 12 [hours] with no warning, not even an apology, the bastards.'⁹

According to incorrect information obtained by Ne'eman from the French (Martin and Barjot in Cyprus), the delay was due to a 'rebellion' by the joint forces' commander General Keightley against his own government (see below). Keightley, who (like the army chiefs in Israel and France) had not been made privy to the Sèvres agreement, refused to attack at first light (on 31 October), maintaining that the timing was wrong from a military point of view. His plan mandated an evening strike, at last light. Keightley refused to budge, even if it meant his removal. The message from Ne'eman, however, did little to allay the fears of Prime Minister David Ben-Gurion and General Dayan. The latter felt himself constrained at this stage to dissuade the Prime Minister from ordering a general withdrawal of Israeli forces from Sinai, a move that would have spelled the end of the Anglo-French plan: without an Israeli presence near the Suez Canal the allies would lack any pretext to invade Egypt in order, supposedly, to 'restore peace' there.¹⁰

The French were worried that Israel would in fact react to a delay in the air attack by pulling its forces out of Sinai. On 31 October, Mangin arrived in Israel for an unscheduled visit, apparently to reassure the increasingly sceptical Israelis. He told his hosts that over and above the principle of night bombing, which Keightley was insisting on, British concern had also been aroused by a high altitude reconnaissance flight carried out by a British Canberra bomber over Egypt on the first night of the war. It was pursued by an Egyptian MiG to an altitude of 50,000 feet, and 'the Canberra pilot had the feeling that there was a foreign pilot in this MiG, not an Egyptian'. The British, said Mangin, were upset about the possibility of encountering East European pilots, and perhaps were also concerned that their involvement would be exposed even before the ultimatum was delivered. On this point, at least, Keightley saw eye to eye with his government.¹¹

Apparently the information that was made available to the French, and passed on to the Israelis, was far from complete. Had Israel been apprised by the British, through the French, about what really transpired that day in Cyprus, Ben-Gurion might have felt less tense. But the British were too deeply enmeshed in their self-made trap of deniability at all costs; there was absolutely no British–Israeli dialogue on military operations. The entire affair remains difficult to reconstruct, because some of the documents involved were destroyed at the time and others are still classified. To this day, Britain is committed to concealing all evidence of an 'Israeli connection'. The British historian Keith Kyle, who spent years trying to uncover the documents in question, discovered that an order had been issued to burn any document (and in some cases part of a document) liable to suggest that Britain had known in advance of the Israeli offensive in Sinai on 29 October.[12]

As noted, the commanders of Operation *Musketeer* task forces, like their IDF counterparts, had received no information about the Sèvres agreement. Nevertheless, on 28 October (Sunday) the air squadrons, located in Cyprus and Malta, were ordered to prepare for their first bombing raid on Egypt at 2.15 A.M. local time on 31 October. They were not told that the reason for the attack was a political commitment to Israel: compartmentalization was not only an IDF phenomenon. The next day they were informed that the raid might have to be launched even earlier than that, and preparations were stepped up.

On 29 October there were two Canberra squadrons, one in Cyprus and one in Malta, capable of lifting off at six hours' notice; H-hour had not been changed. The operational decision was that the first targets would be the Radio Cairo station and four air bases, including Cairo West, where (for Israel) the fearsome Soviet-made Il-28 bombers were based. Under pressure of time, Air Marshal Dennis Barnett, commander of the joint air task force, sent reconnaissance missions over Egypt, though these could have signalled that an attack was imminent. All the same, as of 31 October *Musketeer* forces were authorized only to continue with the execution of a deception manoeuvre, code-named *Boathook*, which had begun on the morning of 29 October with naval movements from Malta to the eastern Mediterranean.[13]

Throughout Tuesday 30 October, British pilots remained on alert, though uncertain that the attack order would in fact be given. The only hint that reached Cyprus from London was that the order might be given only after the planes had already lifted off – a scenario not calculated to raise morale. During the day Egyptian radar picked up the British aircraft involved in the photo-reconnaissance missions, and the Egyptian air force scrambled jets to intercept them. That afternoon, Keightley was ordered to schedule the first strike, which had been planned as a night raid, to a later, daylight hour on 31 October. Apparently London did not want the attack to follow so closely on the heels of the ultimatum, which was issued at 6 P.M. on Tuesday 30 October. Keightley, at Barnett's remonstrations, urged the chiefs of staff in London to avoid a daylight raid, which could be dangerous. Neither officer was aware of the Sèvres agreement.[14]

Keightley's request was addressed in London on the night of 30–31 October during a meeting between Prime Minister Anthony Eden and his inner cabinet circle and the chiefs of staff. As a matter of fact, since the British government wanted to let as much time as possible elapse between the ultimatum and the allies' intervention, Keightley's request was a godsend – not a rebellion, as the French thought. The air strike was put back several hours for political reasons, and then again by several more for operational reasons. Some ministers, says Kyle, noted ironically that there was no sign so far that Israel has attacked Egypt from the air. The upshot was that Keightley was ordered to prepare for a night strike, but also to be ready for immediate action against Egypt 'if Israel suffers a serious air attack that morning [by Egyptian Ilyushins]'. The start of the bombing campaign was delayed by 12 hours altogether.[15]

'The cover story', Kyle observes, 'had to fit not only here and now, but also the history books of tomorrow.' To achieve this end, Eden was ready to renege on his agreement with Israel, although not totally: Britain would have responded immediately if Israel was attacked from the air. Ben-Gurion and Dayan were not aware of this, nor were the French, though they must have seen the preparations that were under way in Cyprus. In the final analysis, the *Musketeer* command structure gave the British the final say in the air as in all spheres of military activity. This episode furnishes additional evidence of the character of the cooperation (or non-cooperation) between Israel and the allies, and between the allies themselves, in the Sinai War.[16]

Ne'eman, having no direct communication with the British, tried to protest to the French and hold them accountable for the delay. He also insisted that French anti-aircraft vessels, which had been ordered to leave Israeli ports that day, be sent back immediately. The French replied that they had left a ship on the Israeli coast but they could not provide any more, since their ships were required to escort the convoys *en route* to Egypt. Ne'eman argued that in the present situation it was better to leave the convoys exposed rather than Israeli cities. Barjot remained unconvinced; he promised to look into the matter, but seems to have done nothing more in practice.[17]

When Ne'eman asked the French for intelligence information, he was told that an Egyptian armoured brigade had crossed the canal eastward. Moreover, the French said that to compensate Israel for the postponement of the air strike they were even ready to consider the possibility of using their squadrons that were secretly based in Israel to attack Egyptian armour, even before the overt allied assault. But it was clear that within the Sèvres framework, and under the constraints of the *Musketeer* command structure, this was out of the question – as impossible as it had been to compel General Keightley to attack on the morning of 31 October. In any event, using French aircraft based in Israel (even if camouflaged) before Britain and France had officially entered the war might have undone the entire 'cover story' of the collusion. How could the Israeli air force operate about 60 French Mystères IV while it had none only a few months before the war?

The French bent over backwards to persuade Israel not to pull out of the agreement because of the delay, but ultimately there was not much they could do. As a conciliatory gesture, Martin placed a special plane at Ne'eman's disposal so that he could fly to Israel whenever he wished.[18]

On the night of 31 October, Ne'eman informed Dayan that the British did not intend to land at Port Sa'id until 6 November. It was Ne'eman's understanding that this issue, too, had generated a sharp dispute between the generals in the field and the government in London, as well as between the British and the French. Ne'eman reported that the French were pressing for a landing as early as 3 November, and 'Martin is blowing his top and bombarding Paris with cables'. Eden's generals lacked 'operational discipline', Ne'eman thought. But the Israeli liaison officer could not have been aware of the seemingly intractable problems faced by the British commanders in view of the ambiguities surrounding Operation *Musketeer*. By the same token, he had no idea that the British officers knew even less than Martin, or than he himself did, about the underlying causes of the equivocal instructions Eden was strafing them with through the chiefs of staff in London. Ne'eman could never have imagined that the decision to land on 6 November was actually an improvement over the original timetable, which had set 8 November for the landing in Egypt.[19]

Later that evening (31 October) Israeli pressure was turned on the Israel-based French liaison officer for land forces Colonel Simon. Gazit was sent to impress upon him that Dayan was seriously contemplating the possibility of asking Ben-Gurion's permission to cable French Premier Guy Mollet that the postponement of the air operation was a breach of the agreement. Gazit told Simon that 'Even though [Dayan] knows that the liaison officer cannot help, it is important that he know that the delay of the operation is a severe setback for us.' The French reported this development immediately, probably to Barjot in Cyprus. Concerned at the Israeli reaction, Barjot ordered his squadrons in Israel to begin providing air support for the IDF in Sinai the next morning. This was in any event necessitated by the opening of the British air offensive in Egypt that night. What was most important from Israel's point of view was the goodwill displayed that day by Martin and Barjot. The French began their attacks in Sinai on the morning of 1 November (actually a few hours after the British air attack on Egypt had 'officially' begun).

In addition to direct offensive support for the IDF in Sinai, the French also assisted Israel in interdiction, transport, attacking targets in Egypt, and supplying intelligence information collected by their air force. These operations were carried out by planes that lifted off simultaneously from Cyprus and from Israel without knowing about one another's activity.[20]

Disruptions in the communications network between Cyprus and Israel, together with French insistence on avoiding overt coordination which would expose their collaboration with Israel, resulted in a number of uncoordinated missions, particularly air drops. Tolkovsky later quoted Brigadier-General Raymond Brouhon, the deputy commander of *Musketeer*'s air mission, as claiming that the British had deliberately jammed radio communications between French air force personnel in Israel and Cyprus. There is no corroborating evidence of this. IAF historians maintain that the French, with their penchant for secrecy, avoided using their radio links to Cyprus, claiming falsely that their equipment was out of order. Be that as it may, during the war transport aircraft from Cyprus arrived in Israel without the knowledge of Israeli air control, and it was only by chance that they were not intercepted by Israeli planes. Due to the confusion, a great deal of equipment (in one case even a French paratroopers force, which landed at Lod) ended up at unscheduled destinations where no one knew how to handle it. For example, on 4 November an Israeli paratroop brigade reported unidentified aircraft – apparently Egyptian planes on a bombing run. However, it soon turned out that the French were unexpectedly dropping supplies, including bottles of wine.[21]

It would not be the last time that the French would operate on two channels (Cyprus–Israel and France–Israel) simultaneously but without coordination between them. The desire to placate both Britain and Israel at the same time extracted a price from the French, mainly in the aerial sphere though after the war in the political–diplomatic sphere as well.[22]

Some of the problems were resolved thanks to the daily shuttle flight of a Dakota plane that the French operated between Cyprus and Israel. At one point there was talk of cancelling the flights, but the French liaison mission in Israel protested and the idea was aborted. It was obvious that the daily flight was the one secure channel of communication that remained between the French missions in Israel and in Cyprus, and between Israel and allied HQ on the neighbouring island.[23] The intelligence and other information that the plane brought back to Israel was usually disappointing in both quantity and in quality. Mostly it was air intelligence (including aerial photographs) about Egypt, obtained in French and British reconnaissance sorties. The French refused to provide Israel with intelligence about Syria and Saudi Arabia, despite repeated requests.

The IAF was unable to reach an agreement with allied HQ on Cyprus on setting up a shared radio frequency with *Musketeer* aircraft, or even a common distress frequency. Nor was there an agreed procedure for search and rescue missions in Sinai (though British and French aircraft could land in Israel in emergencies). The result was that Israeli and *Musketeer* transport planes (including French planes based in Israel) flew missions simultaneously with no communication or coordination.

COOPERATION AT SEA: UNFOUNDED EXPECTATIONS

French naval support to Israel encountered even more hitches and misunderstandings than the situation in the air. Air support had at least involved orderly advance planning, but the joint naval operations suffered from the fact that they were last-minute improvisations. The Israelis found that their expectations were completely unfounded. Compounding the situation, Israel found itself in direct contact with the British in the naval sphere. The chaotic state of affairs caused one direct collision, the combined fault of lack of coordination in the air and the failure of the partners to prepare the naval arena for orderly cooperation between Israeli and *Musketeer* forces. Small wonder, then, that all the naval operations involving any form of cooperation between Israeli and Anglo-French forces remain controversial to this day.

At around noon on Monday, 29 October, Dayan informed the French that Israeli support for their forces at the canal, if required, would be contingent upon their significant naval support for the IDF. French naval activity was implemented as part of Operation Archer, (code-name for French naval support for Israel) according to which two French destroyers would patrol off Haifa Port and a third destroyer off the coast of Tel Aviv. Israeli navy destroyers were to execute similar missions in coordination with the French. The French informed Israel that on the morning of 31 October, with the start of the Anglo-French air offensive against Egypt, two of their destroyers would be diverted to escort the French sea-borne convoys making for Egypt, leaving only one destroyer to patrol off the Israeli coast.[24]

However, it soon became apparent that the Sèvres agreement was insufficient for the French naval officers; they said they required additional authorization. The commander of the French flotilla in Israel asked Dayan to issue a formal request to the French navy for anti-aircraft protection. The bizarre request derived from French reluctance to issue formal orders to their units in Israel, for fear the British would discover their 'off-limits' assignment. But there were other factors as well. For reasons of internal compartmentalization between the two French operations, '700' (*Musketeer*) and '750' (assistance to Israel), the commanding officers of the French naval forces based in Israel (like their air force counterparts) were not briefed on their precise missions in advance. They got their orders only after arriving in Israel, and even then received no explanation of the political background to the mission. At the same time, they were instructed to coordinate naval support (down to the minutest details) and air support (in general terms) with *Musketeer* HQ in Cyprus, prior to implementation. So in addition to the hitches caused by the compartmentalization between Britain and France, further havoc was caused by internal French compartmentalization.[25]

In the first stage, Israel requested naval support for its operation to conquer Rafah, in northern Sinai. Dayan reminded the French that this was not a case of unplanned assistance: 'It was agreed to by Generals Challe and Martin, we were promised execution...The entire operational plan is based on it...We [furthermore] intend to ask for more support as we go along on the Mediterranean coast [eastward along the coast of northern Sinai].' Much to Dayan's surprise, the French had received no prior orders on this point. It was agreed that the French would begin planning their support, and in the meantime one of their officers would fly to Cyprus to get orders from Barjot. It turned out that the French conception called for support on a far smaller scale than Dayan had envisaged. In fact, operational expectations of the French naval bombardment itself were never very high: Dayan saw it as more of a test case to discover the extent of French willingness to support Israel, and to create a precedent to be invoked later if needed.[26]

On 31 October, Ne'eman discussed this problem in Cyprus with Martin, who was willing to meet any Israeli demand in view of the postponement of the allies' air campaign against Egypt. Martin accepted Dayan's request to intensify the Rafah bombardment, but he also made it clear that subsequently the French might be hard-put to provide additional naval support, once their own sea-borne operations commenced (other than in the Straits of Tiran, should this prove necessary). The French adduced two conditions for providing a more massive bombardment: first, two Israeli destroyers must escort the cruiser that would fire the barrage (as two French destroyers had been diverted to protect *Musketeer*'s maritime convoys); and second, Dayan must withdraw his request for a French bombardment of El Arish (the largest town in the Sinai Peninsula, west of Rafah) even though this had already been agreed on.

The original plan called for French shelling of Rafah during the night of 30–31 October, and of El Arish the next night. But the postponement of the British air offensive against Egypt, and the general delay in the timetable as a result, led the French to conclude that a late operation against Rafah and El Arish might interfere with the main operation at the Suez Canal. During the night originally scheduled for the French shelling of Rafah, allied air raids on Egypt were supposed to be in full swing (this actually happened on 5 November). At that stage, *Musketeer* HQ in Cyprus intended to muster all its available naval forces to support allied troop movements towards Egypt. French Admiral Lancelot, deputy commander of *Musketeer*'s naval task force, after consulting with his British superior, Admiral Durnford-Slater, on 31 October, agreed to make his cruiser *Georges Leger* available to French–Israeli collaboration for 40 hours only.[27]

The *Georges Leger* reached Haifa in the afternoon of 31 October and moved south after dark. Beginning at midnight (31 October–1 November) the French bombarded army bases around Rafah for four hours. Dayan and his aide Mordechai Bar-On, who witnessed the shelling with the forces of the 77th Division, were very impressed, and Bar-On later noted in his diary: 'The camps became an inferno. But because of little experience [with international joint operations] there were long pauses between successive barrages, and between the last one (which was rather unimpressive) and the actual assault.'[28] Although ultimately ineffective, the French bombardment of Rafah should be judged by its contribution to bolstering Israeli self-confidence by demonstrating French willingness to cooperate with the IDF. It was not a whim of Dayan's to have invested so much time in coordinating this single action. Moreover, the bombardment, however ineffectual, contributed to the rapid collapse (within 9 or 10 hours) of the Egyptian deployment in and around Rafah.[29]

Admiral Barjot agreed that the barrage was unimpressive but noted that by aiding the IDF to make rapid progress it had effectively supported the Anglo-French move in the northern area of the canal. Barjot went further, claiming that the shelling had strongly impressed the other Arab nations (meaning Syria and Jordan), who remained on the sidelines despite their mutual defence treaties with Egypt. In general, the senior French officer of Operation *Musketeer* viewed the Israeli effort in Sinai, particularly along the northern route, as an integral part of the campaign against Port Sa'id, Port Fuad, and indeed the entire Suez Canal. Before the war Dayan, too, had given thought to the military and political benefits, notably in the form of deterrence, that Israel could derive from the spread of rumours about active French support for the Israeli offensive, although such rumours were a rare commodity in the climate of secrecy and intrigue that enveloped the war.[30]

PREPARATIONS FOR A JOINT FRENCH–ISRAELI OPERATION IN THE SUEZ CANAL

The possibility of the IDF reaching the Suez Canal was discussed on several occasions between Israel and France during October 1956. Although the Israelis made it plain that they had no interest in reaching the canal, and the Sèvres agreement, to which the British were also a signatory, barred Israel from reaching the waterline, the idea constantly recurred, particularly in the discussions between the sides at military level.

One of Yuval Ne'eman's tasks in Cyprus was to ensure that no clashes occurred between the IDF and French or British forces, due to misunderstanding. Two areas that were blatantly prone to such mishaps were the Suez Canal and the Straits of Tiran. However, a combination of factors – including the Anglo-French plans to operate there, and the poor coordination between the IDF and *Musketeer* HQ – made the occurence of such errors almost inevitable.

On the morning of Monday 29 October, just hours before the scheduled start of the Israeli sweep into Sinai, Colonel Jean Simon, the French liaison officer to the ground forces, showed Dayan and several senior officers the main points of the *Musketeer* ground forces' battle plan. Simon told Dayan that General André Beaufre, the deputy commander of the land task force of Operation *Musketeer* (as in the air and on the sea, the French were subordinate to British commanding officers), was worried about the pace of British preparations, and noted that Israeli pressure could give the British a needed push. Specifically, Beaufre requested that by the time of the French landing at Port Fuad, scheduled for 6 or 8 November, the IDF would have decimated the Egyptian forces in Sinai and readied the northern Sinai coast for the landing operation. Beaufre was worried by the fact that the narrow landing site assigned to the forces under his direct command on the east bank of the canal would hinder the effective deployment of his troops. He therefore prepared an alternative invasion plan, without the knowledge of his British superior, involving a joint French–Israeli operation that constituted a sharp deviation from Sèvres.

Beaufre's approach was a purely military one and was based on his perception of military assistance to Israel as part of the general plan for war against Egypt. As he saw it, every operation in support of Israel in the air and on the sea came at the expense of the forces intended for direct action against Egypt; consequently, he, like his colleague Barjot, tended to consider the IDF as part of the French forces operating against Egypt. In his memoirs he maintained that the IDF, which employed three divisions against one Egyptian division (Beaufre exaggerated somewhat, but it was true that the IDF enjoyed overwhelming superiority, qualitatively and quantitatively, against the Egyptians in Sinai), should have been utilized in support of his forces, which faced the bulk of the Egyptian army. He was also concerned that Egyptian troops pushed westward by the IDF would link up with the forces fighting his troops at Ismailiya and Qantara, on the Suez Canal. Anglo-French hopes that the Egyptian army would flee eastward, deeper into Sinai, and become an Israeli problem, were rendered unrealistic once it became clear that the allied landing would occur after the IDF had already conquered most of Sinai.

Still, Beaufre's protestations were not completely off the mark. Beyond the apologetic tone of his memoirs, the truth is that on the eve of the war the French could have justifiably expected much more than they were to get from the IDF, which enjoyed undeniable superiority over the Egyptians in the Sinai and benefited from extensive Anglo-French support. Furthermore, Dayan thought he could turn Beaufre's requests to Israel's advantage. As noted above, for example, he made the pace of IDF progress along the northern route in Sinai contingent on French naval support. Nevertheless, during the first few days of war, there was no reason to expect concrete cooperation in the spirit of these ideas.[31]

In view of the delay in the commencement of the allies' operations, and the presence of IDF units near the Mitla Pass with little capability of defending themselves, the Israeli General Staff decided on the evening of 30 October to examine the possibility of air strikes against the canal bridges in order to prevent the Egyptians from moving reinforcements into Sinai. The problem was that this would have meant encroaching on an area slated for Anglo-French operations. The IDF therefore reconsidered Beaufre's offer of cooperation, made a day earlier: IDF assistance for a French landing east of the canal without coordination with the British.

To begin with, Ne'eman tried to sound out the French in Cyprus about an IDF strike against the canal bridges, using French aircraft based in Israel (and still bearing Israeli insignia). The French, who had already expressed their interest in Israeli support in the area of the canal, did not explicitly object, but explained that the bridges were not on their list of targets. It should be borne in mind that for Britain the main objective was to seize the canal and reactivate it immediately, without taking action liable to block the waterway – such as knocking out the bridges. It is difficult to imagine that the French would have condoned an operation that would have undermined a major British objective. Furthermore, they wanted Egyptian forces to cross the canal eastward; if the IDF could draw the Egyptian army into Sinai, this would facilitate Anglo-French activity in Egypt. In short, neither the French nor the British had good reason to prevent the Egyptians from moving east, but they would not have liked to see them retreating back to the west.

The French therefore explained to Ne'eman that close coordination would be required before the IDF could act in their zone of operations along the canal, but in principle, if Israel so desired, it could deal with the canal bridges later on – after the Egyptians were defeated. At this stage, the French did nothing to further the required coordination. Not even the French desire to placate Israel the next day because of the delay in the start of the British air campaign, induced them to accept Ne'eman's idea; it was put on hold for the time being. Still, Ne'eman found some hope in French willingness to consider the possibility that Israel take control of the harbour at Port Tawfiq, at the southern entrance to the canal and well away from the planned Anglo-French combat zone. Ne'eman quoted Martin as saying that '[we may regard] ourselves free to take Port Tawfiq as well, if we are interested'.[32]

In retrospect, it emerges that what convinced the French to consider a joint operation for the occupation of the entire Canal Zone was not Israel's distress prior to the war – its inability to use the canal – but its success during the early stages of the war. Observing the weakness of the Egyptian army in Sinai (and in particular the incompetence of the Egyptian air force) during four days of allied air strikes and IDF advances, the French decided to re-examine the possibility of making use of Israeli forces stationed near the canal. On Friday, 2 November, Martin arrived in Israel with Ne'eman. In a meeting with senior officers of the IDF General Staff, they discussed possible ways of utilizing the IDF presence near the Suez Canal in order to facilitate the French landing there. Dayan reacted by ordering the IDF not to approach the canal closer than the agreed 10-mile limit; however, he added, when the French reach the canal 'we will send out patrols to make contact with them'.[33]

Immediately afterwards Dayan convened the General Staff and passed on the information that the French would like to see the IDF at the canal by Monday (5 November), so that it could support French operations at Port Sa'id and Qantara. Dayan said that afterwards, as far as the French were concerned, Israel could do as it pleased in Sinai. Although it was not clear whether France would provide explicit diplomatic support for an Israeli take-over of part of the canal, 'the French are even prepared to see us taking Port Tawfiq'. The port was important for Israel, Dayan noted, because 'we have no other route along the Suez, and we have no water in that area'.

Dayan then went with the idea to the Prime Minister. Ben-Gurion hesitated: he did not want to commit Israel to direct military involvement in the Anglo-French war against Egypt. Israel, he insisted, must do nothing in the Canal Zone that was directly linked to the Suez crisis. In general, Dayan and Ben-Gurion both preferred at this stage to dissociate Israel's operations in the Sinai from the Anglo-French operation. Israel had fulfilled its obligations by giving its allies a pretext for war, and should now concentrate on its own interests in Sinai. Occupying Port Tawfiq might be regarded as a move that was not too obviously connected with events in the Canal Zone. Ben-Gurion thus gave Dayan the go-ahead to examine this possibility, and Dayan concluded: 'We would prefer it this way: the [UN General] Assembly meets in New York, while Uri [Colonel Ben-Ari, commander of the 7th Armoured Brigade] and Arik [Lieutenant-Colonel Ariel Sharon, commander of the 202nd Paratroop Brigade] meet on the Suez Canal.'[34]

A renewed French approach on this issue was encouraging. On Saturday night, 3 November, Dayan met with Colonel Simon, who elaborated further on Martin's proposal of the previous day. Simon now preferred to talk about Qantara, which was of greater interest to him. In fact, the orders he received from Martin and Barjot left him very little leeway for independent decision-making. The French, it turned out, were in dire straits in view, on the one hand, of the UN demand for a cease-fire, and on the other, British insistence on sticking to the original plan of a landing only on 6 November. The French wanted to attack at once and were even looking into the possibility of doing it alone. As in previous instances, Israel had a central role in that option, with Martin and Barjot requesting that the IDF support a French landing at Port Sa'id by conquering eastern Qantara and thus creating a concrete threat to the canal. The French were perfectly aware that this was a major departure from the Sèvres agreement: 'Israel has the right to say no', Simon told Dayan.[35]

The French wanted to launch air strikes on Sunday morning (4 November) and effect the landing in the Canal Zone at midday. Simon said his superiors knew that the IDF was reluctant to stage daylight attacks, and were therefore willing to postpone their landing until last light. Without Israel, their operation would be extremely problematic. An embarrassed Simon told Dayan that all this must be kept completely secret: the French government must know nothing about it, to say nothing of the British. As though it were self-evident, he added that the IDF would of course evacuate Qantara as soon as French troops got there. He went on to explain that Barjot himself had conceived the idea of Israeli support for a French landing in order to make it easier for Paris to reach a decision on the matter. Therefore, it was out of the question to appear to depart from Sèvres. Barjot was even willing to lend the IDF French uniforms for the mission, but Dayan rejected the idea out of hand.[36]

Accepting the French plan would have made the assault on Port Tawfiq, already approved by Ben-Gurion, into an Israeli campaign for the entire Canal Zone. Dayan tried to help Simon work out a more realistic plan, which might receive Ben-Gurion's approval. First of all, he pointed out, the Anglo-French ultimatum, which required Israel to stay 10 miles from the canal proper, was still in effect. It would be highly embarrassing if the British, who were supposedly intervening to prevent an Israel capture of the canal, should find Israeli troops already dug in there. Second, the French government obviously did not want Israeli participation in the occupation of the east bank of the canal. Consequently, Dayan maintained, such a move would deeply embarrass the French.

As a more practical solution to the quick capture of the canal, Dayan asked Simon to consider the possibility of the French (and the British too, if they wished) landing at El Arish, which was already in Israeli hands, and then moving on to the canal. 'Anyway, the French may move forces on all our routes, any place they choose.' But if they insisted on their plan, Israel would even agree to a daylight attack, though on two conditions: massive air support, and coordination with Britain. Dayan did not want to create a situation in which 'the English reach Qantara before the French and open fire on us at 200 meters range, and then claim we did not let them know we were there in the first place'.

Dayan insisted on official liaison, including liaison officers on the ground. Simon hesitated. It was agreed finally that the IDF would be ready to assist the French even if they landed on 6 November, but under Dayan's two conditions. The French would also be able to evacuate their wounded to Israel, on routes controlled by the IDF. Dayan went to Tel Aviv to obtain Ben-Gurion's approval, while Simon flew back to Cyprus in order get the go-ahead from Barjot.[37]

By this time Ben-Gurion was 'in a nit-picking state of mind', according to Dayan. He heard him out on the details of the new French idea, but the discussion revolved around his stay at Qantara with the Jewish Battalion in the Second World War. Finally Ben-Gurion approved Dayan's plan, with its qualifications. The 202nd Paratroop Brigade was then ordered to prepare for the recapture of the Mitla Pass (after the 31 October failure) and move on to Port Tawfiq – the 'Israeli objective' in the joint operation with France on the canal.[38]

However, the French decided to avoid taking independent action. Under growing pressure from the United Nations and the United States, France and Britain reached a compromise to attack on 5 November rather than on the 6 November. Because of the abbreviated timetable, *Musketeer* HQ improvised a fast landing plan, called Telescope. *En route* to Port Said another improvisation was made, this one code-named 'Omelette', for a 'light' landing (infantry and paratroopers, without heavier support). By this stage it was obvious that Egyptian resistance would be minimal.[39]

The French now asked Israel to refrain from any activity at all in the Canal Zone. Without authorization, an approach to the canal was ruled out; Dayan was forced to back off. Thus the plan to conquer Port Tawfiq was dropped from the IDF agenda.[40]

BRITAIN AND ISRAEL: HOSTILE COLLABORATION

The cancellation of the joint operation in the Canal Zone had repercussions that went beyond the purely military aspect. British pressure on France to avoid any overt military collaboration with Israel had paid off handsomely for Britain. With Israel having done its part and the two European powers already at war with Egypt, the British demanded that the French henceforth keep Israel out of their operations.

The embarrassed General Martin not only called off the joint French–Israeli action along the canal; on 3 November he sought an understanding with the IDF whereby 'the partnership between Israel and the allies is now liquidated, [Israel] having done its part, so that there is no reason now to continue with military coordination'.[41]

This was not a major military problem for the IDF, provided the allies continued to fulfil the agreement reached at Sèvres to support the IDF's push to Sharm al-Shaykh, which was on the brink of being accomplished. Nor did it represent a significant political problem for Israel. Ben-Gurion and Dayan were willing to end the war even before the *Musketeer* landing. By pulling out of the conflict, Israel would please the British, who could then proceed without fear of being suspected of collaborating with Israel, while Israel would divest itself of mounting international pressure.[42]

Thus, the IDF was not surprised to hear the Israeli ambassador Abba Eban announce at the UN on the evening of 4 November, New York time (early morning of 5 November in Israel) that Israel would accept a cease-fire, provided the Egyptians did likewise. There was in fact little coordination between the Israeli military and the diplomats. It was the foreign ministries of the European allies, which remained outside the real decision-making process, that were behind Eban's statement. Eban, who faced heavy pressure in the General Assembly, asked Foreign Minister, Golda Meir, to sound out her French and British counterparts as to whether their governments would agree to an Israeli declaration of willingness to accept a cease-fire. Meir spoke with the two ambassadors in Israel. She knew the embassies in Israel were unaware of the secret agreements, but it is not clear whether she assumed her question would eventually reach the ambassadors' respective heads of government, who were in the know, or whether she consulted with Ben-Gurion before-hand. Be that as it may, Whitehall and the Quai d'Orsay, which had no knowledge of the military cooperation, responded in the affirmative to her query.

However, a scenario in which Egypt accepted a cease-fire along with Israel was untenable for Britain and France, since their pretext for going to war would disappear even before the first British or French soldier trod on Egyptian soil. The foreign ministries in London and Paris knew nothing of all this.

But when Egypt agreed to a cease-fire, Mollet and Eden found that they still needed Israeli support, after all. Abel Thomas, Director-General of the French Ministry of Defence, called his Israeli counterpart Shimon Peres on 4 November to protest Israel's acceptance of a cease-fire. Then the Defence Minister himself, Maurice Bourgès-Maunoury, accused the Israeli government (also in a phone call to Peres) of overturning the situation in what was tantamount to a betrayal of France. Britain, though, even at this critical moment, said nothing; the principle of deniability was to be guarded zealously.

Peres defended Israel's agreement to a cease-fire by citing the postponement of the Anglo-French invasion of Egypt, and particularly Martin's declaration of 3 November on terminating military cooperation. Still, it was clear that Eban's statement would damage French interests above all, which was the last thing Ben-Gurion and Dayan wanted. Following a series of diplomatic negotiations involving Britain, France and Israel and their representatives in New York, Israel's agreement to a cease-fire was reformulated in a manner that meant a 12-hour delay in its implementation, giving *Musketeer* forces time to launch their landing at Port Said and Port Fuad.

So it came about that on 4 November, Eban stated at the United Nations that he had been misunderstood – he had only wanted to describe the situation in the war zone. At the same time the British and French governments informed UN Secretary-General, Dag Hammarskjöld, that they still considered their intervention necessary, in order to prevent the continuation of the Israeli–Egyptian war. In view of the new military situation in Sinai, they said in their statement, it was essential to ensure the withdrawal of Israeli troops from Sinai as soon as possible. Ben-Gurion reacted furiously, and the French tried to explain that they meant withdrawal from the Canal Zone. Israeli mistrust, particularly of Britain, was intense even before the war ended.

Hammarskjöld demanded Israel's unconditional agreement to a cease-fire, and meanwhile Britain and France moved up their landing in Egypt by 24 hours. Eventually Israel accepted a cease-fire on the evening of 5 November, having accomplished all its objectives in Sinai (apart from occupying the tiny islands of Tiran and Sanapir at the approaches to the Straits of Tiran). In addition, the Anglo-French invasion was already under way, so the allies no longer needed the 'Israeli pretext'. In the final analysis, Israel preferred an Anglo-French force as a buffer between the IDF and the Egyptian army, rather than UN troops (a Canadian proposal, which was adopted that same day by the General Assembly).[43]

Dayan and his aide Bar-On, deeply offended by the British attitude and by French backing for Britain in this episode, noted in conclusion of the cease-fire affair:

What pleas and remonstrations could not accomplish [namely, bringing *Musketeer* D-day forward], this bold, merciless and impartial diplomatic move did [referring to Israel's unilateral agreement to a cease-fire]. The shameless British, who stuck by their rigidly frozen plan like a blinkered horse, now lost their cool and were forced to bring their landing forward by a whole day, when they suddenly realized they needed Israel even after they thought they could drop it by the sidelines.[44]

This was not a completely accurate presentation of the facts, but clearly reflected the feelings about Britain that existed in Israel even in the midst of the joint military move against Egypt.

The disagreements over the Israeli agreement to a cease-fire only heightened Israel's suspicions of Britain. Indeed, Israel was never able to comprehend British policy on the Suez crisis. For example, even during the war, British propaganda broadcasts to the Middle East remained as blatantly anti-Israel (and anti-Zionist) as ever.[45]

Britain sought to lay the foundations for a new relationship with the Arab world after the war and even to create the impression that Egyptian President Nasser was in collusion with Israel. At the height of the war, the Foreign Office in London vetoed a proposal by Britain's ambassador John Nicholls, in Tel Aviv, to seize the opportunity for a *rapprochement* with Israel in order to heighten British influence there. Nicholls was advised not to display too much understanding for Israel's problems. When he tried to explain that Israel was worried about Soviet inroads into Syria, the British Foreign Office replied that Israel was 'trying to make up a story' and that no movement of troops would be tolerated, even if 'intended to save the region from communism. In such an eventuality, it is better that Iraq [which had the dual advantage of being an Arab state and being loyal to Britain] take action.'

This reaction of the Foreign Office was drawn up by Donald Logan, one of the very few officials who knew about Sèvres (he had been one of the two British signatories to the agreement). Even though Eden himself protested that it was wrong to compare Israeli with communist action – in terms of the ostensible hostility of both – the Foreign Office remained adamant. The looming military fiasco in Egypt, compounded by domestic public pressure, gave Whitehall overriding influence even during the war, and this atmosphere was hardly conducive to British collaboration with Israel. Any such collusion continued to be denied after the war as well. On 22 November 1956, the British government insisted, in response to a query in Parliament, that there had been no contacts, direct or in writing, between Britain and Israel about the situation in the Middle East.[46]

The British–Israeli antipathy also had a military aspect. The agreement reached between the two nations before the war was largely a negative one between adversaries. It held that Britain would not help Jordan if that country initiated a war against Israel, and that Israel would not attack Jordan if Britain agreed not to intervene should Jordan attack

Israel. For the British, even during the Sinai War, Israel remained an 'enemy by official definition'. In the various *Musketeer* operational orders, and in the intelligence reviews of the operation, both Israel and Egypt were listed as 'enemies'.[47]

The British received ongoing updates from the French about IDF moves and, equally important, about Israeli intentions. But they wanted more. The Royal Navy monitored Israeli activities by listening and observation. The detailed report that the Israeli envoy conveyed daily to Cyprus on the situation of Israeli forces in Sinai almost certainly reached the British, at least in part. Indeed, it was impossible to keep the French–Israeli collaboration a complete secret. Certainly there was no concealing the fact that two French fighter squadrons had made a brief landing in Cyprus, lifted off again, and never returned; or that a large-scale airlift by French transport planes plied the Cyprus–Israel route daily. Moreover, some French moves – such as the bombardment of Rafah by a French cruiser described above – were undertaken only after consultation with British HQ in Cyprus. Still, only a few British officers were in on the secret. Martin told Dayan afterwards that 'the English [in Cyprus] asked if it was true that Israel was going to take over all of the Sinai, and when he said it was true, general apoplexy broke out there'.[48]

Despite the British refusal to communicate with Israel, necessity dictated otherwise. Early in the war, Britain asked Israel for humanitarian assistance in the search for an Egyptian civilian plane which had disappeared over the eastern Mediterranean early on Monday 29 October, not far from the Israeli coast. The request followed an Egyptian approach to Britain itself, also on a humanitarian basis. The Israeli navy joined in the search. The IAF, which knew nothing of the search effort, discovered the search flotilla late Monday night and asked the High Command to call in the navy to engage the ships. That request went unheeded, of course. What neither the British nor the Israeli navy nor the IAF – apart from a few top officers – knew was that the missing plane had been shot down by an IAF fighter. On the night of 28–29 October, two Egyptian aircraft were on their way to Egypt after having taken off from Syria. One of them carried Egyptian Chief of Staff, Field Marshal Amer, who was returning from coordination meetings in Jordan and Syria. Knowing of Amer's presence, the Israelis shot down one of the planes – but the wrong one. Amer reached Cairo safely.[49]

On 3 November the Egyptians shot down a British plane; the pilot bailed out and landed east of Qantara. A unit from the IDF's 27th Brigade in the area tried to assist in the rescue mission, but HQ at Cyprus ordered the rescue force that was dispatched to the site not to draw on Israeli assistance, as this could be misconstrued if reports leaked out. According to Air Marshal Barnett, the commander of the allied air task force, the rescue mission chief needed no such cautioning, since he knew nothing of the collusion and viewed the Israelis as enemies no less than the Egyptians. Nor did *Musketeer* forces have any liaison arrangements with the Israelis for such eventualities. On top of this, British aircraft circled the area to ward off Israeli troops. The rescue itself was executed by a helicopter – one of the first operations of its kind.[50]

Britain continued to ignore its Israeli ally. In a report on a successful French air strike at Luxor on 4 November, the British failed to mention the fact that the attacking aircraft, F-84s, lifted off from and returned to an Israeli air base twice that day. Indeed, the strike itself was an Israeli idea, approved by the joint HQ in Cyprus and carried out by the French. Israel, as related above, was much concerned about Egyptian Ilyushin-28 bombers, which had the range to bomb Israeli cities (the MiG G-15 turned out not to have this capability). The bombers had been hastily evacuated from their regular base, Cairo West, to remote Luxor in Upper Egypt. A first raid on Luxor by British planes was executed from too great an altitude to be effective. The return raid was carried out by the French following pressure by IAF Commander General Dan Tolkovsky, on the basis of intelligence provided by the IAF. But the results of the initial French effort, launched from Lod air base at 6 A.M., did not satisfy Tolkovsky. The French agreed to carry out another strike that same afternoon. Altogether, 18 Ilyushins were destroyed on the ground, and those that survived were evacuated by the Egyptians to Saudi Arabia.[51]

Several other mishaps occurred during the war due to the absence of direct British–Israeli military liaison. On Saturday, 3 November, at about 4 P.M., IAF planes attacked the British frigate HMS *Crane*, inflicting light damage. The incident was hushed up, as neither Israel nor Britain had an interest in making it public, and the details are still a matter of controversy. The IAF version is that the attack on the frigate, which had General Staff authorization, was the result of mistaken identity. The vessel sustained only minor damage because no armour-piercing rockets were used. The frigate immediately left the area.[52] Piecing together the available evidence, we emerge with the following picture: a mixed Anglo-French flotilla, under British command, was operating in the Straits of Tiran within the framework of Operation Toreador, which had been mounted to support the main *Musketeer* effort from the south, to prevent the Egyptians from sending reinforcements to the straits or north to the Canal Zone. On 30 October, the Toreador flotilla, which got to the scene before the Israeli navy, sank an Egyptian ship that was carrying reinforcements from Suez to Sharm al-Shaykh. The IDF was concerned about the implications of the incident, and with good reason. Until at least 5 November, the British – for it was one of their ships that had sunk the Egyptian troop carrier – were determined to seize the Straits of Tiran if Israel failed to do so. In this sector, the Israeli advance was far slower than elsewhere.

Once the British discovered that Israel was in control of the straits, Toreador HQ was ordered not to interfere. The Israeli move, they were told, was taking pressure off *Musketeer* forces. However, Israel knew nothing of this order, and Dayan, as noted, issued orders to prepare for a possible British attack against Sharm al-Shaykh. Under these circumstances of unclear intentions, the fog of war, mutual suspicions, and proximity of operations, mistakes were inevitable.

The British version of the *Crane* incident appeared in the summarizing report made by the ship's captain on 5 November. He said he was attacked off Ras Nasrani in three sorties, though only minor damage had been caused. The ship had returned fire and shot down one of the attacking planes. He thought his attackers were Egyptians.[53]

On 2 November, about 24 hours before the air strike against HMS *Crane*, the plane flown by the commander of the IAF's 101st Squadron of Mystères, Major Benjamin Peled, was shot down above Ras Nasrani. Tolkovsky claimed that Peled (afterwards the commander of the IAF) had been hit by Egyptian anti-aircraft fire from Ras Nasrani. Bearing in mind the proximity in time, British identification problems (the British opened fire at Ras Nasrani that day), and Israel's flat denial of any such attack the next day – an attack that could have been taken as retaliation for the downing of the Mystère – the possibility cannot be ruled out that the only Israeli Mystère lost in the war was actually brought down by the British.[54] In any event, the IAF took precautions to avert similar incidents. No one wanted to engage the British army. Thus the tangled relations between Israel and Britain that had existed on the eve of the Suez crisis and throughout its unfolding, continued to manifest themselves even during the course of the war itself.

In conclusion, basic differences in the motivation of each of the three partners were clearly apparent in the prosecution of the war. The problem was made even more acute by the absence of a joint command. Moreover, the sharp compartmentalization and the three-way mutual mistrust made even seemingly simple operations, such as the rescue of a downed pilot, exceedingly difficult. The coalition that attacked Egypt in 1956 was weak and disunited; its existence was heavily conditioned. The speedy collapse of the coalition effort against Egypt was therefore due not only to the effective threats issued by the two superpowers; it was also the result of the inherent fragility of the triple coalition.

THE 1956 WAR

NOTES

1. See, for example, K. Kyle, *Suez* (London: Weidenfeld & Nicolson, 1991); M. Bar-On, *The Gates of Gaza*, (New York: St Martin's Press, 1994); M. Golani, *Israel in Search of a War* (Brighton: Sussex Academic Press, 1998).
2. D. Tolkovsky, *Operation Kadesh: The Air Force Final Report* (in Hebrew) November 1957, Israel Air Force History Branch Archive.
3. Ibid.
4. Chief of Staff Diary (CoSD), IDF Archives (IDFA), Ne'eman's report to Dayan, 31 October 1956; 'Minutes of a meeting with the French Held on 1 November 1956', CoSD.
5. CoSD, 29 October 1956; J. Nicholls (the British ambassador to Israel) to Foreign Office, No. 567, 29 October 1956, Public Record Office, London (PRO), FO371/121782.
6. Dayan's instructions to Ne'eman are quoted in CoSD, 30 October 1956.
7. Y. Ne'eman's report to Dayan, CoSD, 31 October 1956.
8. Y. Ne'eman, 'Connection with the British and the French During Sinai Campaign', *Ma'arahot* 306–7 (1986), p. 36 (in Hebrew); CoSD, 2–6 November 1956; Tolkovsky, *Operation Kadesh*.
9. CoSD, 30 October 1956.
10. CoSD, 31 October 1956.
11. Ibid.; 'Minutes of Meeting with the French Held on 1 November 1956', IDFA 532/73/179.
12. Author's interview with Keith Kyle, London, 10 December 1991; see also Kyle, *Suez*, p. 372.
13. Report of Bomber Wing, Cyprus, on Operation *Musketeer*, PRO AIR20/9967.
14. Compartmentalization was not a problem for Israel only. See correspondence between General Keightly (CNC Operation *Musketeer*) and the military in London. Chiefs of Staff to Keightly, 30 October 1956, PRO, AIR8/1490; Keightly to Chiefs of Staff, 30 October 1956: PRO, AIR8/2111.
15. Interview, see note 12; Kyle, *Suez*, pp. 372–5.
16. Kyle, *Suez*, p. 374.
17. CoSD, 31 October 1956.
18. Ibid.
19. Ibid. On the uncertainty in planning Operation *Musketeer*, see, M. Golani, *There Will Be War Next Summer... The Road to the Sinai War, 1955–1956*, (in Hebrew) (Tel Aviv: Marakhot, 1997), ch. 20.
20. Golani, *There Will Be War*, chs 29–33.
21. Tolkovsky, *Operation Kadesh*; Joint Report (in Hebrew), written by Col. N. Eldar, Israeli liaison officer with the French Air Force mission in Israel, November 1956, Israel Air Force Branch Archive, File 15.
22. CoSD, 30-31 October 1956; Report of Lt-Col. Souvier, operation officer of the French Air Delegation in Israel, Service Historique de L'Armeé de L'Air (SHAA), Paris, C2496; War Dairy of the French Delegation in Israel, SHAA, G5255/Y2.
23. Tolkovsky, *Operation Kadesh*; Joint Report 1956; author's interview with Gen. (then Lt-Col.) Souvier, Paris, 18 April 1991.
24. CoSD, 29 October 1956; internal report of the French Navy (not for circulation at the time); Phillipe Masson, *La Crise de Suez* (Vincennes: Marine Nationale Service Historique, 1966), pp. 118–20.
25. CoSD, 29 October 1956; Masson, *La Crise de Suez*, p. 120.
26. CoSD, 29 October 1956.
27. Masson, *La Crise de Suez*, pp. 120–1.
28. CoSD, 1 November 1956.
29. Ibid.; Masson, *La Crise de Suez*, p. 121.
30. CoSD, 29 October 1956; A. Beaufre, *The Suez Expedition 1956* (London: Faber & Faber, 1969), pp. 64, 74, 79–80.
31. Ne'eman's report to Dayan from Cyprus, CoSD, 31 October 1956.
32. CoSD, 2 November 1956.

33. As Israeli Prime Minister David Ben-Gurion made no diary entries while he was ill this is based on CoSD, with obvious limitations.
34. CoSD, 3 November 1956; for a general description of the situation in the French army at the time, see 'Rapport sur l'operation d'Egypt', Force A, Julliet–Décembre 1956, SHAA C2307.
35. CoSD, 3 November 1956.
36. IDF General Staff Branch, 'War Diary', operative order 'Advance to the Canal and Deployment', 3 November 1956, IDFA; DoSD, 3 November 1956.
37. Ibid.
38. Ibid.
39. Final report by Air Marshal D. Barnett, the *Musketeer* aerial task force Commander, 27 November 1956, PRO ADM116/6133.
40. CoSD, 3 November 1956; M. Dayan, *The Sinai Campaign Diary*, (in Hebrew) (Tel Aviv: Am ha-sefer, 1966), pp. 142–4; Discussion of the entire affair (including possible French–Israeli collaboration at the Suez Canal) can be found in M. Bar-On, *Etgar ve-tigra* [Challenge and Quarrel], (Sde Boker: Ben-Gurion University, 1991), pp. 318–20.
41. CoSD, 4 November 1956.
42. For the Background to the British role at the Sinai Campaign see Golani, *Israel in Search of a War*.
43. Ibid. Concerning international developments, see report by UN Ambassador Abba Eban, 'The Political Campaign in the UN and the US Following the Sinai Operation, October 1956–March 1957', Washington, June 1957, Ben-Gurion Archive at Sde Boker, Israel (BGA); see also Bar-On, *Etgar ve-tigra*, pp. 321–5.
44. CoSD, 4 November 1956.
45. Kyle, *Suez*, pp. 238–40.
46. Correspondence between Nicholls in Tel Aviv and Logan in London and a final report by Ross, head of the Levant Department at the Foreign Office in, PRO FO371/121696, 3 November 1956; for background material on Foreign Office responses to questions in Parliament see, PRO, FO371/121706.
47. See, for example, 'Military Intelligence about the Enemy', PRO, AIR20/9677, 30 October 1956.
48. CoSD, 2 November 1956; report by Chief of Naval Intelligence to the Admiralty, 30 October 1956, PRO, ADM/205/19. On this subject, see also a paper by the head of History Branch, French Air Force, L. Robineau, 'Les Port-a-faux de l'affaire de Suez', *Revue Historique des Armées*, 4 (1986), pp, 44–6.
49. CoSD, 28–29 October 1956.
50. Bar-On, *Etgar ve-tigra*, p. 320; Barnett's final report (see note 35); Joint Report, 1956.
51. Daily report by the *Musketeer* aerial task force HQ, 4 November 1956, PRO, AIR/9675; Tolkovsky, *Operation Kadesh*.
52. Daily report by the *Musketeer* aerial task force HQ, 3 November 1956, PRO, AIR/9675.
53. CoSD, 30 October, 4 November 1956. On Operation Toreador see, PRO, ADM116/6103 vol. VII of a 10-volume report by the Royal Navy; Masson, *a Crise de Suez*, pp. 121–4; M. Dayan, *Avnei derekh: otobiografiya* (Jerusalem: Idanim, 1976), p. 307.
54. Report to the Admiralty and Commander, Mediterranean Theatre, PRO, ADM205/141, 6 November 1956.

9

Egyptian Perspectives on the Suez War

YORAM MEITAL

The Suez War has occupied a dominant position in the national historiography of Egypt. During the last four decades, numerous articles, books, literary works and cultural artifacts have dealt with this event. Most of them regarded the Tripartite Aggression (*al-ʿUdwan al-Thulathi*), as the Suez War has been called in Egypt, as a pivotal phase in the country's long-standing struggle for independence, especially after the July 1952 revolution.[1] This description is based on the argument that since the inauguration of the Suez Canal in November 1869, its control became the object of several states, particularly Britain. After British occupation of Egypt in 1882, British leaders defined control of the Suez Canal as a vital imperial interest, and held large forces on its banks. Even when Britain issued the unilateral declaration of Egypt's independence in February 1922, it reserved for itself, among other things, responsibility for the control and security of the Suez Canal. The Anglo-Egyptian treaty of August 1936 reaffirmed this stipulation.

On 23 July 1952 a group of military officers launched a successful military coup in Egypt. One of the main objectives of the new regime was to find a solution to the country's most acute national problem – hammering out an agreement for the evacuation of British forces from Egypt (most of which were stationed in the canal area). When negotiations with Britain opened on April 1953, Egyptian–US relations drew substantially closer. The United States called for the complete evacuation of British troops from Egypt and was ready to provide civilian aid for the new regime. On 19 October 1954 an agreement was signed, according to which British forces would evacuate the Suez Canal Zone within 20 months. However, in Article 4 of the agreement, the parties agreed that in case of an attack by an outside power against any Arab League state or against Turkey, Egypt would allow British forces to return to the Suez Canal area. In conformity with this agreement the last British troops left Egyptian soil on 13 June 1956.[2]

The main objectives of Egypt's revolutionary regime, especially the need to secure full national freedom and socio-economic development, were manifest in the process which led to the Suez crisis and war. A prime indication of this can be found in the controversy surrounding the construction of the Aswan High Dam project. This huge project was designed to serve as a fundamental lever for the regime's agricultural and industrial plans. However, the lack of financial resources and technological capability brought Egypt, in 1954–55, to apply for Western aid. Initial reactions were positive, as the United States, Britain and the World Bank expressed their willingness to support the project and provide it with substantial financial aid. This goodwill on the part of the international community was reversed, however, following the strengthening of Egypt's image as a central leader of the anti-imperialist struggle. This image emerged largely as a result of Egypt's objection to Western efforts to consolidate regional military pacts (such as the Baghdad Pact), along with its support for national liberation movements (such as the Algerian *Front de Libération Nationale*). Some Western governments followed Egyptian activities within the non-alignment group of states with much concern. Egypt's recognition of the People's Republic of China on 16 May 1956, its growing contacts with the Soviet Union, and the increasing prestige of Egyptian President Gamal 'Abd al-Nasser, especially after the role he played in the Bandung Conference (18–24 March 1955), only exacerbated existing Western anxiety.

The signing of the Czech–Egyptian arms deal had a crucial effect on Egypt's image in many Western states, as well as in Israel, since it was seen in the West as an expression of a fundamental change in Egypt's foreign policy orientation. The deal, which was negotiated between Egypt and the Soviet Union during the summer of 1955 and announced in 27 September, was immediately perceived as an event with enormous regional and international implications. Egypt emphasized the direct impact of the IDF raid on Gaza in February 1955 as the main motivating force for this arms deal.[3] The 38 Egyptian officers and soldiers who had been killed during the raid symbolized the poor condition of the Egyptian armed forces, and ultimately injured the national pride of its revolutionary regime. In view of these circumstances, Egypt decided to intensify its efforts to seek modern arms abroad.[4] However, the political circumstances of the Cold War made the issue of an arms deal a complicated one. The United States, for one, opposed Egypt's request for modern arms arguing that it ran counter to the United States' commitment to restrain the arms race in the Middle East. The arms that Britain was willing to sell Egypt were limited both in quantity and in quality. The

Egyptian leadership thus felt increasingly frustrated, and on several occasions they even considered the possibility of approaching the Eastern bloc. They were well aware of the broad implications and risks that such a move could entail, especially Egypt's relations with the Soviet Union. This can be learned, for example, from Egypt's foreign minister at the time, Mahmoud Fawzi, who noted in his memoirs, 'When the Egyptians and the Americans were alone together, 'Abd al-Nasser said, "You know, I've had a lot to do with the Russians, and I don't like the Russians. I've had a lot to do with your people, and basically I like your people."'[5] However, as hope for acquiring arms from Western sources declined, the sensitive decision to turn to the Eastern bloc was ultimately taken.

The United States and Britain feared that Egypt's reorientation towards the Eastern bloc could harm their efforts to secure their interests in the Middle East, specifically the attempts to circumscribe Soviet penetration of the region. Consequently, on 19 July 1956, the United States announced the withdrawal of its offer to provide financial aid for the High Dam project. Britain and the World Bank soon made similar announcements. This development reflected the fact that the United States and Britain, as well as Israel and France, had reassessed their policies towards Egypt – and this had a direct effect on the evolution of the Suez crisis. From 'Abd al-Nasser's perspective, Western reactions were bound to undermine some of his most vital policy issues, i.e. arms supply, economic development and political manoeuvre). First and foremost, however, he felt that the steps that had been taken by the West could jeopardize the position of Egypt as a sovereign and independent state. 'Abd al-Nasser thus reacted unequivocally and vigorously: he declared the nationalization of the Suez Canal. Hence, the Suez crisis was born, during which the concerned parties took some unanticipated steps that were destined to have substantial implications for the history of the Middle East.

The announcement of the cancellation of Western financial aid for the High Dam project reached Egypt only a few days before the fourth anniversary of the July revolution. After discussions regarding the options left for Egypt, 'Abd al-Nasser decided to go ahead with the idea of declaring the nationalization of the Suez Canal Company. According to Muhammad Hasanayn Haykal, at that point 'Abd al-Nasser summarized his thoughts on the issue in a handwritten paper dated 22 July 1956. He wrote that nationalization of the Suez Canal would give Egypt the financial resources required to cover the costs which it needed for the construction of the High Dam. He described his decision as an act that would gain the support of all Egyptians who dreamt of the day when the canal would be under direct Egyptian rule. He thus considered nationalization to be a true expression of Egypt's full independence – including its freedom of political manoeuvre. 'Abd al-Nasser estimated that the vast majority of Arabs would support his decision; and he considered this support a message for the West in general and for the United States in particular.[6] 'Abd al-Nasser had carefully calculated his steps in that sensitive situation. He therefore decided to announce the nationalization of the Suez Canal Company in his traditional speech on the occasion of King Faruq's exile. It was the first appearance in public of Egypt's president since Western aid for the High Dam had been cancelled. Many had therefore expected 'Abd al-Nasser to disclose his country's reaction during his speech in Alexandria on 26 July. In it, he described at length Egypt's national struggle for true independence and freedom. He reviewed the history of the Suez Canal, emphasizing that it had been planned all along to serve and secure the interests of Western imperialism. 'We dug the canal with our lives, our skulls, our bones, our blood', he told his audience, but:

> Instead of the canal being dug for Egypt, Egypt became the property of the canal...It is no shame for one to be poor and to borrow in order to build up one's country; what is a shame is to suck the blood of a people and usurp their rights...Does history repeat itself? On the contrary! We shall build the High Dam and we shall gain our usurped rights...Therefore I have signed today and the government has approved a resolution for the nationalization of the Universal Company of the Suez Maritime Canal.[7]

Although many were aware of the growing tension between Egypt and the West, it seems that no one was prepared for such a dramatic statement. The connection between the content of 'Abd al-Nasser's announcement, i.e. nationalization of the Suez Canal, and the occasion at which it had been made, i.e. the anniversary of Faruq's exile, was pregnant with symbolic meaning for the Egyptian public. This linkage was fully exploited by 'Abd al-Nasser, to the point that when he reached the last part of his speech he reiterated that: 'In the same way as Faruq left on 26 July 1952, the old Suez Canal Company also leaves us on the same day.'[8]

Soon enough, the surprise of the Egyptian public had changed into deep feelings of rejoicing, although signs of concern were also expressed. The Egyptian leadership spent the next few days in long discussions on several scenarios. The general evaluation was that the Egyptian armed forces were not yet ready for a full-scale war, and that only a small portion of the Czech arms deal had been received by the army units. Therefore, the main objective for Egypt was to secure its control over of the Suez Canal, to assert its own ability to manage the

Suez Canal Company, and to guarantee freedom of navigation in this important waterway. From the sources at hand we have found two versions regarding the chances that a war would break out. According to the first, most commonly cited, Egypt's leadership was deeply concerned with the West's reactions, but thought that under the circumstances neither Britain nor France would risk their interests in the Arab world by launching a full-scale war against Egypt. Egypt assumed that if it were able 'to buy time', the chances of war would decline substantially. At this initial stage of the crisis, 'Abd al-Nasser believed that in the first week after the nationalization of the canal there was an 80 per cent risk of war, and that by the end of October it would decline sharply to about 20 per cent.[9] Another version was offered in subsequent research conducted by the Defence Ministry of Egypt. According to this study, throughout the summer of 1956 the army predicted that Britain and France were planning an attack on Egypt. This estimation was conveyed on several occasions to the country's top leadership.[10] From the two versions we can deduce that during that stage of the crisis, Egypt's decision-makers considered Britain as the key factor in any war scenario; but it ruled out the possibility of military cooperation between Britain, France and Israel.

At about this time Egypt's leaders came to the conclusion that if they wanted to gain time and prevent war, they also had to exhaust fully all diplomatic and intelligence channels. They assumed that, in time, the outcome of the crisis would be determined on the political front. Egypt was encouraged by the support it had received from the Soviet Union, China and several Arab states. After it had invested heavy diplomatic efforts, Egypt also gained the support of Saudi Arabia, India and many states within the non-alignment group. The basic US stand, which was rather sympathetic to Egypt's right to nationalize the canal, and especially the US administration's appeal to solve the crisis by mutual understanding, was also received with satisfaction by the Egyptian leadership.[11]

In its diplomatic campaign from July to October Egypt had made use of several legal, political and moral arguments. Its fundamental claim was that

> the Suez Canal Company was an Egyptian Company subject to Egypt's laws and customs . . . Consequently, the nationalization of the Egyptian Suez Canal Company by the government of Egypt is a decision emanating from the Egyptian government according to the right of sovereignty. Any endeavour to attribute to the Suez Canal Company an international status is but a pretext for intervening in Egypt's internal affairs . . . The nationalization of the company has not interfered with the freedom of navigation in the canal.[12]

Egyptian officials argued that the act of nationalization was a legitimate legal procedure, which evolved from the initial status of the canal as 'an Egyptian public company' subjected to Egyptian law. This legal argument was fully presented in Law 285 (26 July 1956) which regulated the legal procedures of the Suez Canal Company. This law described the special status which the company had enjoyed for several decades, a status granted to it by the Egyptian authorities. The current government therefore had the legal right to cancel all previous agreements regarding the status of the canal. It also mentioned that Egypt promised to pay fair compensation to the company shareholders.[13]

Official sources stressed that Egyptian society and resources had been exploited both fiscally and economically during the construction of the canal as well as after it had been opened as a waterway with international importance. The special supplement to Law 285 reads as follows: 'The Suez Canal was dug with Egyptian blood to serve maritime navigation.' It was also mentioned in this regard, that more than 100,000 Egyptians had died in forced labour during the construction of the canal, and that their families had never been paid any compensation. This document also said that nearly the entire economic infrastructure of the country had been mobilized for this project, and that the Egyptian authorities had invested huge amounts of money and taken extremely large foreign loans for its completion.[14] The Suez Canal Company exploited the fact that since 1882 Egypt had been under British occupation and it 'behaved as a state within a state. It considered itself immune from Egyptian law and behaved in the Canal towns as if it, and not the Egyptian government, were the real authority.'[15]

Further clarification of Egypt's position was expressed in a personal message which President 'Abd al-Nasser sent to President Eisenhower in mid-August, in which 'Abd al-Nasser emphasized the need to differentiate between the on-going management of the Suez Canal and the issue of securing freedom of navigation through this important waterway. He declared that Egypt was fully obliged to respect freedom of navigation, but insisted that this principle should not be confused with the issue of managing the canal or responsibility for its security. As an independent and sovereign state, Egypt had the right of and the responsibility for managing and securing the canal, which was located within Egyptian territory. 'Abd al-Nasser asked Eisenhower not to ignore the fact that the Suez Canal Company had never been given the authority to secure the physical security of the canal; and that the company liaison had been limited only to the management and operation of the navigation in the canal. Therefore, he concluded, Egypt rejected in principal the proposal for international supervision of the management or security of the canal, and rendered any suggestions to that effect as a violation of international law and conventions.[16]

On 29 October 1956, the IDF launched a full-scale military operation against Egypt with the aim of conquering the Sinai Peninsula. The attack took Egyptian society and its military and political leadership by surprise. During the Sinai operation, and in accordance with the Sèvres agreement, Britain and France issued an ultimatum proclaiming that the outbreak of hostilities in the Sinai 'threatens to disrupt the freedom of navigation through the Suez Canal', and that Britain and France 'are resolved to do all in their power to bring about the early cessation of hostilities and to safeguard the freedom of passage of the canal'. The two powers thus called on Egypt and Israel: 'a) to stop all warlike action; b) to withdraw all Egyptian/Israeli military forces to a distance of ten miles from the canal; and c) in order to guarantee freedom of transit through the canal...to accept temporary occupation by the Anglo-French forces of key positions at Port Said, Ismailiya and Suez.' In the final sentence of this ultimatum it was said that Britain and France demanded the compliance of both Egypt and Israel within 12 hours; and that 'if at the expiration of that time one or both governments [of Egypt and Israel] have not undertaken to comply with the above requirements, United Kingdom and French forces will intervene with whatever strength may be necessary to secure compliance'.[17]

After urgent consultations, Egypt's decision-makers decided to reject the ultimatum and to prepare the country for the expected Anglo-French attack. At this stage, they became aware of the possibility that Egypt would have to face a complicated situation whereby Britain, France and Israel cooperated in accordance with a plan that had been agreed upon well before the outbreak of hostilities. Against this background, Egypt decided to withdraw its armed forces from the Sinai. Conflicting explanations are given for this decision in the sources. In the West in general, and in Israel in particular, the withdrawal is described as an unorganized retreat by Egyptian forces after their defeat by the IDF. Egyptian sources portray a totally different picture. The order of withdrawal is described as part of an organized plan, which was accepted only after the Anglo-French ultimatum had been announced, and after it become obvious that Egypt was facing a tripartite act of aggression. According to this line of reasoning, the logic behind the withdrawal decision was to prevent the risk of splitting Egypt's forces in the Sinai from the canal area and to concentrate all troops for the defence of the Suez Canal, the Nile Delta and the capital, Cairo.[18]

When the withdrawal decision was taken, the regime embarked on a campaign to enlist the support of Egyptian public opinion, and of the Arab world. The first expression of this can be found in 'Abd al-Nasser's speech on 2 November. The president presented the outbreak of the war as yet another phase in Egypt's struggle for independence and sovereignty. He described the British and French actions as crimes designed to re-occupy the Suez Canal area and to dictate degrading conditions that would jeopardize Egypt's liberties and national pride. We have now to decide, 'Abd al-Nasser emphasized, 'shall we fight or surrender?... We shall fight in defence of Egypt's honour, freedom, and dignity... We shall fight a bitter war. We shall fight from village to village and from place to place... Let our motto be: We shall fight, not surrender.'[19] The campaign to win public support was successful. This was reflected in the increasing number of citizens who were ready to take up arms and fight the invading forces. The recruitment centres for the new National Liberation Army (Jaysh al-Tahrir al-Watani), which was established at the beginning of the Suez crisis (9 August), were packed with volunteers. This military organization, which included forces from the National Guard and new volunteers, was trained in guerrilla warfare methods. Egyptian sources stressed that nearly half a million weapons were allocated by the government to support semi-military activities during the Suez crisis. The authorities decided also to close the country's high-schools and universities in order to encourage the enlistment of volunteers. An atmosphere of national emergency unfolded all over the republic, and the general mood was of a fateful fight for the survival of the state.[20]

At the beginning of November 1956, the Egyptian leadership found itself in a vulnerable situation. Militarily, the state's armed forces were unable to contain the three attacking armies, and updated intelligence reports warned that Britain and France had ordered their forces to move towards Cairo with the aim of toppling the regime. At that stage, 'Abd al-Nasser estimated that only intervention by a superpower could turn the grave situation in his favour. He felt that because of substantial influence on Britain and Israel, the US had to be addressed. On 1 November, 'Abd al-Nasser summoned US Ambassador Raymond Hare and asked him to deliver a special message to the US president. Although this event is not mentioned in most Egyptian sources, we find evidence for it in the following words of 'Abd al-Nasser in an interview with Kenneth Love:

I sent a message to President Eisenhower... telling him... that we ask the help of the United States... Then the answer came to me, next day, that of course America cannot go to war against their allies but that they will do all they can to solve the problem in the United Nations.[21]

And indeed, the diplomatic activities of the superpowers, especially the United States, brought the war to an end after seven days of fighting. On 7 November, the guns fell silent, but not before the IDF had occupied the Sinai Peninsula and British forces held sway over several areas along the Suez Canal. The agreement that terminated the war included a complete withdrawal of the forces of Britain, France and Israel from all the territories that they had occupied; UN peace-keeping forces were called upon to take positions within the Sinai Peninsula, and to guarantee freedom of navigation in the Gulf of Aqaba. During the war the Egyptian armed forces had suffered a heavy blow. Yet, a place of honour was reserved in the country's national historiography for the courageous Egyptian stand against the Tripartite Aggression, and in particular for the battle at Port Said. Although large parts of the city were occupied during the war, the civilian and military resistance was described as an expression of the glorious spirit that prevailed in Egypt during the Suez crisis.[22]

The common assumption of most Egyptian primary and secondary sources is that the real cause of the outbreak of the Tripartite Aggression was neither nationalization of the Suez Canal Company nor the issue of freedom of navigation. In extensive research carried out by Egypt's Defence Ministry it was stated that the main reason for the Suez war had been to punish Egypt for its revolutionary policy, especially after Egypt adopted an anti-imperialist policy and was prepared to assist national liberation movements.[23] In their research into the Suez War Hasanayn Haykal and Rif'at Sa'id Ahmad reached similar conclusions. Both argued that the general background to the war was the omnipotent struggle for domination over the Middle East, in which Egypt under 'Abd al-Nasser represented the most radical local challenge to Western plans to gain control over this region.[24]

Any balanced inquiry into the Suez War should take into consideration the objectives of the interested parties at the beginning of the crisis. Egyptian sources emphasized the extraordinary goals which Britain, France and Israel attempted to achieve, i.e. re-occupation of the Suez Canal area; the destruction of Egypt's armed forces; the overthrow of 'Abd al-Nasser's revolutionary regime; and the imposition on Cairo of a peace agreement with Israel, which would guarantee the latter freedom of navigation through the Gulf of Aqaba and the Suez Canal. An official source that examined the overall implications of the war maintained that although the invaders achieved 'limited military victories', they did not accomplish their main goals. Thus, when the war ended, Egypt maintained exclusive control of the Suez Canal; its armed forces, although harmed, were not completely destroyed; the invading forces withdrew all their forces from Egypt; the efforts by Western propaganda to isolate Egypt regionally and internationally ended in complete failure;

and most importantly, not only had 'Abd al-Nasser's revolutionary regime not been overthrown, it had become stronger. All in all, at the end of the crisis, Egypt's regime and society felt that they had achieved a great national victory.[25]

The Suez War had a significant impact on both the domestic and foreign policies of revolutionary Egypt. On 1 January 1957, the government issued a law stating that in view of Britain's involvement in the Tripartite Aggression, Egypt no longer considered as valid ,the agreement which the two states had signed on 19 October 1954. Furthermore, the Suez War impaired severely the efforts made in the direction of establishing regional pro-Western alliances, such as the Baghdad Pact. Another pertinent implication of the war involved Israel. Following Israel's collusion with Britain and France, the negative image of Israel in the eyes of many Arabs intensified. Generally, the Arabs now looked upon Israel as merely a pawn of imperialism that aimed to harm Arab efforts to achieve unity and development.[26]

Nevertheless, the most important outcome of the Suez crisis was reflected in what can be characterized as the decade of Nasserite domination. From 1956 to 1967 the ideological framework of Nasserism was consolidated, and several steps were taken in Egypt and other Arab states to implement it. In this regard, we should recall the centrality of the Suez crisis and the war in Arab nationalist consciousness. During the crisis 'Abd al-Nasser demonstrated his extraordinary ability to express the deepest nationalist sentiments of wide sectors of the Egyptian population and even to create the impression that his political agenda was determined by these sentiments. Using symbols and images, 'Abd al-Nasser gave the Suez crisis a meaning that went far beyond the military confrontation in the battlefield. From the outset of the crisis he tended to describe the causes of its outbreak, as well as Egypt's position in it, as a struggle for the revolutionary regime's ideology. In a certain way, these tactics reflected a persistent effort to present the revolutionary ideology as a practical concept which could be applied in the political, social and cultural spheres. Thus, many other events notwithstanding, the Suez War was used as an all-encompassing symbol through which official sources and supporters tried to expose large sectors of the population to a conceptual package – Nasserism as a revolutionary alternative.

Since 1956 phrases such as the Suez War (*Harb al-Suwis*) and the Tripartite Aggression (*al-'Udwan al-Thulathi*) have been used in Egypt as metaphors encompassing most of the national and cultural challenges which Egypt and the rest of the Arab states faced. These included the struggle for national liberation and the establishment of political and economic infrastructures. Such usage can be found in poetry, popular songs, novels, dramatic plays, movies and the arts; and of course in textbooks, and in countless official statements and sources.

Egypt's policy during the Suez crisis brought to a climax the reputation and popularity of President 'Abd al-Nasser in Egypt and beyond. In the eyes of many Arabs, 'Abd al-Nasser and his policies presented both a conceptual and practical alternative. The expectations from 'Abd al-Nasser and Egypt were enormous. Thus, several parties and senior officers in Syria called for immediate unification with Egypt. These efforts eventually led to the announcement of the United Arab Republic in February 1958. At the same time, several Arab regimes viewed the consolidation of revolutionary ideas and increasing mass support for them with much concern. The rulers of Saudi Arabia, Jordan, and Lebanon, to mention but a few, were worried about the implications of Egypt's endeavour to forge Arab unity through revolutionary methods. The evidence that the Nasserite regime had given support to opposition groups and subversive elements all over the Middle East distressed them. This was the background to the sharp deterioration of inter-Arab relations, or to the period which Malcolm Kerr so pointedly described as 'The Arab Cold War'.[27]

The centrality of the Suez crisis in Egypt's ethos did not disappear when the Nasserite era came to its end following the defeat of Egyptian forces in the 1967 Arab–Israeli war. Current evidence for the durability of the Suez crisis as a symbol and a focal element in Egypt's ethos can be found in the film *Nasser 56*. Apart from unaminous acclaim for the exquisite role played by Ahmad Zaqi (as 'Abd al-Nasser), a heated debate erupted regarding the historical accuracy of the script, and the meaning of the massive audiences in the cinema houses. What is more important is the fact that when it was decided to produce (with unprecedented investment) a film sympathetic to 'Abd al-Nasser, it was understood that it would concentrate on his policy during the Suez crisis and the war.

NOTES

1. Jumhuriyyat Misr al-'Arabiyya, *Nazhrat 'ala intisarat al-'asqariyya al-wataniyya al-misriyya* [Arab Republic of Egypt, Ministry of Information, Views on the nationalist military victories of Egypt] (Cairo: 1992), pp. 283–9. It is no surprise that out of the 927 pages of Haykal's book on the Suez War (in the Arabic version), only 81 pages are devoted to the military confrontation, while the crisis that preceded the war, with all its extensive diplomatic activities, is discussed at length. Muhammad Hasanayn Haykal, *Milafat al-suwis* [The Suez files] (Cairo: Markaz al-Ahrain lil-Tarjamah wa-al-Nashr, 1986).
2. For a detailed description of the negotiations and of the agreement, see Mahmoud Fawzi, *Suez 1956: An Egyptian Perspective* (London: Shorouk International, 1986), chapters 2–3; Haykal, *Milafat*, pp. 185–7, 240–51. Wm. Roger Louis and Roger Owen (eds), *Suez 1956: The Crisis and its Consequences* (Oxford: Clarendon, 1989), Ch. 3.

3. The arms deal produced a wide range of arguments with regard to its timing, quantity and consequences. For an early expression of this controversy, see Karen Dawisha, *Soviet Foreign Policy towards Egypt* (London: Macmillan, 1979), pp. 10–14. Ginat, who recently claimed that Egyptian deliberations with the Soviet Union had predated the IDF's raid on Gaza, raised a novel argument. See Rami Ginat, *The Soviet Union and Egypt* (London: Frank Cass, 1993), pp. 207–19. The historical process that led to the conclusion of the Egyptian–Czech arms deal is described at length in Rami Ginat, 'The Origins of the Egyptian–Czech Arms Deal: A Reappraisal', in this volume.

4. In extensive research conducted by Egypt's Defence Ministry, it was argued that following the Gaza raid, Cairo decided to invest much more effort and resources in the purchase of arms. Jumhuriyyat Misr al-'Arabiyya, *Harb al-'udwan al-thulathi* [Arab Republic of Egypt, Ministry of Defence, The Tripartite War] (Cairo: n.d.), pp. 11, 21. The causes that motivated Israel's decision-makers during 1955–56 are discussed in: David Tal, 'Israel's Road to the 1956 War', *International Journal of Middle East Studies (IJMES)* 28, 1 (February 1996), pp. 59–81.

5. Fawzi, *Suez*, p. 31.

6. Haykal, *Milafat*, p. 459. It was claimed in some sources that the idea of the nationalization of the canal had been discussed in Egypt several times before 1956. See Fawzi, *Suez*, pp. 38–40; Ahmad Hamrush in *M'araqat al-suwis – thalatun 'aman* [The Suez Campaign – Thirty Years] (Cairo: 1988), pp. 9–10. For the perspective of those who were charged with the management of the canal after it was nationalized see *Qanat al-suwis w-al-ayam alathi hazat al-dunia* [The Suez Canal and the Days that Had Shook the World] (Cairo: 1987).

7. *Al-Ahram*, 27 July 1956.

8. Ibid.

9. Haykal, *Milafat*, pp. 459–61.

10. Jumhuriyyat Misr al-'Arabiyya, *Harb al-'udwan al-thulathi*, Appendix 4, pp. 266–74.

11. For a detailed account of the diplomatic struggle, especially during the London conference, see Mohamed Hassanein Heikal, *Cutting the Lion's Tail: Suez through Egyptian Eyes* (London: André Deutsch, 1986), Chs 12–15; Fawzi, *Suez*, Ch. 5.

12. Fawzi, *Suez*, p. 52.

13. Jumhuriyyat Misr, *al-Kitab al-abyad fi ta'mim shariqat qanat al-suwis* [The Republic of Egypt, Foreign Ministry, White paper on the nationalization of the Suez Canal Company] (Cairo: 1956), pp. 7, 63–4.

14. Ibid., p. 6. The argument that 120,000 Egyptians died during the construction of the canal was first mentioned by 'Abd al-Nasser during his announcement of the canal's nationalization. However, Love's research on this subject found no evidence for such a claim. Drawing on documents of the Suez Canal Company, Love found that 1,394 Egyptians and 1,314 foreigners had died during the digging of the canal. Kenneth Love, *Suez: The Twice-Fought War* (New York: McGraw-Hill, 1969), p. 349.

15. Heikal, *Cutting the Lion's Tail*, pp. 22–3; 'Abd al-Rahman al-Rafe'i, *Thawrat 23 julyu sanat 1952* [The Revolution of 23 July 1952] (Cairo: Maktabut al-Nahdat al-Misriyah, 1989), p. 261.

16. For the text of this message, see Haykal, *Milafat*, pp. 803–4.

17. For the complete text of the ultimatum, see Love, *Suez*, p. 464.

18. Jumhuriyyat Misr al-'Arabiyya, *Nazhrat 'ala intisarat*, p. 289.

19. Love, *Suez*, p. 558.

20. *M'araqat al-suwis*, pp. 48–50; al-Rafe'i, *Thawrat 23 julyu*, pp. 272, 293–302; Jumhuriyyat Misr al-'Arabiyya, *Harb al-'udwan al-thulathi*, pp. 253–4. It can be assumed that the timing of 'Abd al-Nasser's declaration of the establishment of the National Liberation Army was intended as a message to the participants attending the first session of the London Conference (16 August 1956).

21. Love, *Suez*, p. 557.

22. See for example the memoirs of Major-General (ret.) Muhammad Kamal 'Abd al-Hamid, *Ma'raqat sina wa qanat al-suwis* [The Sinai Campaign and the Suez Canal] (Cairo: Jamiyat al-Way al-Qawmi, 1964), chapters 4, 5, 6.

23. Jumhuriyyat Misr al-'Arabiyya, *Harb al-'udwan al-thulathi*, pp. 37, 52.

24. Haykal, *Milafat*; Rif'at Sa'id Ahmad, *Thawrat al-general* [The General's Revolution] (Cairo: 1993), pp. 351–5.
25. Jumhuriyyat Misr al-'Arabiyya, *Nazhrat 'ala intisarat*, p. 284; Jumhuriyyat Misr al-'Arabiyya, *Harb al-'udwan al-thulathi*, p. 63; Cf. 'The first victory', in Sa'id Ahmad, *Thawrat al-general*. Haykal presented a document showing that as early as the spring of 1955, senior intelligence officers from Britain and the United States had discussed the option of getting rid of 'Abd al-Nasser and his regime. Haykal, *Milafat*, pp. 925–7. Egyptian sources attribute only minor importance to Israel's achievements following the war, especially the assignment of UN forces in the Sinai and the guarantee of freedom of navigation in the Red Sea and the Gulf of Aqaba.
26. al-Rafe'i, *Thawrat 23 julyu*, pp. 342–50; Rif'at, *Thawrat al-general*, p. 398.
27. See Malcolm Kerr, *The Arab Cold War: Gamal 'Abd al-Nassir and his Rivals, 1958–1970* (London and New York: Oxford University Press for Royal Institute of International Affairs, 1971).

10

Regaining Lost Pride: The Impact of the Suez Affair on Egypt and the Arab World

ELIE PODEH

'Today we need a hero like Gamal 'Abd al-Nasser who can resurrect the Egyptian people.'

Anushka, an Egyptian singer, 1996[1]

More than 40 years after the Suez affair, Egypt is rediscovering this episode. A film released in August 1996 and called *Nasser, 1956*, has been received enthusiastically by the Egyptian people.[2] Faced with a harsh reality, they tend to identify with 'Abd al-Nasser's boldest challenge against the West – the nationalization of the Suez Canal Company, which took place on 26 July 1956. Through this movie, many young Egyptians rediscovered 'Abd al-Nasser – the charismatic leader whose memory has largely faded during the last two decades as a result of an intensive process of de-Nasserization by the Sadat and Mubarak regimes. Both the old and new generations came to realize that it was the Suez affair which had partially restored the dignity (*karamah*) of the individual Arab, which had been lost during decades of Ottoman and Western domination, and after the humiliating defeat by Israel in 1948. From our present perspective, this is perhaps the most important consequence of the Suez affair.

This chapter analyses the inter-Arab dimension of the Suez affair – the nationalization and the subsequent war. From an Arab perspective, the 1956 war – known in Egyptian historiography as 'the Tripartite Aggression' (*al-'Udwan al-Thulathi*) – has been largely neglected. In spite of the wealth of material existing in Western archives, there is no thorough research, either in English or in Arabic, on the developments in the Arab world during the Suez affair. In contrast, Arab conduct during the 1948, 1967 and 1973 wars has been studied extensively. The existing literature, which has made little use of US, British and Israeli archives, is therefore based primarily on secondary sources, Arab

209

memoirs and the press.[3] This chapter attempts partially to fill that gap in the literature by using British archival material as well as Arab sources.

This chapter advances three arguments: First, in contrast to the war that preceded it (1948) and followed it (1967), the Suez affair did not constitute a watershed in terms of the Arab state system. It merely accelerated existing processes, some of which Britain and France aimed to arrest when launching the war. Still, the Suez affair was highly instrumental in elevating 'Abd al-Nasser to a leadership role in the Arab world, though this position would be challenged persistently by other Arab rulers. Second, in spite of the frequent display of verbal solidarity, Arab divisions remained basically unchanged, reflecting antagonistic state interests. And, finally, the Suez affair, both in the short and the long run, enabled the Arabs, at least psychologically, to regain some of their lost dignity that resulted from long subjugation under, and in their struggle with, foreign powers.

The fate of the Baghdad Pact was the main focus of the struggle between Egypt and Iraq before the Suez crisis. On 24 February 1955, Iraq and Turkey signed a military pact, which served as the basis for the formation of the Baghdad Pact, which also included Britain, Pakistan and Iran.[4] Originally, the pact was part of a Western build-up (in conjunction with NATO and the South-East Asia Treaty Organization (SEATO)), designed to 'protect' the Middle East from the Soviet menace. However, 'Abd al-Nasser saw Iraq's central role in the pact as a challenge to Egypt's perceived leadership of the Arab world, and relentlessly attempted to dissuade the Arab states from joining it. In the struggle that ensued between Egypt and Iraq, the former succeeded in winning over Syria and Saudi Arabia; Syria vacillated for a short period before yielding to Egyptian pressure; Saudi Arabia enthusiastically supported Egypt, owing to the age-old rivalry between the Hashemites and the Saudis. This coalition was further consolidated when Egypt signed two interlocking military agreements with Syria and Saudi Arabia in October 1955.

Meanwhile, Britain and Iraq tried to persuade Jordan to join the Baghdad Pact. Such a venture – so it was hoped – would tip the scales in favour of Iraq, stimulating other Arab states to join as well. The struggle reached its climax in December 1955, when Britain, Iraq and Turkey pressed King Husayn not to succumb to Egyptian and Saudi pressure but to adhere to his former decision to join the pact. The riots which spread across Jordan, fuelled by the Egyptian media and Saudi money, convinced Husayn that by adhering to the pact he would seal his own fate. His refusal proved to be a fateful turning point for the Baghdad Pact; for, even though the struggle in the Arab world over the pact did not cease, it was clear that no Arab state would dare join it.[5]

The 'Jordanian episode' led to the isolation of Iraq in the Arab world against an Arab tripartite coalition, while Jordan and Lebanon were still straddling the fence. Yet, while the Egyptian–Syrian bond was tightening, the Egyptian–Saudi axis was gradually disintegrating owing to the different nature of the two regimes. With Western encouragement, Iraq attempted to erode 'Abd al-Nasser's influence by detaching Saudi Arabia from Egypt. However, the nationalization of the Suez Canal Company temporarily suspended this process.

ARAB RESPONSES TO NATIONALIZATION

On 26 July, in the main square of Alexandria, 'Abd al-Nasser made public for the first time his decision to nationalize the Suez Canal Company in front of an enthusiastic crowd. Anthony Nutting, a British Minister of State for Foreign Affairs and shrewd observer of current events, claimed that the nationalization was 'defiance in the grand style and it won for its author an acclaim from Arab nationalists everywhere greater than any he ['Abd al-Nasser] had ever achieved before'.[6] Indeed, many perceived it as an astonishingly bold move by a brave Arab leader who was not intimidated by the Western powers and was willing to confront them. After a hundred years of Ottoman rule and more than 70 years of British 'occupation', this act of defiance symbolized Arab independence. Throughout the Arab world people roamed the streets, demonstrating and shouting the name of 'Abd al-Nasser.

Arab leaders, however, received the news with mixed emotions: jubilant Syrian leaders, for example, called for a meeting of the Arab League to endorse a declaration of unequivocal support for Egypt.[7] Iraq, on the other hand, vehemently opposed the Syrian initiative. Ironically, the news of the nationalization reached Iraqi King Faysal II, Crown Prince 'Abd al-Illah and Prime Minister Nuri al-Sa'id as they were dining with the British Prime Minister, Anthony Eden. Nuri's spontaneous reaction, recorded by Hugh Thomas, the *Sunday Times*' correspondent, was 'hit him, hit him hard and hit him now'.[8] Indeed, Nuri and the Royal Hashemites perceived the nationalization as a pretext for the British to eliminate the Egyptian leader once and for all. They considered his downfall as the only remedy for their predicament and the problems besetting the Middle East in general. Nuri did not suggest any specific name to replace 'Abd al-Nasser, but he hoped that the former leader of the Free Officers, Muhammad Nagib or other army members would topple 'Abd al-Nasser. Crown Prince 'Abd al-Illah was more specific, advocating the restoration of the monarchy in Egypt. His preferred candidate for the throne was Prince 'Abd al-Muni'm, the eldest son of Egypt's last Khedive, 'Abbas Hilmi.[9] Publicly, however, Iraq was forced to yield to public opinion in the Arab world. Accordingly, the Iraqi cabinet issued a public statement declaring, *inter alia*, that the nationalization was Egypt's 'indisputable right', and expressing hope for a reasonable settlement of the dispute.[10]

While Syria was exerting its efforts to convene the Arab League, Nuri was working furiously to undermine Syria's draft proposal.[11] His diplomatic skill was manifested by his success in convincing Lebanon, Saudi Arabia, Libya and Sudan to accept a more moderate resolution.[12] Considering the circumstances, the resolution of the Political Committee of the Arab League, issued on 12 August, was an impressive victory for Iraq. First, the Syrian proposal which was supported, if not initiated, by 'Abd al-Nasser, was successfully blocked. Second, the resolution did not support explicitly nationalization, but expressed support generally of Egypt's policy. Finally, even if the severance of diplomatic relations with the West and the imposition of an embargo had been discussed in the proceedings, these proposals were excluded from the final resolution.[13] This compromise satisfied both Egypt, enabling it to claim 'wide Arab support', as well as Iraq, which was not compelled to pay more than lip service to Egypt.[14]

On 16 August, Anthony Eden opened the London Conference, convened by the Western Powers in order to find a diplomatic solution to nationalization. The Arab world marked the occasion with five minutes of silence and a general strike. The protest was meant to express their contempt for what 'Abd al-Nasser called an 'imperialist conspiracy against freedom'.[15] This unprecedented demonstration of solidarity was a genuine expression of the widespread support 'Abd al-Nasser enjoyed among the masses. Another expression of support was the creation of the Arab–Syrian Committee for Aiding Egypt, formed by representatives from various political parties in Syria to coordinate aid for Egypt.[16] The committee invited delegations from various Arab organizations and political parties who supported Egyptian nationalization to attend a conference in Damascus. The assembly, which met on 18 September at the Syrian Parliament building, chose the Lebanese, Hamid Faranjiyya, as its president, and decided to open branches in the Arab states, with a central liaison committee in Cairo. The conference, however, succeeded in extracting only verbal declarations of support for Egypt.[17]

In contrast to the vast support among the Arab masses, many Arab leaders saw the nationalization as a dire threat to their survival and the stability of their regimes. They were apprehensive lest the waves of enthusiasm created by 'Abd al-Nasser's stunning move led to their eventual downfall or undermined their legitimacy. Yet, unable to publicly voice their criticism of 'Abd al-Nasser, they denounced his move behind the scenes. The most vehement opposition, as was to be expected, came from Nuri al-Sa'id and the Iraqi Hashemites. Great anxiety concerning the Egyptian president's rising prestige was also expressed by Saudi King Sa'ud, Lebanese President Sham'un and to a lesser extent by Jordan's King Husayn. Even Syrian President Shukri al-Kuwatly, Egypt's staunchest ally, seemed to be occasionally dissatisfied with 'Abd al-Nasser's independent decisions. This contradiction was a permanent feature of Arab politics: as a result of their precarious legitimacy, Arab rulers were forced to respond to public opinion by an overt expression of solidarity with Egypt, even though such a position could have undermined their own interests.

Of the Arab states to oppose Egypt, Iraq was the most critical. Its reluctance to accept any compromise with Egypt was expressed unequivocally to British officials. The key sentence frequently repeated was that 'Abd al-Nasser should not 'get away with it', or rather be able to 'save his face'. The issue at stake was not just the fate of the Baghdad Pact or the leadership of the Arab world, but the very survival of the Iraqi ruling élite and British influence. Nuri emphatically claimed that the operation against 'Abd al-Nasser should be 'swift, short and successful.' He argued that the latter was profiting from the passage of time as the possibility of a military response was gradually diminishing. He added that if the Egyptian president were to reject the proposals offered by the London Conference then Britain should resort to force (with or without the United States), compelling him either to surrender or to wage war. Perhaps having in mind the Israeli attempt at sending a ship through the Suez Canal (the Bat-Galim incident in 1954), Nuri and 'Abd al-Illah suggested that the interception by Egypt of a British ship carrying arms for the Iraqi army could serve as a *casus belli*. In case of hostilities against Egypt, they averred, Iraq could maintain internal order by imposing martial law.[18]

Nuri's political machinations were not confined solely to Britain. He also attempted to diminish 'Abd al-Nasser's stature in the Arab world by detaching Saudi Arabia from Egypt and by drawing Jordan closer to Iraq. The idea of separating Saudi Arabia from Egypt was proposed by the US State Department as early as March 1956. The underlying assumption was that Egypt's ties with the Soviet Union, coupled with the disturbing influence of radical Arab nationalism, would create a solid basis for cooperation between Iraq and Saudi Arabia.[19] The nationalization gave greater impetus to the Iraqi–Saudi *rapprochement*, which had begun in spring 1956. Although Sa'ud was compelled publicly to support 'Abd al-Nasser's move, he was irritated by the decision which, in contravention of their 1955 military agreement, had not been coordinated with him. As Sa'ud was dependent on Western aid, he was anxious lest the nationalization forced him to support Egypt against the West.[20]

Quick to take advantage of the widening rift between Saudi Arabia and Egypt, Nuri dispatched Prince Zayd, Iraq's ambassador in London, to Riyadh.[21] Sending Zayd, the fourth and only surviving son of King Husayn, who was evicted by the Saudis from the Hijaz, was intended to open a new era between the two dynasties.[22] The Iraqi–Saudi *rapprochement* was further consolidated after the meeting between the two kings in September 1956. During the deliberations, Sa'ud promised the Iraqi King Faysal not to be drawn into hostilities against the West, nor to rely on 'dictators and presidents', but rather to base his future policy on 'cooperation with the sister monarchy, Iraq'.[23] As soon as Faysal concluded his visit, the Syrian and Egyptian presidents arrived in Riyadh.[24] The timing of their visit was planned carefully. It was undoubtedly intended to water down the tremendous impact of the meeting between the two kings; indeed, as the British ambassador in Jedda lamented: 'I am afraid that the good effect from King Faysal's visit, if not entirely lost, was heavily overlaid.'[25] Nevertheless, the meeting between Faysal and Sa'ud was a handsome victory for Iraq, and later served as the basis for the royalist axis in inter-Arab politics.

Simultaneously, Iraq attempted to patch up differences with the Hashemites in Jordan. Jordan's refusal to join the Baghdad Pact and its insistence on maintaining a neutral position between the Egyptian and the Iraqi camps had soured relations between Iraq and Jordan. A major obstacle in the way of improving relations was the amount of military and financial aid Iraq was willing to allocate to Jordan.[26] The nationalization, however, made Iraq more forthcoming in its willingness to aid Jordan; thus, when Husayn, alarmed by Israel's latest incursions into his territory, invited, on 14 September 1956, an Iraqi division, his request met with approval.[27] Although the reply was considered an expression of Arab solidarity against the common enemy, Nuri made it plain to Israel through the British ambassador in Baghdad that his primary goal was to detach Husayn from 'Abd al-Nasser.[28] The Israeli Foreign Office estimated therefore, that the dispatch of Iraqi forces was 'initially to prevent Egyptian domination of Jordan, and, at a later stage, to draw it into the Baghdad Pact'.[29]

'Abd al-Nasser, however, was not deceived: in his conversation with the US ambassador he remarked that he did not believe that the entry of Iraqi forces was aimed at defending Jordan from Israel, but was part of a combined British–Iraqi conspiracy to detach Jordan from Egypt.[30] Despite the favourable Iraqi response, negotiations with Jordan were stalled over the question of the force's command. Consequently, 'Abd al-Illah left for Amman on 14 October; his arrival was a genuine expression of Iraq's concern over the Jordanian question. Eventually, Jordan rescinded its request, after it was agreed that Iraqi forces would stay near the Jordanian frontier, and move in only if Jordan were attacked and upon a formal request.[31] The withdrawal of Jordan's request for the entry of Iraqi forces was a direct result of the changing atmosphere in Jordan. On 21 October, the National–Socialist Party, headed by Sulayman al-Nabulsi, won the elections. Nabulsi became Prime Minister, while 'Abdallah al-Rimawi, the Ba'th leader, became Minister of State for Foreign Affairs. Three days later, Jordan joined the Egyptian–Syrian military command.

THE IMPLICATIONS OF THE WAR

No sooner had Israeli forces invaded Sinai, than Syria, Saudi Arabia and Jordan offered Egypt military support. While expressing his appreciation, 'Abd al-Nasser – who had already ordered his troops to retreat from Sinai – declined the offer, fearing that it might serve as a pretext for the Western powers to invade Syria and inflict further humiliation. The Egyptian president preferred that Syrian President al-Kuwatly would proceed with his planned visit to Moscow (1–3 November) in order to ensure Soviet assistance, if that should be required.[32] However, when the transmitting stations of *Sawt al-'Arab*, the main Egyptian propaganda station, were destroyed by the British Royal Air Force, Radio Damascus replaced the Egyptian radio.[33] Meanwhile, in response to a formal invitation, Syrian, Saudi and Iraqi units entered Jordan in order to protect it from a possible Israeli attack. In addition, Egypt, Syria and Saudi Arabia severed their diplomatic relations with Britain and France.

The main focus of criticism in the Arab world during and after the war was turned against Iraq. From the beginning of the war, anti-Western demonstrations were held in Syria and Jordan, calling on Iraq to withdraw from the Baghdad Pact and demanding Nuri's resignation. However, the most significant action was the explosion by a Syrian army unit of three pumping stations in Syria along the Iraqi pipeline from Kirkuk to the Tripoli and Banyas terminals in Lebanon. The operation, according to Haykal, was carried out upon the orders of Colonel 'Abd al-Hamid Sarraj, the head of Military Intelligence in the Syrian army, probably without the knowledge of either the Syrian President or his Prime Minister. Haykal further claims that the sabotage operation was coordinated with Mahmud Riad, the Egyptian ambassador in Damascus, but without the knowledge of 'Abd al-Nasser. 'In those days [of the war]', says Haykal, 'everybody in the Arab world was acting on his own initiative; any attempt to coordinate strategy or tactics would have been impossible.' Moreover, 'Abd al-Nasser would be reluctant to issue such an order since it might have triggered undesired British or Iraqi intervention in Syria.[34] However, there was no doubt that the sabotage was aimed solely against Iraq and Britain, since the Tapline pipeline running in Syria (a Saudi–US venture) remained intact. Riad feared that Britain and Iraq would pump oil through the Kirkuk–Haifa pipeline, which had not been used since the establishment of Israel in 1948. Consequently, he convinced Amin al-Hussayni, head of the Palestinian Arab Higher Committee, to send a *fedayeen* unit to discover whether it was indeed being used.[35] Financially, the operation caused the interruption of the oil flow for six months and severely damaged Iraq's economy (while also proportionately decreasing Syrian royalties).[36] Under British pressure, the Iraqi Petroleum Company (IPC) allocated a credit of £25 million, which enabled Iraq to overcome the budget deficit caused by the loss of oil revenues.[37]

From the beginning of the war, the Lebanese president had made efforts to convene an all-Arab conference. Sham'un's motives were unclear; he either wanted to become a moderating power in the Arab world, or he strove to strengthen his position at home.[38] Eventually, the conference was convened on 13 November, with the participation of all Arab heads of state, except 'Abd al-Nasser who empowered the Egyptian ambassador in Beirut to represent him. The main topic on the agenda was the question of Arab diplomatic relations with Britain and France. Syrian President al-Kuwatly claimed that all the Arab states should follow Egypt, Syria and Saudi Arabia, by severing their diplomatic relations with Britain and France. Iraqi's King Faysal was adamantly opposed to severing relations with Britain, although he had done so with France. Lebanon, Libya and Sudan supported the Iraqi position by displaying a moderate stance. Egypt did not share Syria's enthusiastic attitude since it was apprehensive of further alienating the Western powers. The resolution adopted by the conference was relatively mild; it declared general support of Egypt's policy, denounced the Tripartite Aggression and insinuated that each Arab state could take any political step it deemed necessary. At the conclusion of the conference, the general feeling of the participants was that its results 'could have been worse' and that in spite of Syria's declared radical position, the Lebanese president had succeeded in riding out the storm.[39]

As a consequence of the war, Britain's allies in the Arab world found themselves in an extremely difficult position: not only had a Western power attacked a sister Arab state, but the attack was carried out in collusion with their arch-enemy – Israel. Of all the Arab states, Iraq's situation was the most difficult; its special ties with Britain as well as its joint membership in the Baghdad Pact made Iraq, and its rulers, the target of Arab attacks. The grave situation in Iraq led Western officials to believe that a coup was inevitable, and that its withdrawal from the Baghdad Pact was imminent. Nuri and the Hashemites were not so much disturbed by the British attack as by the unexpected involvement of Israel in the operation. In order to withstand a deterioration in the domestic situation, the Iraqi cabinet decided on 31 October to declare martial law, jail the nationalists, suspend parliament and close down schools and colleges.[40] Nevertheless, Nuri remained sceptical as to his ability to maintain the internal order; he told British Ambassador Michael Wright that it was impossible to ensure Iraq's stability for more than 'five or six days', emphasizing that Britain must achieve a cease-fire and demand Israel's retreat within this period. Shocked by the repercussions of the war, the ambassador exclaimed: 'almost all we have built up here over many years and with such pains has been shaken nearly beyond repair'.[41]

Troubles at home notwithstanding, Nuri did not neglect the Arab world. He hastened, for instance, to respond to Husayn's request to send troops ('up to a division') to Jordan.[42] The question of command was one of the problems that had hindered the entry of troops into Jordan; now, however, both parties were too troubled to disagree on this point. Nuri was wary of possible Arab accusations that he had refrained from assisting a sister state, while Husayn was perturbed by the possibility of an Israeli attack. Therefore, it was hastily agreed that the Iraqi forces would enter Jordan under joint command, headed by Jordan's Deputy Chief of Staff, 'Ali al-Hiyari. Nuri assured Britain that the Iraqi units would not fight Israel, unless the latter attacked Jordan, and that they would be stationed in Mafraq, far from the Israeli border.[43]

Arab criticism of Iraq focused on its membership in the Baghdad Pact, alongside Britain. Yet, Nuri refused to surrender to demands, voiced in Iraq and the Arab world, which called for withdrawal from the pact; moreover, he tried to use the pact as a lever to enhance Iraq's position in the Arab world. On 3 November, Nuri left for Tehran in order to participate in a conference of Muslim members of the pact. His visit, in spite of the tense situation in his country, clearly indicated the importance he attached to the results of the conference. In Tehran, Nuri hoped to play an active role in ending the war, and to advance a solution for the Palestine problem – the ever-lasting panacea for shifting Arab attention. He arrived with a draft proposal approved by his cabinet, which demanded the return of Egypt's sovereignty and territorial integrity; a guarantee of Israel's retreat to the cease-fire lines; the repatriation of all prisoners of war; and a comprehensive solution of the Palestine problem.[44] Nuri's purpose was two-fold: first, to prove that the Baghdad Pact had played a crucial role in ending the war; and second, to shift public attention from the Suez crisis to the Palestine issue in which Iraq could play a major role. Much to his chagrin, the conference opened only on 8 November, by which time a cease-fire had already been declared. Nevertheless, in the final communiqué it was stated that the appeal of Muslim member states to Britain had influenced Israel's decision to accept a cease-fire.[45]

Following the conference Iraq decided to sever its diplomatic relations with France and to restrict meetings of the Baghdad Pact to its Muslim members (i.e. exclude Britain from its activities).[46] These decisions indicated that the Tehran conference had achieved little in terms of resolving Iraqi domestic and regional problems. The first move was primarily symbolic, as Iraq's ties with France were negligible; while the second move, made without prior consultation with the other members of the pact, was rather surprising and revealed the sinister implications of the Suez crisis on Iraq. Britain and Turkey were reconciled to the Iraqi decision out of understanding for its predicament, but assumed that the suspension would be temporary (as Iraq privately admitted); Pakistan and Iran protested strongly against Iraq's unilateral decision but were unable to change it. By presenting the pact as a seemingly genuine regional defence organization, ostensibly composed of Muslim states and aimed against Israel, Iraq averted public criticism.[47]

There was another drastic twist, however, in Iraqi foreign policy. On 13 November, Iraq adopted a radical new position concerning the Palestine question by calling for the liquidation of the State of Israel and the return of Palestinian refugees.[48] This marked a definite shift from a fairly moderate stance, which accepted the Partition Plan (November 1947) as a basis for the solution of the Arab–Israeli conflict, to a more uncompromising attitude intent on eliminating Israel. The timing of this change was highly significant; Iraq exploited the fact that the Palestine problem had not been discussed at the Beirut conference, thus demonstrating that it was the genuine representative of the Palestinians who had been neglected by the Arab states. Once again, the Palestine problem was used as a lever in inter-Arab politics in order to achieve internal and regional gains.

On 17 November, the Muslim members of the Baghdad Pact reconvened in Baghdad to discuss its future. They concluded that Britain should remain a member despite its involvement in the war. They also agreed to invite the United States to join, an offer that was politely rejected by the US State Department. As before, Nuri hoped to utilize the conference to promote Iraqi interests, yet it proved to be a disastrous mistake; student demonstrations, fuelled by Egyptian propaganda, spread across the country.[49] At the same time, Syria announced the uncovering of an Iraqi plot to depose the Syrian government. Ineptly planned and doomed from the start, the conspiracy had a devastating effect on Iraq. The very fact that it had colluded with Western allies against an Arab state, and especially the timing of the coup (planned innocently for 29 October, the day the Suez operation began), justified unprecedented attacks by Syria and Egypt.[50]

Nuri effectively subdued domestic strife in Iraq, but only for a short period of time. His abortive manoeuvres led to Iraq's isolation in the Arab world. The announcement of the Eisenhower doctrine, in January 1957, temporarily strengthened the Iraqi regime. Nuri also succeeded in building a counter-coalition, which consisted of pro-royalist forces in Jordan and Saudi Arabia and was supported tacitly by Lebanon and the North African countries. Yet, the Israeli withdrawal from Sinai and the humiliating British and French withdrawal from Port Said further bolstered 'Abd al-Nasser's position in the Arab world.[51] Thus, neither the new US policy, nor the new Arab alignment, could change or arrest the long process that eventually brought about the collapse of the Iraqi regime. On 14 July 1958, 'Abd al-Karim Qasim instigated a military coup, which annihilated the Hashemite dynasty and ushered in a new era in Iraqi and Arab politics.

CONCLUSION

In terms of the Arab state system, the Suez affair did not signal a major turning point, yet it did accelerate several trends. It is commonly believed, as Rashid Khalidi claimed, that the war enabled 'Abd al-Nasser firmly to establish himself as 'the pre-eminent Arab until the end of his life, and Arab nationalism as the leading Arab ideology for at least that long'.[52] No doubt, the nationalization of the Suez Canal and the results of the war turned 'Abd al-Nasser into an Arab hero. Yet, it would only be fair to note that this process had commenced in 1955, with his successful struggle against the Baghdad Pact, his ostentatious participation in the Bandung Conference and the signing of the Czech arms deal. Moreover, though 'Abd al-Nasser became the recognized leader of the Arab world (certainly in Western eyes), he was persistently challenged by some Arab leaders. Qasim in Iraq, Faysal in Saudi Arabia and Bourguiba in Tunisia were among the main protagonists who did not accept 'Abd al-Nasser's leadership as a foregone conclusion.

In ideological terms, the Suez affair strengthened Egypt's commitment to pan-Arabism. In his booklet 'The Philosophy of the Revolution', published in late 1953, 'Abd al-Nasser offered for the first time his interpretation of this ideology, which established a justification for Egyptian hegemony of the Arab world. Publicly, however, 'Abd al-Nasser spoke of Egypt's role in Arab affairs only in July 1954, the second anniversary of the revolutionary regime. During 1955, pan-Arabism became an important instrument designed to strengthen his legitimacy at home and establish a credible claim for Arab hegemony. The Suez affair solidified this trend, substantiating his thesis that the Arab states should unite against the common enemy – imperialism and Israel. By strengthening 'Abd al-Nasser's hitherto hesitant commitment to pan-Arab ideology, the Suez affair contributed to the formation of the United Arab Republic (UAR) – the Egyptian–Syrian union – which was established in February 1958.[53]

The Suez affair was also instrumental in ending the Saudi–Hashemite dispute. Fearing the growing wave of Arab radicalism led by Egypt and Syria, the Hashemites both in Iraq and Jordan, as well as the Saudi dynasty, formed a tripartite coalition. The emergence of the new monarchic coalition signalled the disappearance of the age-old rivalry between the Hashemites and the Saudis, which had gravely affected inter-Arab relations since the mid-1920s. This development commenced, in fact, in late 1955, when Saudi Arabia came to realize that in spite of its military agreements with Egypt and Syria, 'Abd al-Nasser's policy constituted a threat to the kingdom's stability. This realization served as the basis for the Saudi–Hashemite *rapprochement* that culminated in 1957.[54]

On the international and regional levels the Suez affair also accelerated the break-up of the Baghdad Pact. Not only was Britain suspended (at least temporarily) from its activities, but the United States too was unwilling to join the organization as a full member, preferring to base its policy on the Eisenhower Doctrine. Moreover, from an Arab point of view the war substantiated the Egyptian allegation that the pact was no more than an 'imperialist device' and a substitute for the old treaties between the Western powers and the Arab states. In regional terms, it was clear that no Arab state would join the pact. Yet, it should be emphasized that the decline of the Baghdad Pact commenced in December 1955, when Britain and Iraq failed to draw Jordan into it. The fact that Jordan – a declared British ally and a Hashemite state – had declined to join as a result of Egyptian and Saudi pressure sealed the fate of the pact in the Arab world.

The Suez affair accelerated the course of events that led to the Iraqi revolution. The military coup of July 1958 was a result of social, economic and political processes, but the perceived close association of the Iraqi Hashemites and Nuri al-Sa'id with the British gave them further impetus. The Suez affair, observed the US ambassador in Baghdad, 'came close to being Nuri's undoing'. The Iraqi historian Khaldun al-Husri also thought that 'Suez was to be the last storm that Nuri and the ruling class were able to ride.'[55] Indeed, though the Hashemites survived the war and even seemed to consolidate their position during 1957, this short-term development did not change the long-term process that eventually brought about the downfall of the monarchy and the execution of the king, the crown prince and Nuri al-Sa'id.

The Suez affair was also a factor in the awakening of Palestinian self-awareness. One of the Palestinian leaders, Salah Halaf (Abu Iyad), claimed that the nationalization of the canal was a 'major turning point' since 'Abd al-Nasser restored the Palestinians' self-confidence in their ability to stand up against the imperialist powers.[56] Yet, apart from sporadic acts of solidarity with Egypt, the Palestinians as a group remained dormant. It was only after their disenchantment with the first Arab unity experience, the UAR – as Halaf himself admitted – that many Palestinians flocked to the newly formed al-Fatah movement in the late 1950s and the beginning of the 1960s.[57]

But perhaps the most significant result of the Suez affair was its positive psychological impact on the Arab world. On 1 August 1956, an Egyptian journalist published an article entitled 'The Leader Who Resurrected the Spirit', which glorified Mustafa Kamil, the legendary national hero who stood up to the British at the beginning of the twentieth century.[58] Written at the height of the Suez crisis, the Egyptian reader could not fail to make the inevitable link between Kamil and 'Abd al-Nasser. This perception was even strengthened at the end of the Suez affair. From an Arab perspective, the three colluding leaders – British Prime Minister Anthony Eden, French President Guy Mollet and Israeli Prime Minister David Ben-Gurion – were all deposed sooner or later, while 'Abd al-Nasser remained firmly seated until his death in 1970. For Egyptians (and Arabs in general), the military débâcle of 1956 was a moral and political victory over Israel and imperialism. It was a far cry from the humiliation inflicted upon the Arabs in 1948. Unsurprisingly, the historical narrative of the Suez affair in Egyptian school textbooks has emphasized the heroic struggle of the Egyptian people in general, and of the people of Port Said in particular, against the Tripartite Aggression. Egypt, according to its national narrative, did not lose Sinai but voluntarily withdrew its armed forces so as to defend the homeland from the Suez Canal line.[59] Egyptian historiography has successfully turned the Suez affair into a myth, denoting the Arab world's heroic stand against imperialism, Zionism and Israel. The date British and French forces eventually evacuated Port Said, 23 December, has become a national Egyptian holiday and an occasion for a major speech delivered by the president. Thus, the Suez affair was highly instrumental in elevating the somewhat tarnished Arab self-image, a result of debilitating 'subjugation' to Ottoman control and British imperialism. Forty years later, the enthusiastic public response to the movie *Nasser, 1956* indicates that many still cherish this legacy.

NOTES

1. *Ruz al-Yusuf*, 30 September 1996.
2. *Middle East Times*, 11 August 1996; *Ruz al-Yusuf*, 30 September 1996; *Ha'aretz*, 2 September 1996; *Yediot aharonot*, 3 September 1996.
3. See, in particular, R. Khalidi, 'Consequences of the Suez Crisis in the Arab World', in

Wm R. Louis and R. Owen (eds), *Suez 1956: The Crisis and its Consequences* (Oxford: Clarendon, 1989), pp. 377–92; I. Rabinovich, 'The Suez-Sinai Campaign: The Regional Dimension', in S. I. Troen and M. Shemesh (eds), *The Suez–Sinai Crisis 1956: Retrospective and Reappraisal* (New York, NY: Columbia University Press, 1990), pp. 162–71.

4. On the Baghdad Pact, see E. Podeh, *The Quest for Hegemony in the Arab World: The Struggle over the Baghdad Pact* (Leiden: E. J. Brill, 1995).

5. On this episode, see ibid., chapter 8.

6. A. Nutting, *Nasser* (New York: Dutton, 1972), p. 145.

7. *Al-Hayat*, 1 August 1956; K. al-'Azm, *Mudhakkirat Khalid al-'Azm,* (Beirut: al-Dar al-Muttahidah lil-Nashr, 1972), Vol. II chapter 12.

8. H. Thomas, *The Suez Affair* (London: Weidenfeld & Nicolson, 1986), p. 38. Nutting wrote that 'their reaction was more angry than cautious and Nuri, in particular, expressed the hope that Britain would respond resolutely to Nasser's act of defiance.' See A. Nutting, *No End of a Lesson: The Story of Suez* (New York, NY: C. N. Potter, 1967), p. 47. See also the description in Lord Birdwood, *Nuri As-Said: A Study in Arab Leadership* (London: Cassell, 1959), p. 240.

9. Public Record Office (PRO), Wright's Minute, 30 July 1956, VQ1051/43, FO 371/121662; Dodds-Parker's Minute, 30 July 1956, JE14211/327, FO 371/119088; Amery to Lloyd, 1 August 1956, VQ1051/45, FO 371/121662. See also K. S. al-Husry, 'The Iraqi Revolution of July 14, 1958. Part II', *Middle East Forum*, 41 (1965), p. 26; G. De Gaury, *Three Kings in Baghdad, 1921–1958* (London: Hutchinson, 1961), p. 177; F. al-Jamali, *Dhikriyyat wa-'Ibar* (Beirut: 1964), pp. 77–8.

10. *Al-Hayat*, 7 August 1956.

11. PRO, Gardner (Damascus) to FO, Tel. 452, 11 August 1956, JE14211/632, FO 371/119100. See also *al-Hayat*, 10 August 1956.

12. PRO, Wright to FO, Tel. 876, 11 August 1956, JE14211/632, FO 371/119100.

13. *Al-Hayat*, 14 August 1956; PRO, Trevelyan (Cairo) to FO, Tel. 1526, 12 August 1956, JE14211/660, FO 371/119100; Tel. 1551, 13 August 1956, JE14211/691, FO 371/119101.

14. For more details on the Arab League's meeting, see PRO, Trevelyan to FO, Tel. 1545, 13 August 1956, JE14211/687, FO 371/119101.

15. *Al-Hayat*, 17 August 1956.

16. Ibid., 15 and 25 August 1956.

17. For the names of the delegates, see ibid., 19 September 1956.

18. PRO, Wright to FO, Tel. 914, 20 August 1956, JE10393/5, F) 371/118857; Tel. 951, 29 August 1956, ES1021/53, FO 371/120756; Rose to Hooper, 8 August 1956, VQ1051/45, FO 371/121662.

19. W. Gallman, *Iraq under General Nuri: My Recollections of Nuri al-Sa'id, 1954–1958* (Baltimore, MD: Johns Hopkins University Press, 1964), p. 151; Shuckburgh's Minute, 6 March 1956, VQ10325/3, FO 371/121655.

20. PRO, Parkes (Riyadh) to FO, Tel. 249, 8 August 1956, JE14211/474, FO 371/119094; Parkes to Lloyd, Dispatch 57, 11 August 1956, ES10316/10, FO 371/120759; M. H. Heikal, *Cutting the Lion's Tail: Suez Through Egyptian Eyes* (London: 1986), pp. 133, 155–7.

21. PRO, Parkes to FO, Tel. 249, 18 August 1956, ES1021/49, FO 371/120756; Parkes to Lloyd, Dispatch 65, 3 October 1956, ES1021/102, FO 371/120758.

22. PRO, Wright to FO, Tel. 951, 29 August 1956, ES1021/53; Tel. 954, 30 September 1956, ES1021/55; Tel. 970, 1 September 1956, ES1021/57, FO 371/120756.

23. For accounts concerning the Sa'ud–Faysal meeting, see PRO, Wright to FO, Tel. 1049, 15 September 1959, ES1021/72; Tel. 1085, 23 September 1956, ES1021/81; Parkes to FO, Tel. 303, 23 September 1959, FO 371/120757; Parkes to Lloyd, Dispatch 65, 3 October 1956, ES1021/102, FO 371/120758.

24. Heikal, *Cutting the Lion's Tail*, pp. 158–9.

25. PRO, Parkes to FO, Tel. 318, 2 October 1956, ES1021/94, FO 371/120757.

26. PRO, Duke (Amman) to FO, Tel. 1138, 18 August 1956, VJ10393/54; Wright to FO, Tel. 945, 28 August 1956, VJ10393/55, FO 371/121486.

27. PRO, FO to Baghdad, Tel. 1948, 28 September 1956, VJ10393/69, FO 371/121486.

28. PRO, Wright to FO, Tel. 1097, 27 September 1956, VJ10393/68, FO 371/121486.
29. 'Israel and the Entrance of Iraqi Army to Jordan', 18 October 1956, Israel State Archives, 2453/10.
30. PRO, Trevelyan to FO, Tel. 2480, 17 October 1956, JE1053/87, FO 371/118865.
31. PRO, Wright to FO, Tel. 1187, 17 October 1956, VJ10393/146; Duke to FO, Tel. 1490, 18 October 1956, VJ10393/161, FO 371/121489.
32. M. Riad, *Mudhakkirat Mahmud Riad: al-Amn al-Qawmi bayna al-Injaz wa-al-Fashl*, Vol. II (Cairo: 1986), p. 155.
33. BBC, British World Broadcasters/The Middle East, No. 92, 8 November 1956, p. II.
34. Heikal, *Cutting the Lion's Tail*, p. 191; M. H. Haykal *Milaffat al-Suis* (Cairo: 1986), pp. 548–9. See also Riad, *Mudhakkirat Mahmud Riad*, pp. 155–7.
35. Riad, *Mudhakkirat Mahmud Riad*, p. 157. Ultimately, no oil was found in this pipeline.
36. For data, see B. Shwadran, *The Middle East: Oil and the Great Powers* (New York, NY: Wiley, 1973), p. 270. See also *al-Hayat*, 4 and 7 November 1956.
37. PRO, Wright to Lloyd, Dispatch 181, 11 July 1957, VQ1051/34, FO 371/128057.
38. PRO, Middelton (Beirut) to FO, Tel. 1074, 8 November 1956, VL1022/8, FO 371/121608.
39. On the conference, see PRO, Middleton to Lloyd, Dispatch 188, 27 November 1956, VL1022/13; Wright to FO, Tel. 1416, 17 November 1956, VL1022/11, FO 371/121608.
40. BBC, British World Broadcasts/The Middle East, No. 87, 2 November 1956, p. II. See also Husry, 'The Iraqi Revolution', p. 27
41. PRO, Wright to FO, Tel. 1287, 4 November 1956, VR1091/523, FO 371/121786. See also Tel. 1263, 2 November 1956, VQ1015/94, FO 371/121646; Tel. 1250, 2 November 1956, VR1091/484, FO 371/121785.
42. PRO, Wright to FO, Tel. 1238, 1 November 1956, VJ10393/176, FO 371/121489.
43. PRO, Wright to FO, Tel. 1268, 3 November 1956, VR1091/557, FO 371/121787; Tel. 1280, 3 November 1956, VJ10393/182, FO 371/121489.
44. PRO, Stevens (Tehran) to FO, Tel. 871, 4 November 1956, VR1091/590, FO 371/121788; Stevens to Lloyd, Dispatch 125, 15 November 1956, V1073/405, FO 371/121266.
45. For the text, see PRO, Stevens to FO, Tel. 920, 8 November 1956, VR1091/766, FO 371/121793.
46. *Al-Hayat*, 10 November 1956; PRO, Wright to FO, Tel. 49 Saving, 10 November 1956, VQ1094/3, FO 121682; Tel. 1476, 26 November 1956, VQ1015/108, FO 371/121647.
47. PRO, Stevens to FO, Tel. 932, 10 November 1956, V1073/387; High Commissioner (Karachi) to Commonwealth Relations Office, Tel. 1878, 13 November 1956, FO 371/121265.
48. *Al-Hayat*, 14 November 1956; BBC, No. 98, 15 November 1956, pp. 7–8.
49. BBC, No. 105, 23 November 1956, p. 8; No. 106, 24 November 1956, p. I.
50. For details on the Iraqi plot, see P. Seale, *The Struggle for Syria: A Study of Post-War Arab Politics, 1945–1958* (London: I. B. Tauris, 1986), pp. 270–82; W. C. Eveland, *Ropes of Sand: America's Failure in the Middle East* (New York, NY: Norton, 1980), pp. 181–233; D. Little, 'Cold War and Covert Action: The United States and Syria, 1945–1958', *Middle East Journal* 44 (1990), pp. 51–75; A. Gorst and W. S. Lucas, 'The Other Collusion: Operation Straggle and Anglo-American Intervention in Syria, 1955–56', *Intelligence and National Security*, 4 (1989), pp. 576–95.
51. Twenty-three December (1956) – the day British and French forces left Egypt – remains a public holiday in Egypt.
52. Khalidi, 'Consequences of the Suez Crisis in the Arab World', p. 377.
53. For more information, see E. Podeh, *The Decline of Arab Unity: The Rise and Fall of the United Arab Republic* (Brighton: Sussex Academic Press, 1999).
54. Further on this issue, see E. Podeh, 'Ending an Age-Old Rivalry: The Rapprochement between the Hashemites and the Saudis', in A. Susser and A. Shmuelevitz (eds), *The Hashemites in the Modern Arab World, Essays in Honour of the Late Professor Uriel Dann* (London: Frank Cass, 1995), pp. 85–110.
55. Both quotations taken from Husry, 'The Iraqi Revolution', p. 27. On the importance of Suez in this connection, see also P. Marr, *The Modern History of Iraq* (Boulder, CO: Westview, 1985), p. 153.

56. Abou Iyad, *Palestinien sans Patrie: Entretiens avec Eric Rouleau* (Paris: 1978), taken from the Hebrew edition (Tel Aviv: 1983), p. 50.
57. Ibid., pp. 68–9.
58. Anwar Ahmad, '*al-Za'im Alladhi Ba'atha al-Ruh*', *al-Musawwar*, No. 1661, 1 August 1956.
59. See, for example, *al-Mu'allam fi al-Dirasat al-Ijtima'iyya, lil-Saff al-Thalith al-I'adadi* (Cairo: 1998), pp. 125–6; Amin Husni Radwan, *al-Awwal fi al-Muraja'ah al-Nihai'yya lil-Ta'arikh, lil-Marhala al-Thanya lil-Thanawiyya al-'Amma* (Cairo: 1998), p. 177.

Notes on Contributors

ISAAC ALTERAS is professor of History at Queens College of the City University of New York, author of *Eisenhower and Israel, US–Israeli Relations, 1953–1960* (1993); 'The Oslo Accords of 1993', in *The Dictionary of American History* (1995); and is currently working on a book entitled *US–Israeli Relations, From Truman to the Camp David Accords, 1948–1979.*

PAUL GAUJAC was a colonel in the French army and director of the Military Center of Archives and History (1990–94). He is the author of numerous volumes of military history, among them: *La bataille et la libération de Toulon* (Paris, 1994), *Suez 1956* (Panazol, 1986), *La guerre en Provence* (Lyon, 1999), and *Les forces spéciales de la liberation* (2000).

RAMI GINAT is a senior lecturer in the Department of Middle Eastern History, Bar Ilan University. He is the author of *The Soviet Union and Egypt, 1945–1955* (1993) and *Egypt's Incomplete Revolution: Lutfi al-Khuli and Nasser's Socialism in the 1960s* (1997). He is currently working on a new book entitled *The Rise and Fall of Neutralism in the Arab World.*

MOTTI GOLANI is a senior lecturer in the Department of Israeli Studies, University of Haifa. His book on the Sinai campaign (*Tiheyeh milhamah ba-kayits . . .: ha-derekh le-milhemet Sinai 1955-1956* (1997) has been translated into English (*Israel in Search of a War*, 1998) and French (*La Guerre du Sinai*, 2000).

KEITH KYLE was visiting professor of History at the University of Ulster (1993–1999). At the time of the Suez crisis he was Washington correspondent of *The Economist*, and has since worked for the Royal Institute of International Affairs (Chatham House, London). He is the author of *Suez* (1991), *The Politics of the Independence of Kenya* (1999) and joint editor of *Whither Israel?* (1993).

YORAM MEITAL is the Chair of the Department for Middle East Studies at Ben-Gurion University. He is the author of *Egypt's Struggle for Peace: Continuity and Change, 1967–1977* (1997).

ELIE PODEH is senior lecturer in the Department of Islam and Middle Eastern Studies at the Hebrew University of Jerusalem and coordinator of the Middle East Unit at the Harry S. Truman Institute for the Advancement of Peace. He is also the co-editor of the journal *Hamizrah Hehadash* (The New East). Among his publications are *The Decline of Arab Unity: The Rise and Fall of the United Arab Republic* (1999) and *The Arab–Israeli Conflict in Israeli History Textbooks, 1948–2000* (forthcoming).

LAURENT RUCKER holds a PhD in political science. He is a lecturer at the Institut d'etudes politiques de Paris and the author of numerous articles about Soviet and Russian foreign policy. His book *Staline, Israel et les Juifs* will be published in 2001.

ARON SHAI is the Shoul N. Eisenberg Professor of East Asian Affairs at Tel-Aviv University. He is a professor in the Departments of History and East Asian Studies. He has published several books on Britain, China and East Asia among them *Britain and China 1941–1947: Imperial Momentum* (1984) and *The Fate of British and French Firms in China 1949–1954: Imperialism Imprisoned* (1996).

AVI SHLAIM is a fellow of St Antony's College and a professor of International Relations at the University of Oxford. He is currently the Director of Graduate Studies in International Relations at Oxford. Professor Shlaim is the joint author of *British Foreign Secretaries since 1945* (1977); *The United States and the Berlin Blockade 1948–1949: A Study in Crisis Decision-Making* (1983); *Collusion across the Jordan: King Abdullah, the Zionist Movement and the Partition of Palestine* (1988); *The Politics of Partition* (1990); *War and Peace in the Middle East: A Concise History* (1995); and *The Iron Wall: Israel and the Arab World* (2000).

DAVID TAL is a lecturer in the Department of History, Tel Aviv University. He teaches Diplomatic and Military History, and is the author of *Israel's Conception of Current Security: Origins and Development, 1949–1956*, published in 1998. He has written various articles on Israel's security and foreign affairs, and is currently completing a book on the 1948 war in Palestine.

Index

INDEX

Kuwait, 98
al-Kuwatly, President Shukri, 79, 82, 213, 215, 216
Kyle, Keith, 11–12, 120, 173–4, 175

Labour Party, 20, 75, 95, 112
Lancelot, Admiral, 57, 179
Laqueur, Walter, 146
Lawson, Edward, 27
Lebanon, 2–3, 124–5, 145, 211, 212, 213, 215, 216, 219
Lenin/Leninism, 86, 87, 89, 101
Libya, 51, 212, 216
Litani River, 124
Lloyd, Selwyn, 67, 106, 112, 120, 121–2, 125–6, 127, 129, 135
Lod, 190
Lodge, Henry Cabot, 33, 38, 39, 42
Logan, Sir Donald, 120–1, 125–6, 129, 131, 132, 136, 188
London, 49, 51, 68, 74, 79, 99, 106, 108, 127, 129, 174, 176, 188; first conference (August 1956), 68–72, 75, 212, 213; second conference, 73 *see also* Britain
Louis, Wm Roger, 21
Love, Kenneth, 202
Luxor, 190

Macmillan, Harold, 23, 99, 101, 114
Mafraq, 217
Makins, Sir Roger, 97
Malenkov, Georgii, 84, 85, 86, 150, 155
Malta, 51, 52, 100, 102, 106, 107, 108, 174
Malin, Vladimir, 83, 85
Mangin, Colonel Louis, 53, 54, 124, 128, 171, 173
Mapai party, 10
Mar'i, Hasan, 158
Martin, General André, 170, 171, 173, 176, 179, 182, 183, 184, 186, 187, 189
Massu, General, 57
Mediterranean, 40, 111, 174
Meir, Golda, 10, 30, 42, 72, 186
Meital, Yoram, 13
Menderes, Adnan, 156
Menzies, Robert, 72, 73
MID (Soviet Ministry of Foreign Affairs), 68, 71, 73, 75, 76
Middle East, 1, 6, 7, 8, 9, 12, 13, 21, 25–6, 27, 32, 33, 37, 39, 65, 70, 71, 89, 95, 97, 98, 115, 124, 125, 145, 146, 148, 149, 150, 196, 197, 203, 205, 210 *see also* individual countries
Middle East Command, proposal for, 147, 149
MiG aircraft, 111, 152, 158, 159, 161, 173, 190

Mikoian, Anastas, 86–7
Mikunis, Shmuel, 78
al-Misri, 152
al-Misri, 'Aziz 'Ali, 154
Mitla Pass, 58, 79, 128, 132, 182, 185
Mixed Armistice Committees, 3
Mollet, Guy, 8, 42, 53, 54, 55, 56, 79, 80, 98, 99, 108, 114, 122, 123, 124, 129, 133, 136, 137, 176, 186, 221
Molotov, Viacheslav, 85, 86, 87
Monde, Le, 98
Morocco, 59
Moscow, 66, 67, 68, 71, 72, 74, 75, 76, 78, 79, 80, 81, 82, 83, 84, 89, 148, 153, 154, 215 *see also* Soviet Union
Mossad (Israeli intelligence service), 34
Mountbatten, Lord, 101, 102, 103, 106, 108, 111
Mubarak, Hosni, 209
Musketeer/Musketeer Revise, 52, 76, 100, 101, 102, 105, 109, 170, 172, 174, 175, 176, 177, 178, 179, 180, 181, 185, 186, 187, 189, 190, 191
Mystère fighters, 6, 8, 9, 53, 137, 175, 191

al-Nabi, Kamil 'Abd, 154
al-Nabulsi, Sulayman, 215
Nagib, Muhammad, 5, 152–3, 211
Nahhas Pasha, 149
Nahmias, Yosef, 170–1
Nakhl, 129
al–Nasser Gamal 'Abd, 1, 5, 6, 7, 8, 9, 10, 11, 13, 14, 22, 23, 29, 31, 32, 37, 42, 43, 53, 59, 66, 67, 68, 69, 71, 72, 73, 75, 77, 78, 80, 84, 86–7, 96, 97, 98, 99, 101, 103, 104, 105, 110, 111, 113, 119, 121, 123, 124, 125, 126, 127, 129, 130, 138, 146, 148–9, 152, 153, 154, 155, 157, 158, 159, 160, 161, 188, 196, 197–8, 199, 200, 201–2, 203, 204, 205, 209, 210, 211, 212, 213, 214, 215, 216, 219, 220, 221
Nasser, 1956 (film), 205, 209, 221
National Assembly (France), 79
National Guard (Egypt), 202
National Liberation Army (Egypt), 202
National Security Council (US), 31, 67
National-Socialist Party (Jordan), 215
NATO (North Atlantic Treaty Organization), 21, 29, 30, 31, 40, 49, 50, 56, 59, 60, 75, 210
Near East, 70, 71, 82, 85, 86, 87, 89, 149 *see also* Middle East
Ne'eman, Colonel Yuval, 170, 171–2, 173, 175, 176, 179, 180, 182, 183
Nehru, Jawaharlal, 71
New York, 55, 113, 122, 187